Lecture Notes in Computer Science   10790

Commenced Publication in 1973
Founding and Former Series Editors:
Gerhard Goos, Juris Hartmanis, and Jan van Leeuwen

More information about this series at http://www.springer.com/series/8277

Zhigeng Pan · Adrian David Cheok
Wolfgang Müller (Eds.)

Transactions on Edutainment XIV

 Springer

Editors-in-Chief
Zhigeng Pan
Hangzhou Normal University
Hangzhou
China

Wolfgang Müller
University of Education
Weingarten
Germany

Adrian David Cheok
Graduate School of Media Design
Keio University
Yokohama-shi
Japan

ISSN 0302-9743   ISSN 1611-3349 (electronic)
Lecture Notes in Computer Science
ISSN 1867-7207   ISSN 1867-7754 (electronic)
Transactions on Edutainment
ISBN 978-3-662-56688-6   ISBN 978-3-662-56689-3   (eBook)
https://doi.org/10.1007/978-3-662-56689-3

Library of Congress Control Number: 2017933073

Printed on acid-free paper

This Springer imprint is published by the registered company Springer-Verlag GmbH, DE
part of Springer Nature
The registered company address is: Heidelberger Platz 3, 14197 Berlin, Germany

Editorial

In this issue, we selected 19 papers, which are divided into four sections. In the first section, there are five papers. In the first paper, Cao et al. describe the application of 2D/3D visualization in the process of clothing thermal computational design. The computational 2D visualization is employed to compare the key parameters between target cases and select appreciate case design. In the second paper, Wang et al. discuss the application of computer simulation and 3D modeling technology for e-fitting. They focus on analyzing and selecting key parts and characteristic parameters that influence the effect of dressing, and study how to create the contour of the human body's key parts by leveraging these key characteristic parameters. In the third paper, a novel dynamic hierarchical-layout algorithm is proposed to visualize hierarchical information on mobile devices. This layout algorithm tries to represent the hierarchical dataset with a more balanced aspect ratio for the rectangles, which is closely related to the aesthetics of treemaps. In the fourth paper, the special structure of an indoor environment was applied to accelerate home video cameras for 3D collection and identification of the indoor environment. There are two stages in this method: (a) the learning stage, for the 3D model of objects; (b) the identification stage, to determine the objects that were seen before. In the fifth paper, Liu et al. present a robust watermarking algorithm for 3D point cloud models based on feature vertices.

The second section comprises four papers. In the first paper, Li et al. propose an algorithm related to customers based on image gradient orientation (CS-IGO-LDA), where they represent the original samples by using image gradient orientation rather than the pixel intensity. In the second paper, Gao et al. train and test the aforementioned five-layer convolutional neural network on the pavement crack dataset. The experimental results show that this five-layer convolutional neural network performs better than the classic conventional machine learning method. In the third paper, an image zooming model was proposed based on image decomposition. The model decomposed the image into cartoons and textures; it analyzed the features of the isotropic model and anisotropic model, the cartoon part was zoomed by the isotropic model, and the texture part was zoomed by anisotropic model. In the fourth paper, Guo et al. propose an algorithm of salient object detection based on the fusion of foreground coarse extraction and background prior, which uses the prior information of the image boundary, as well as local and global information to extract the saliency map to construct the coarse saliency map.

In the third section, there are five papers. In the first paper, Pan et al. discuss a novel way to generate the customized couplet from the name-embedded couplet. The two-gram word graph technology is used to generate the first sentence that contains the given word. In the second paper, Lv et al. use computer simulation technology to build a virtual exhibition system for traditional costumes, so as to modify the public learning approach to traditional culture, to express and spread the culture meanings of Tang Dynasty costumes through text, images, and music, and to realize interaction with users by means of interactive effects. In the third paper, Hu et al. use simulation techniques to reproduce animation game quake scenes, as well as secondary disasters caused by earthquakes, in which participants can be drilled for evacuation through virtual roles. Controlling the virtual character, participants can try out various escape plans. In the fourth paper, Huang et al. analyze and screen players in online games to quickly capture game bots, and let game operators perform the subsequent processing. First, they analyze game log data and arrange user behavior sequences to form a matrix with user information. Second, an extreme learning machine is used for classification and screening. In the fifth paper, Wang et al. present an algorithm that uses head posture, gaze, eye closure, and mouth opening, as well as facial expression features as attention observation attributes. Then machine learning classifiers are applied to code behavior features. Finally the time sequential statistics of behavior features evaluate the attention level and emotional pleasure degree.

The fourth section includes five papers. In the first paper, the authors expound on the connotation of the collaborative innovation research platform and its requested functions, and then illustrate the principles of building the collaborative innovation research platform. In the research, they take the Jilin Animation Institute as an example to study the structure. In the second paper, the author presents a bibliometric analysis of the papers published in the journal of *Technology Enhanced Foreign Language Education*, a core professional academic journal in China, during the period 2006–2015. The result aims to provide a clear view of the evolution of literature in the research field of technology-enhanced foreign language learning over the past decade. In the third paper, the authors establish a performance evaluation system for rural public sports services as the basis for setting up a scientific administrative control system for public sports services. In the fourth paper, the author elaborates on processes of the production and development of ink deckle-edged paper-cutting animation and summarizes its artistic style. In the fifth paper, the authors describe a CAD usability study for teaching and learning clothing thermal computational design for university students of fashion and textiles.

February 2018   Zhigeng Pan

Transactions on Edutainment

This journal subline serves as a forum for stimulating and disseminating innovative research ideas, theories, emerging technologies, empirical investigations, state-of-the-art methods, and tools in all different genres of edutainment, such as game-based learning and serious games, interactive storytelling, virtual learning environments, VR-based education, and related fields. It covers aspects from educational and game theories, human–computer interaction, computer graphics, artificial intelligence, and systems design.

Daniel Thalmann   EPFL, Switzerland
Kok-Wai Wong   Murdoch University, Australia
Gangshan Wu   Nanjing University, China
Hyun Seung Yang   KAIST, Korea
Xiaopeng Zhang   IA-CAS, China

Contents

3D Modeling and Visualization

Image

E-learning and Games

Miscellaneous

3D Modeling and Visualization

Application of Visualization in Clothing Thermal Computational Design

Mingliang Cao[1](✉), Lu Jin[2], Yi Li[2], and Zhigeng Pan[3]

[1] Guangdong Academy of Research on VR Industry,
Foshan University, Foshan 528000, China
merlin.cao@connect.polyu.hk
[2] School of Materials, The University of Manchester, Manchester M13 9PL, UK
jinlul0ll@hotmail.com, henry.yili@manchester.ac.uk
[3] Digital Media and Interaction (DMI) Research Center,
Hangzhou Normal University, Hangzhou 310012, China
zgpan@cad.zju.edu.cn

Abstract. Computational design provides a scientific and quantitative way for designers to conduct clothing functional design. In this study, the authors describe the application of 2D/3D visualization in the clothing thermal computational design process. The computational 2D visualization is employed to compare the key parameters between target cases and select appreciate case design. The computational 3D visualization can provide more detail supplementary information to demonstrate the final effects of the selected case design.

Keywords: 2D/3D visualization · Clothing thermal computational design

1 Introduction

Apparel products require speedy development which can be achieved through effective and efficient operations. Computer Aided Design (CAD) technology is becoming increasingly apparent in textiles and apparel industries due to the competitive nature of businesses in the sector [1, 2], with the aim of saving on production time and improving quality [3]. Although CAD programs have been developed specifically for apparel industry and apparel CAD training, fashion designers mostly used basic CAD design programs. These basic CAD programs were also available to fashion and textiles designers and included CorelDraw, and Adobe Illustrator and Photoshop which allow designers to communicate their designs professionally. In the apparel industry, with its growing development and creation of new fibers, new machines and new processing, and the increasing demand for new designs, there are bigger challenges in apparel design than ever before. The adoption of computational design CAD technology makes it possible to meet new consumer requirements. Consumers are increasingly concerned about the thermal functions and performance of clothing, which in turn encourage universities and companies to conduct research in this area. With the development of mathematical modeling and computational technology, computational design CAD technology provides a potential way for designers to design for clothing thermal functions and performance.

© Springer-Verlag GmbH Germany, part of Springer Nature 2018
Z. Pan et al. (Eds.): Transactions on Edutainment XIV, LNCS 10790, pp. 3–13, 2018.
https://doi.org/10.1007/978-3-662-56689-3_1

Design for clothing thermal functions and performance is a functional design process for creating conceptual or prototype apparel that achieves desirable thermal functions and performance for people living in a range of climates and weather conditions. Traditional practices of this functional design process include user surveys, user requirements, garment design, garment assembly, testing & analysis (bench scale testing or field trials) and production [4]. The conventional procedure for the functional design process without CAD technology is based largely on the designers' experience and intuition, which have the following disadvantages [5]: experience-based design; long-term process of making interactive decisions; and incapability in predicting parametric design before real product. In consideration of the above-mentioned problems, the computational design CAD software [6], based on mathematical models, was developed as an engineering design tool for technicians and designers as well as educators to conduct clothing thermal computational design (CTCD) in a scientific and quantitative way. The development process of computational simulations and graphics for clothing thermal computational design can be described in Fig. 1.

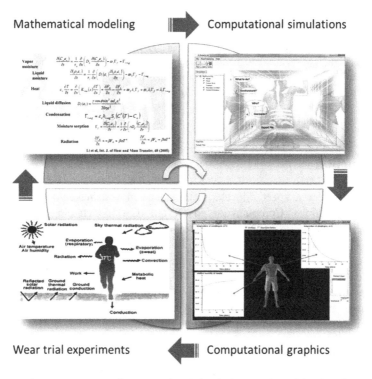

Fig. 1. Development process of computational simulations and graphics for clothing thermal computational design

2   Clothing Thermal Computational Design

Computational design process for apparel development (see Fig. 2) describes an engineering process for designers to conduct function/performance-oriented clothing design with computational simulations and graphics under the context of a real-life situation. There are three features of the CTCD.

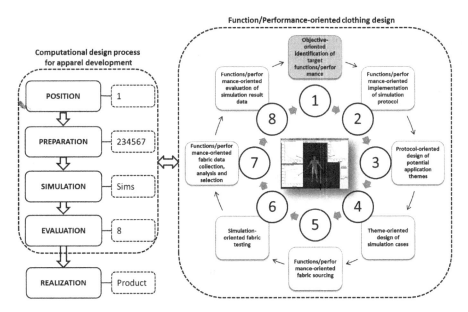

Fig. 2. Computational design process for apparel development

2.1   Engineering Based Design

Clothing thermal computational design is engineering based design. It employs computational simulation technology to design apparel products with the aid of engineering design methods. The engineering design process is a multi-step process including the research, conceptualization, feasibility assessment, establishing design requirements, preliminary design, detailed design, production planning, and tool design, and finally production. The engineering design process involves a number of steps, and parts of the process may need to be repeated many times before the production of a final product can begin. In this study, the process of computational design for apparel development includes 5 steps: position, preparation, simulation, evaluation, and realization.

2.2   Function/Performance Oriented Design

Clothing thermal computational design is function/performance oriented design. This is a design process for achieving the target clothing thermal functions and performance. The key difference between the computational design in this approach and the traditional fashion design is that the former focuses on functions and performances influenced by technology and engineering, while the latter focuses on appearance and aesthetics influenced by cultural and social latitudes.

2.3 Quantitative Guided Design

Clothing thermal computational design is quantitative guided design. The overall structure of the quantitative design is based on scientific methodology. It employs deductive reasoning, with the designers forming a hypothesis, collecting data in an investigation of the problem, and then using the data from the investigation, after the analysis is done and the conclusions shared, to investigate the hypotheses.

3   Clothing Thermal Computational Design CAD

With the computational design CAD software, users can perform multi-layer CTCD to simulate and preview the thermal performance of the clothing wearing system at the whole level, and to identify and improve their designs before making any real garments. Through the software, the user can consider fundamental physical/chemical properties and structured features of fibers, yarns, and fabrics in the computational design simulation to generate solutions that are very close to practical situations. As an engineering tool for the users to conduct CTCD, the software has several advantages compared to the traditional trial-and-error design method, such as speeding up the design process, saving time and money, and increasing productivity. A typical computational design simulation case includes three modules: pre-processing, computation, and post-processing. Several steps need to be followed to get a pre-processing case file (see Fig. 3).

4   Computational Design Simulations for HCE System

The key difference between computational design and traditional design in fashion and textiles is that the former employs model-based quantitative simulations while the latter employs experience-based qualitative trials. Therefore, the unique part of the CAD based computational design is that it provides an engineering approach which enables the designer to locate, evaluate and decide the specific design plan according to quantitative comparisons of the target thermal functions and performances. In other words, it helps to design apparel with quantitative scientific data based support. There are many factors which have more or less influence on thermal functions and performance in human body-clothing-environment (HCE) system. This means that there is a factor space which the designer should consider. It is impossible to think about all factors in the practical problem-solving situations. There were several considerations to be taken into account before developing the computational design simulations: covering whole areas (human body, clothing and environment) of the HCE system; covering the key factors for each area of the HCE system; and, being a factor-control design. Figure 4 shows the relationship between the computational design simulations and HCE system.

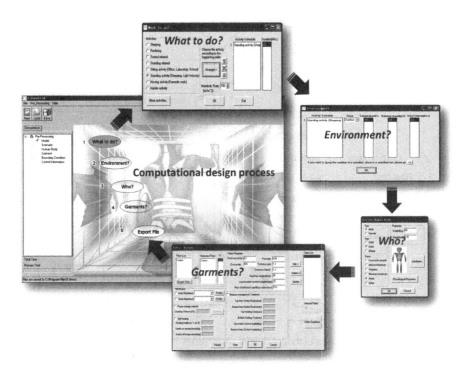

Fig. 3. Clothing thermal computational design process. "What to do" to select the activity and the duration time of the activity; "Environment" to specify the environment for the activity; "Human body" to set up basic information about the human body; and, "Garment" to design the style, fitness, fiber and fabric properties of the garment

5 Clothing Computational Parametric Design

In order to conduct the CTCD in a more scientific way, a clothing computational parametric design (CCPD) method was developed according to the physical scale of properties (see Fig. 5): human body & garments – m scale, fabric & yarns scale – mm scale, and, fibers – nm/μm scale.

The following are the target properties for the clothing computational parametric design:

- *Physical activity* - three physical activities (i.e. walking on the level at 2 km/h, gymnastics, wrestling) with different metabolic rates (i.e. 110 W/m^2, 319 W/m^2, 506 W/m^2) were selected to investigate the influence of physical activity on the results of CTCD;
- *Environment* - three places (i.e. Vancouver, Hong Kong, Basra) with different climatic conditions (in Autumn) and the four seasons (i.e. Spring, Summer, Autumn, Winter) of Hong Kong were selected to investigate the influence of the environment on the results of CTCD;

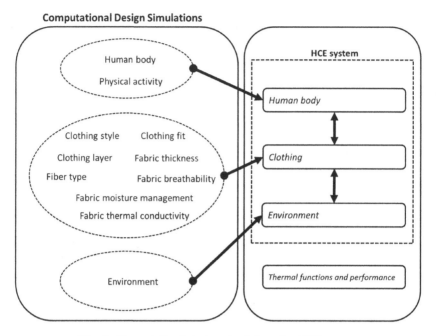

Fig. 4. Computational design simulations for HCE system

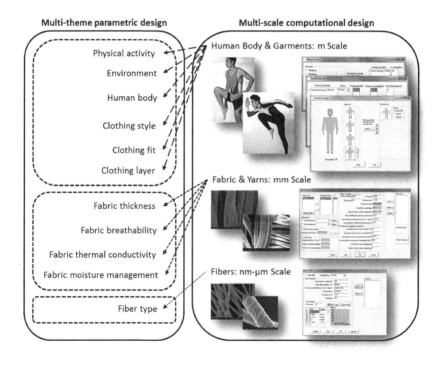

Fig. 5. Clothing computational parametric design

- *Human body* - three groups of cases (i.e. same weight, different height; different weigh, same height; different weight, different height) were designed to investigate the influence of human body properties on the results of CTCD.
- *Clothing style* - three clothing styles with different cover ratios (i.e. 30%, 55%, 90%) were selected to investigate the influence of clothing style on the results of CTCD;
- *Clothing fit* - three clothing fits (i.e. loose fit, just fit, tight fit) were selected to investigate the influence of clothing fit on the results of CTCD;
- *Clothing layer* - four garments with two layers were included to investigate the influence of clothing layers on the results of CTCD;
- *Fabric thickness* - three fabric thicknesses (i.e. 1 mm, 5 mm, 10 mm) were selected to investigate the influence of fabric thickness on the results of CTCD;
- *Fabric breathability* - three fabrics with different water vapor diffusion coefficients (i.e. 0.3, 3, 60) were selected to investigate the influence of fabric breathability on the results of CTCD;
- *Fabric thermal conductivity* - two fabrics with different thermal conductivities (i.e. 7.8E-5, 1.95E-3) were designed to investigate the influence of fabric thermal conductivity on the results of CTCD;
- *Fiber type* - four fabrics with different fibers (i.e. cotton, polypropylene, polyester, wool) were designed to investigate the influence of fiber type on the results of CTCD.
- *Fabric moisture management* - three kinds of fabrics (i.e. hydrophobic, hydrophilic, moisture management fabric) with different moisture management abilities are tested and simulated to investigate the influence of fabric moisture management ability on the results of CTCD.

6 Visualization of Computational Simulations

After the computational simulation, the simulation result data can be achieved. There are three kinds of visualization graphics (see Fig. 6) can be generated: 2D visualization, Microsoft Excel and 3D visualization graphics. The 2D and 3D visualization can be generated by the CAD software automatically and the Microsoft Excel graphics can be generated by manual based on the simulation data.

7 Application of Computational Simulations and Visualization

According to many physiological studies, keeping core temperature within 37 ± 0.5 °C is essential for human survival. Beyond this range, humans will feel substantial discomfort. The maximum deviations of the core temperature are approximately 2 °C from the normal level. Beyond this range, serious physical threats, such as hyperthermia and convulsions in case of high core temperature; and hypothermia and cardiac fibrillation in

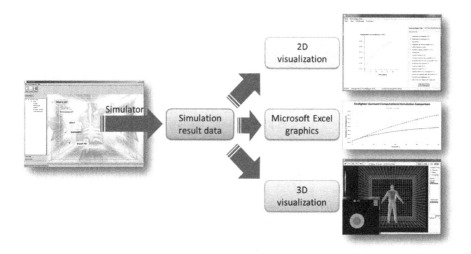

Fig. 6. Visualization for clothing thermal computational simulations

case of low core temperature, may occur. The application of the computational simulations and graphics for clothing thermal computational design follows these steps:

(1) Design and simulate cases according to the target thermal function/performance.
(2) Compare the core temperatures (within 37 ± 2 °C) during target wearing period between the target design cases using the computational 2D images. Step 1 and Step 2 will be repeated if no case data satisfy the normal core temperature range during target wearing period.
(3) Visualize the core temperature images of the required cases using Microsoft Excel graphic by manual and confirm appreciate case design.
(4) Select the time point during the target wearing period and add the 3D graphics as supplementary information to demonstrate the temperature status of core, human body skin and all layers of trial wear.

8   Case Study

This case study is to compare the thermal comfort caused to firefighter between two combinations of firefighters' protective clothing assemblies. Due to the high responsibility and dangerous working task, firefighters always suffer the high intensity of the physical and psychological stress from work. However, firefighter protective clothing with high heat-insulation property in turn hinders the process of dissipating sufficient metabolic heat to the environment, resulting in heat-related illness and heart disease. To be specific, firefighter's tasks such as fire suppression, search and technical rescues work demand a high physical burden and entails a large of energy consumption. Among this energy expenditure, part of energy is actually used in muscles as external work, but most of energy is liberated as heat to be accumulated in the body and increase the core temperature. Consequently, the combined effect of high demanding work and inefficient heat loss on firefighters may lead to heart diseases that have been identified as the top cause of fatality for firefighters as reported in many countries. In fact, firefighters spend only a small percentage of time on firefighting; about 95% of their tasks are technical rescue work that often has a relatively low level of danger and heat exposure. They have to wear a full set of the protective gear in most of their working time. It is anticipated that reducing the heat resistance of firefighter protective clothing may increase thermal comfort.

Firefighter protective clothing assembly is comprised of three layers of fabrics to provide the desired thermal protection. Normally, this includes an outer layer, a moisture barrier and a thermal barrier. In this case study, one kind of outer layer (O1), two types of moisture barrier (M1, M2) and two types of thermal barriers (T1, T2) were employed to conduct two different combinations of assemblies, considering the actual demand for the performance and cost.

The "maximum allowable exposure time" cited from ISO7933, is defined as the time to reach a subject's core temperature of 38.5 °C at a certain condition. To predict the thermal comfort performance of each firefighter protective clothing assembly directly, the maximum allowable exposure time of each assembly was estimated through the clothing thermal computational design CAD software. The CAD software was used as a tool to estimate the core temperature of a firefighter wearing two different firefighting protective clothing assembles.

The core temperature of the mannequin was predicted when wearing firefighter protective clothing made of two different combinations assembles through the CAD software in condition 35 °C and 86% relative humidity at intensive work load with metabolic rate of 400 W/m^2.

As for the thermal comfort indices, the time to a core temperature rise of 38.5 °C at a certain condition is a vital factor directly affecting the thermal comfort performance of firefighter protective clothing directly. In this case study, we adopted a core temperature of 38.5 °C as a tolerate temperature to calculate the maximum allowable exposure time of each assembly. The application of the computational simulations and graphics for this case study follows these steps (see Fig. 7):

(1) Design and simulate two cases according to the protocol and testing data.
(2) Compare the time to a core temperature rise of 38.5 °C between case G1 (21 min) and case G2 (12 min) using individual computational 2D images of core temperature.
(3) Visualize the core temperature images of the required cases using Microsoft Excel graphic by manual and confirm the case G1 as appreciate case design.
(4) Select the time point (i.e. 1 min 5 min 20 min) during the target 20 min wearing period and add the 3D graphics as supplementary information to demonstrate the temperature status of core, human body skin and three layers of the selected G1 firefighter protective clothing.

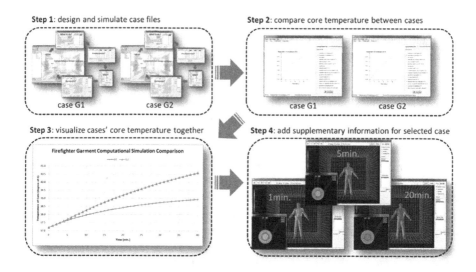

Fig. 7. Computational design process for firefighter protective clothing

9 Conclusion

The application of computational simulations and visualization makes clothing thermal computational design as an engineering-based design process. It provides a scientific and quantitative way for designers to explore their trial conceptual design before real production. In previous study, we have discussed a visualization application of virtual wear trial effects for educational purpose based on the combined technologies of virtual try-on and computational simulations [7, 8]. We also proposed a customized body-mapping visualization approach to facilitate the design of sportswear ergonomics [9]. Combining the research experience of applying visualization in clothing thermal computational design in this study, in the future, we will conduct the research in VR/AR technology based clothing thermal functional wear trials.

Acknowledgments. We thank the Hong Kong Innovation and Technology Commission and HKRITA for funding support of this research through projects ITP/014/08TP and the sponsorship of Hong Kong Jockey Club Sports Medicine and Health Science Center. We would like to thank the support of the EU Horizon 2020 and University of Manchester through projects with project codes 644268-ETEXWELD-H2020-MSCA-RISE-2014 and AA14512. Also, we acknowledge the support of the key national NSFC project under grant 61332017.

References

1. Hardaker, C.H., Fozzard, G.J.: Toward virtual garment: three dimensional computer environment for garment design. Int. J. Cloth. Sci. Tech. **10**(2), 114–127 (1998)
2. Glock, R.E., Kunz, G.I.: Apparel Manufacturing: Sewn Product Analysis, 4th edn. Prentice Hall, Upper Saddle River (2005)

3. Hunter, A., King, R., Lowson, R.H.: The Textile/Clothing Pipeline and Quick Response Management. The Textile Institute International, Manchester (2002)
4. Gupta, D.: Design and engineering of functional clothing. Indian J. Fibre Text. **36**(4), 327–335 (2011)
5. Li, Y., Dai, X.Q.: Biomechanical Engineering of Fashion and Textiles. Woodhead Publishing Limited, Cambridge (2006)
6. Li, Y., et al.: P-smart - a virtual system for clothing thermal functional design. Comput. Aided Des. **38**(7), 726–739 (2006)
7. Cao, M.L., et al.: Creative educational use of virtual reality: working with second life. IEEE Comput. Graph. Appl. **34**(5), 83–87 (2014)
8. Cao, M.L., et al.: Educational virtual-wear trial: more than a virtual try-on experience. IEEE Comput. Graph. Appl. **35**(6), 83–89 (2015)
9. Cao, M.L., et al.: Customized body mapping to facilitate the ergonomic design of sportswear. IEEE Comput. Graph. Appl. **36**(6), 70–77 (2016)

The 3D Human Body Modeling for Virtual Fitting Based on the Key Characteristic Parameters

Meiliang Wang[(✉)] and Yang Shen

Engineering Institute, Lishui University, Lishui, Zhejiang, China
wml@lsu.edu.cn

Abstract. With the development of Internet and e-commerce in recent years, it has become an urgent need for e-commerce users to buy satisfactory clothes through virtual fitting. Therefore, it is of great significance to research and develop a virtual fitting system that can help users create 3D human models to express their personality quickly and effectively by simply entering key characteristic parameters. By using computer simulation and 3D modeling technology, we focus on analyzing and selecting key parts and characteristic parameters that affect the effect of dressing, and study how to create the contour of human body's key parts by leveraging these key characteristic parameters. And then, the contour is used to create 3D human surface model, based on which personalized 3D human body model for virtual fitting can be quickly and effectively created through users' modification of key characteristic parameters.

Keywords: Characteristic parameters · Virtual fitting · 3D human model
Modeling research

1 Introduction

With the progress of the society and the improvement of people's living standard, tailor-made and personalized clothing has become the common needs of both consumers and apparel makers [1]. Especially with the development of Internet and e-commerce in recent years, more and more people tend to buy their favorite clothes online by e-commerce [2]. But many other people hesitate about online purchase because no appropriate technology is available for them to try on clothes through the Internet. This has greatly restricted the further development of e-commerce. Thus the creation of a virtual fitting system, namely, to create a virtual 3D human body model with computer graphics and virtual simulation technology and then introduce it into a computer-generated virtual environment for simulation and interaction of fitting, has not only become a hot spot in researches of international computer graphics, but also an issue demanding urgent solution in the e-commerce industry, automatic clothing design industry and others.

Human body is the carrier of clothing and the 3D human body model is the subject of virtual fitting. After obtaining the metrical data of human bodies, how to quickly build a vivid digital human body model would be the key point to realize virtual fitting [3].

© Springer-Verlag GmbH Germany, part of Springer Nature 2018
Z. Pan et al. (Eds.): Transactions on Edutainment XIV, LNCS 10790, pp. 14–26, 2018.
https://doi.org/10.1007/978-3-662-56689-3_2

2   Main Technical Analysis of 3D Human Body Modeling at Home and Abroad

Researchers have put forward the following representative technologies and methods for 3D human body modeling:

(1) The 3D human body modeling based on anatomy. Foreign scholars such as Scheepers [4] proposed the algorithm of digital human body modeling technology from the anatomical point of view, while domestic researchers such as Zhong [5] carried out researches on 3D reconstruction of digital human body from the perspective of medical research. These modeling techniques, due to the complexity of the modeling process and the low efficiency of modelling as well as the unavailability of users' effective control of the 3D human body model, can hardly realize personalized 3D human body modelling.

(2) The 3D human body modeling based on 3D scanning. This method uses 3D scanners to obtain lots of point cloud data of human bodies, and then reconstructs 3D human body surface. With the gradual popularization of Kinect depth camera, this method has been adopted by more researchers at home and abroad. For example, Weiss et al. [6] and Tong et al. [7] respectively proposed to obtain 3D point cloud data of human body under multiple perspectives with a single Kinect camera and 3 Kinect cameras and then get contour information through modelling of these data to estimate human bodies' posture and shape; Yu [8] and other domestic scholars [9–11] proposed to measure different parts of human body with Kinect, then process the point cloud data by a reasonable coordinate transformation formula, and, finally, align the point cloud data of different parts and reconstruct a 3D human body model with methods such as the three-point alignment method. The human body model based on 3D scanning technology is much more accurate, and can be used to build personalized model of human body, but it is not easy due to the large amount of data needing to be processed and the complicated time-consuming algorithm.

(3) 3D human body modeling based on image sequence. Chen et al. [12] obtained 3D human body model by stereoscopic vision measurement and binocular vision principle; Zhu et al. [13] proposed to obtain finite size characteristics from three-view photos of research subjects and then reconstruct detailed 3D geometry characteristics of the subjects' bodies. However, in the 3D human body model created in this way, it is difficult to achieve the balance between accuracy and modeling speed.

(4) 3D human body modeling based on 3D modeling software. 3D model of human body is drawn by using Maya, 3DMAX, CINEMA 4D [14] and other general modeling software. This modelling method is simple and the model obtained by this method is good looking and convenient. But the high cost of creating a single model, the poor model controllability and low fidelity make it difficult to integrate such 3D human body model into actual application software.

(5) 3D human body modeling based on parameterization. Seo et al. [15] at the MIRALab Laboratory of the University of Geneva in Switzerland proposed to modify the standard model with users' personalized parameters such as body fat

ratio and waist-to-hip ratio, to obtain a real, user-friendly digital model. However, the personalized parameters that need to be provided by users should be obtained and calculated by professionals with professional medical equipment, which is difficult for ordinary users.

To sum up, the existing 3D human modeling techniques are more or less unsatisfactory, with shortcomings ranging from weak modeling of the dynamic deformation process of personalized human body, failure in realizing personalized 3D human body model, to inability to be integrated into practical applications. Such techniques lack support for establishing a large number of personalized human models and suffer from low efficiency. Therefore, there is an urgent need to develop technologies and methods that can rapidly generate a highly realistic 3D human body model according to the user's individual body size so as to be suitable for virtual clothing fitting and other application fields.

3 The 3D Human Body Modeling Based on Key Characteristic Parameters

3.1 The Basic Ideas and Method of Research

The literature review above shows that, although there have been several different methods for 3D human body modeling, they all have their defects, basically not meeting the requirements of virtual fitting system for modeling of human body.

For the convenience of users to purchase clothes online, the basic flow of virtual fitting that we propose is as follows: at any node on the Internet, a user just clicks the clothing style he/she likes and input their familiar daily dress size (key parameters); then the computer would generate a 3D human body model close to the user's body figure by parametric modeling technology; beyond this, the user can select clothes of their favorite brands, styles and designs to "try on" and the user's 3D dressing effect can be displayed in virtual reality environment. Specific flow chart is shown in Fig. 1 below.

In order to complete the virtual fitting process of the above-mentioned users, we propose a technique and method for constructing a personalized 3D human model by using key parameters related to human body's characteristics that affect the users' dressing effect. First, the relationship between human body structure and clothing is analyzed. Human body is viewed as a columnar structure composed of a number of cross-sections, and the key parts affecting the dressing effect of human body are identified. Secondly, 3D modelling is done to the contour lines of the key parts according to key characteristic parameters obtained through measurement and reflecting human body size. And then a 3D human body surface model is constructed based on these contour lines. Finally, a 3D human body model of adult men and women expressed by standard body shape data is established as a general model. In this way, the users only need to adjust the relevant body size parameters and modify the two general models so as to obtain the 3D model that expresses the users' body characteristics. Basic ideas and research method is shown in Fig. 2.

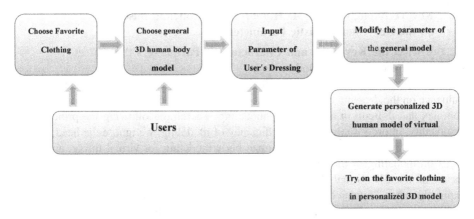

Fig. 1. The flow chart of virtual fitting

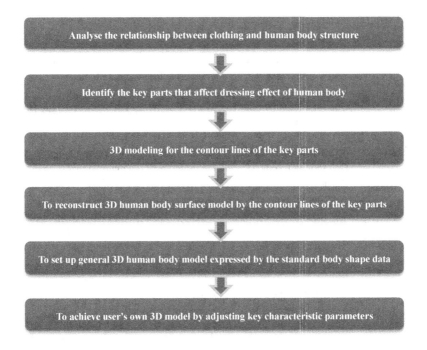

Fig. 2. Basic ideas and research method of 3D human body modeling based on key feature parameters

3.2   Key Technology in the 3D Human Body Modeling Based on the Key Characteristic Parameters

3.2.1   Select the Key Parts and Characteristic Parameters that Affect Dressing Effect of Human Body

Usually when people try on some clothing, the head, hands and feet have small influence on the dressing effect, while modeling of the head, hands and feet is the most complex and difficult in human body modeling. Therefore, following the principle of practicality, in order to improve the efficiency of modeling, we ignore the head, hands and feet in this research of the 3D human body modeling for virtual fitting, and only focus on modeling of the torso and limbs of human body. According to the requirements of the 3D virtual dressing, we choose those parameters that can not only explicitly express human body characteristics and clearly affect dressing effect, but also facilitate user-friendly measurement and modification. The following characteristic parameters of human body are carefully selected to be researched, as is shown in Table 1 below.

Table 1. The human characteristic parameters that affect dressing effect

Parameter	Description	Parameter	Description
Height	The total length from heel to the top of the head	Chest circumference	The longest length of chest circumference
Shoulder height	The total length from the top of the shoulder to the ground	Waist circumference	The shortest length of waist circumference
Shoulder breadth	The length between the two shoulder vertexes	Hip circumference	The longest length of hip circumference
Chest height	The length from the bust point to the ground	Thigh circumference	The longest length of thigh circumference
Loin height	The length from the loin to the ground	Shank circumference	The longest length of shank circumference
Thigh height	The length from the base of the thigh to the heel	Upper arm circumference	The longest length of upper arm circumference
Knee height	The length from the knee to the heel	Forearm circumference	The longest length of forearm circumference
Upper arm length	The length from the shoulder apex to the elbow	Shoulder depth	The maximum thickness from the scapula to the ipsilateral clavicle
Forearm length	The length from the elbow to the wrist ulna	Chest depth	The maximum thickness of side chest
Inframammary distance	The lateral length between the two nipples	Loin depth	The maximum thickness of the side loin
		Hip depth	The maximum thickness of the side hip

In order to reflect the body structure of a small group of people with special body shape, such as pregnant women, fat people and so on, we also define the special characteristic parameters such as thoracic thickness, waist thickness and buttock thickness in the process of selecting the characteristic parameters so as to generate models of special body shapes. The schematic diagram of parameters in the human body models is shown in Fig. 3.

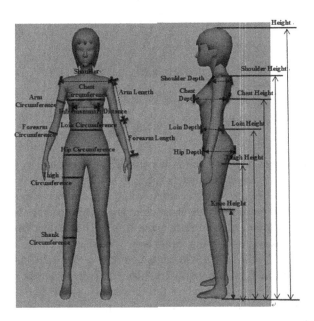

Fig. 3. The schematic diagram of the human characteristic parameters that would affect dressing effect

3.2.2 Modeling of the Contour Lines of Key Parts in Human Body by Characteristic Parameters

Like other objects, the human body surface can also be composed of a series of contour lines from numerous flat cuttings parallel to the horizontal plane, as is shown in the schematic chart of human body trunk contour in Fig. 4 below. We can construct 3D model of the contour lines of key parts of human body through previously measured characteristic parameters of human body, and then use these contour lines as the equipotential lines to model the human body surface. In this way, a 3D model based on characteristic parameters of human body can be obtained and such characteristic parameters can be changed to modify the human body model. Therefore, the key to achieve 3D human body modeling for virtual fitting based on key characteristic parameters is to find out how to use the characteristic parameters to model the contour lines of key parts of human body that affect the dressing effect.

In order to achieve the modeling of the contour lines of key parts, the first thing is to get the key size of each part and the height of human body, as well as their proportional relationship. Let's take a look at the contour modeling of the most

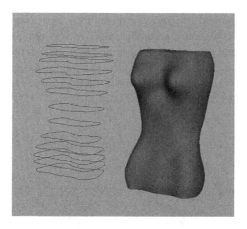

Fig. 4. The sketch of human trunk contour lines

complex part in human body structure, namely, female's chest. The first step in the modeling of the chest is to get parameters such as chest circumference (XiongS), chest height (XiongH) and height (SH). According to a large number of previous statistics and findings [16], the ratio of female chest circumference to height r1 is about 0.548, and the chest height to height ratio r2 is about 0.749. The contour of female chest is rather complicated, as is shown in Fig. 5(a) below. The shape seems to be composed of two tangential ellipses, ellipse A and B, and another two ellipses, C and D, which are tangential to both A and B, as shown in Fig. 5(b). The horizontal axis A, B, and D can be adjusted easily to change the depth of the chest cleavage, the horizontal axis A, B, and C can be adjusted to change the smoothness of the chest and back, the horizontal axis of A and B can be adjusted to change chest breadth, while the vertical axis of A and B can be adjusted to change the depth of the chest. So it would be convenient for later simulation calculation of computer, graph drawing and modification of contour shape through modifying parameters.

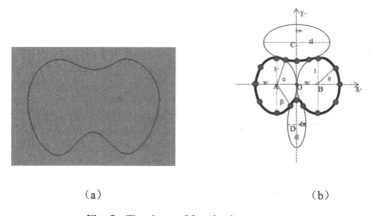

(a)   (b)

Fig. 5. The shape of female chest contour

To achieve the chest contour modeling with fitted curves, the first step is to determine the coordinates of multiple characteristic points on the curve. The more characteristic points are selected, the smoother the curve is, but the speed and efficiency of modeling will be reduced. However, if there are not enough data points, the curve will be rough and the modeling accuracy will drop. Therefore, in order to balance the efficiency and accuracy of modeling, and for meeting users' high requirements for real-time property in virtual fitting, 16 characteristic points are selected in the modeling of the chest contour, among which 12 points are the protruding points of the chest and the inflection points of the convex portion and the concave portion (i.e., the tangent points between the ellipses), while the other 4 points are chosen to make the curve as smooth as possible, as shown in Fig. 5(b). We make the following assumptions: the minor semi-axis of ellipses A and B is w, while the major semi-axis is l; the minor semi-axis of ellipse C is cw, while the major semi-axis is cl; the minor semi-axis of ellipse D is dw, while the major semi-axis is dl; the tangent point of ellipse A and B is the coordinate center; in ellipse A, the included angle formed by the line connecting the tangent point of A and C to the center of the ellipse and the x-axis is α, the included angle formed by the line connecting the tangent point of A and D to the center of the ellipse and the x-axis is β, while the included angle formed by the line connecting any point in ellipse A, B, C or D to the center of the ellipse and the x-axis is θ; the distance between ellipse C and the coordinate center is OC, while the distance between ellipse D and the coordinate center is OD. On such assumptions, the minor semi-axis w and the major semi-axis of ellipses A and B can be easily calculated according to the known length of the chest circumference, namely, the length of the chord of ellipses A and B plus the distance between the upper and lower two fixed points (equivalent to 4w). In addition, the tangent point of ellipses C and D and that of ellipses A and B can be deduced from their equations. The points in ellipse A is in line with the following equation:

$$\frac{(x + w)^2}{w^2} + \frac{y^2}{l^2} = 1 \tag{1}$$

The points on ellipse C are in line with the following equation:

$$\frac{x^2}{cw^2} + \frac{(y - OC)^2}{cl^2} = 1 \tag{2}$$

The tangent points are in line with:

$$\frac{\partial\left(\frac{(x + w)^2}{w^2} + \frac{y^2}{l^2}\right)}{\partial y} = \frac{\partial\left(\frac{x^2}{cw^2} + \frac{(y - OC)^2}{cl^2}\right)}{\partial y} \tag{3}$$

We can deduce the coordinate x and y of the tangent points between ellipse A and ellipse C according to above formula (1), (2), and (3):

$$x = \frac{(w * cw^2 - w^2 * cw)}{(cw^2 - w^2)} \tag{4}$$

$$y = \frac{1 * \sqrt{w^2 - (x + w)^2}}{w} \tag{5}$$

The distance between the center point of ellipse C and the far point of coordinate:

$$OC = y + \sqrt{1 - \frac{x^2}{cw^2}} * cl \tag{6}$$

In addition,

$$\text{Angel } \alpha = \tan^{-1}\left(\left|\frac{y}{w - x}\right|\right), \quad \beta = \tan^{-1}\left(\left|\frac{y}{w - x}\right|\right) \tag{7}$$

According to the above formula and parameters of key parts, we can easily get the coordinates of the 16 characteristic points on the contour line of the chest:

The points in ellipse A (x, y, z):

$$x = w * \cos(\theta) - w; \ y = 1 * \sin(\theta); \ z = XiongH$$

The points in ellipse B (x, y, z):

$$x = w * \cos(\theta) + w; \ y = 1 * \sin(\theta); \ z = XiongH$$

The points in ellipse C (x, y, z):

$$x = cw * \cos(\theta) - w; \ y = cl * \sin(\theta) + OC; \ z = XiongH$$

The points in ellipse D (x, y, z):

$$x = dw * \cos(\theta) - w; \ y = dl * \sin(\theta) - OD; \ z = XiongH$$

The tangent points between ellipse C and ellipse A (x, y, z):

$$x = w * \cos(\alpha) - w; \ y = 1 * \sin(\alpha); \ z = XiongH$$

The tangent points between ellipse C and ellipse B (x, y, z):

$$x = w * \cos(\alpha) + w; \ y = 1 * \sin(\alpha); \ z = XiongH$$

The tangent points between ellipse D and ellipse A (x, y, z):

$$x = w * \cos(\beta) - w; \; y = 1 * \sin(\beta); \; z = \text{XiongH}$$

The tangent points between ellipse D and ellipse A (x, y, z):

$$x = w * \cos(\beta) + w; \; y = 1 * \sin(\beta); \; z = \text{XiongH}$$

From the above analysis, we get the coordinate of 16 characteristic points in the contour line of chest, so that we can draw the contour line of human chest and achieve the modeling of chest contour line. The way of contour modeling for other parts is similar to this one.

3.2.3   Using Contour Line of Key Parts in 3D Human Body Modeling

After establishing the contour model of the key parts of human body, how to reconstruct these contour lines into 3D human body surfaces is the key problem to be solved in the 3D human body modeling for virtual fitting. At present, there are many algorithms in this area, but none is perfect. Here in our research of reconstructing surfaces with 3D contour lines, we mainly focus on the requirements of practical application, namely, the high efficiency of human body modeling required by virtual fitting, the convenience of modifying model through parameters and low demand for modeling accuracy.

Assume there are two adjacent parallel planes, each with a chest contour line, respectively M and N. Fixed points have been selected in the same order in both contours, respectively $m_1, m_2, \ldots m_i$ and $n_1, n_2, \ldots n_j$. Take two adjacent vertexes respectively on the upper and lower contours, such as m_i and m_{i-1}, and another vertex n_j on the lower contour, and connect them with lines, we can get a triangular patch formed by $m_i m_{i-1}$, $m_i n_j$ and $m_{i-1} n_j$, as shown in Fig. 6(a) below. Connecting all the vertexes on the two contours in this way, we can get the surface between the two contour lines, as shown in Fig. 6(b). Of course, in the process of connecting the triangular facets, the following conditions must be met: first, the line segment connecting every two adjacent vertexes must appear in one basic triangular facet once and only once; secondly, the line

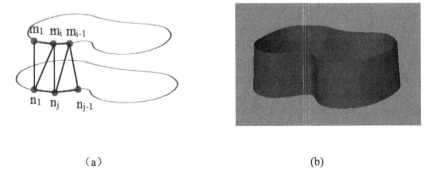

(a)   (b)

Fig. 6. The sketch of surface modeling between contours lines

connecting two adjacent vertexes must be common to two adjacent basic triangular facets. Only those triangular facets satisfying the above conditions are reasonable. But there are many ways to get such triangle facets. In the specific design and implementation of the modeling process, an optimal method must be chosen to solve this problem. Here we use the shortest diagonal algorithm to select vertexes on the two contours for connection [17], for this algorithm enjoys a relatively smaller amount of computation, fast computational speed, and local optima.

4 The Design of 3D Human Body Modeling System and Example of Model Modification

According to the above research findings, we use OpenGL graphics development kit under VC ++ development environment to design and develop the 3D human body modeling system based on key characteristic parameters. The main interface of the developed system is shown in Fig. 7.

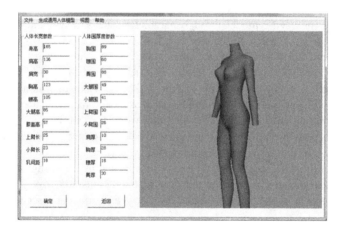

Fig. 7. The main interface of the 3D human body modeling system

The left side of the system is a parameter panel, used to set the body characteristic parameters that affect the dressing effect. The system, based on standard human body characteristic parameters, first generates general models for adults or children. And then the user modifies these parameters according to their actual size and changes the general models into a personalized 3D human body model. For example, a 3D model of a pregnant woman can be generated by modifying parameters such as chest circumference, loin circumference, hip thickness, loin depth, etc., as is shown in Fig. 8 below.

The experimental result shows that the 3D human body model based on key characteristic parameters can more quickly and effectively generate the 3D human body model suitable for virtual fitting.

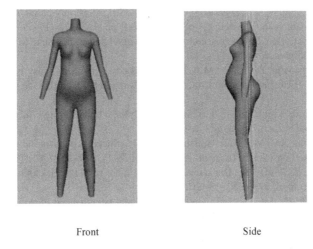

Front   Side

Fig. 8. The 3D Human Body Model of a Pregnant Woman

5 Conclusion

This paper studies the 3D human body modeling based on key characteristic parameters for virtual fitting. The key technology is to establish the contour line model of the key parts of human body based on parametric description of the relevant dimensions of human body that affect the dressing effect, and then to model the entire human body surface through these contour lines. The main idea is to control the shaping of the 3D human body model with key measurable parameters of human body, enabling users to change the body shape simply by modifying the key characteristic parameters. In his way, personalized 3D human body model can be created quickly and users can conveniently get a virtual model in line with their own body size to try on clothes virtually. It finally gives a wonderful solution for e-commerce users to try on clothes before buying proper pieces.

Acknowledgement. This paper is supported by Zhejiang Provincial Natural Science Foundation of China (Grant No. LY17F020003) science and technology funding project (Research on efficient image and video editing methods for preserving semantics, No. 2017RC10) in Lishui and Lishui University University-level research projects (Grant No. KY201333).

References

1. Magnenat-Thalmann, N., Kevelham, B., Volino, P., et al.: 3D web-based virtual try on of physically simulated clothes. Comput. Aid. Des. Appl. **8**(2), 163–174 (2011)
2. Chen, L., Zhao, S., Zhang, L., et al.: History and research hot spot of 3D virtual garment display. J. Text. Res. **32**(10), 153–160 (2011)
3. Chen, M.: Parametric 3D Human Body Modeling and System Implementation. Nanjing University, Nanjing (2014)

4. ScheePers, F., Parent, R.E., Carlson, W.E., May, S.F.: Anatomy-based modeling of the human musculature. In: Proceedings of SIGGRAPH, pp. 163–172 (1997)
5. Zhong, Z., Li, H., Luo, S.: The research of digital virtual person in China. In: The Memoir of Xiangshan Conference, pp. 4–12 (2001)
6. Weiss, A., Hirshberg, D., Black, M.J.: Home: 3D body scans from noisy im-age and range data. In: 2011 IEEE International Conference on Computer Vision (ICCV), pp. 1951–1958. IEEE (2011)
7. Tong, J., Zhou, J., Liu, L., et al.: Scanning 3D full human bodies using ki-nects. IEEE Trans. Visual. Comput. Graph. 18(4), 643–650 (2012)
8. Yu, S., Yu, X., Xu, W., et al.: Splicing 3D body blocking point cloud data and model rebuilding based on Kinect. Comput. Appl. Softw. 33(1), 219–221 (2016)
9. Yang, Z., Yu, Z., Yang, Y.: The standardized treatment of 3D point cloud data. J. Beijing Inst. Cloth. Technol. 37(3), 12–18 (2017)
10. Zhang, K., Liu, H., Lu, T., et al.: High precision and personalized human body modeling method based on single Kinect. Acquis. Process. Data 30(5), 1085–1090 (2015)
11. Yang, Y., Yang, Z., Ye, L.: The identification of human trunk characteristic points based on 3D point cloud data. J. Beijing Inst. Cloth. Technol. 35(2), 29–34 (2015)
12. Chen, L.: Research and Implementation of 3D Clothing Modeling Technology. Wuhan Textile University, Wuhan (2013)
13. Zhu, S.Y.: A Method of Efficient Human Model Customization Based on Monocular Orthogonal Image. The Hong Kong Polytechnic University (2013)
14. Wang, W., Dong, H., Zhang, H.: The 3D Internet clothing display technology for mass customization. Silk 53(12), 29–35 (2016)
15. Seo, H., Cordier, F., Thalmann, N.M.: Synthesizing animatable body models with parameterized shape modifications. In: Proceedings of ACM SIGGRAPH/Eurographics Symposium on Computer Animation, pp. 120–125 (2003)
16. Hu, X.: Research on Key Technologies of Dynamic Simulation of Fabrics Used for Clothing. Huazhong University of Science and Technology, Wuhan (2008)
17. Wang, X., Chen, Y., Wang, J.: Research on 3D human body modeling based on human body slices. Softw. Guide 10(8), 145–146 (2011)

Hierarchical-Layout Treemap
for Context-Based Visualization

Jingtao Wang[1], Yinwen Shen[2], Dingke Kong[2], and Jing Hua[2($\boxtimes$)]

[1] School of Computer Science, Harbin Institute of Technique, Harbin, China
[2] School of Computer Science and Information Engineering, Zhejiang
Gongshang University, Hangzhou 310018, China
xwang@zjgsu.edu.cn

Abstract. In order to represent hierarchical information more efficiently and aesthetically on mobile devices, many researchers have adopted the space-filling method—Treemap. In this article, a novel dynamic hierarchical-layout algorithm is proposed to visualize hierarchical information on mobile devices. This layout algorithm tries to represent the hierarchical data set with more balanced aspect ratio for the rectangles which is closely related to the aesthetics of treemap. Furthermore, a focus+context fisheye distortion algorithm is introduced to help users understand details by increasing the size of the interested items while decreasing the others. Experimental results show that the proposed method can provide a suitable resolution for visualizing hierarchical information with high efficiency and give focus+context views on mobile devices in real time.

Keywords: Treemap visualization · Hierarchy navigation
Dynamic context-based layout · Focus+context distortion

1 Introduction

As is well known, most information in the world is hierarchical information and the most common form of hierarchical representation is the so-called treemap, which is capable of representing hierarchical data [1]. It works by dividing the display area into rectangles whose areas correspond to an attribute such as a value or proportion of the hierarchical data set. Spatial positions between rectangles indicate the relationship of nodes. Treemap can make efficient display of space, thereby representing more hierarchical data sets. Now treemap has been widely applied in this world due to its advantages [2].

Previous methods on treemap can be categorized into two general categories: layout algorithms and interaction algorithms. The first category consists of the layout algorithms for browsing hierarchy structures through space-filling visualizations [1]. The second relates to the techniques that have been specially developed for browsing the details and the context in treemap.

1.1 Layout Algorithms

The original treemap layout algorithm uses parallel lines to divide a rectangle into smaller ones to represent the node and its children [1]. This method creates the layout

© Springer-Verlag GmbH Germany, part of Springer Nature 2018
Z. Pan et al. (Eds.): Transactions on Edutainment XIV, LNCS 10790, pp. 27–39, 2018.
https://doi.org/10.1007/978-3-662-56689-3_3

that contains rectangles with high aspect ratio which leads to the loss of aesthetics and becomes hard to detect the details.

Shneiderman and Wattenberg proposed a novel layout algorithm, namely ordered treemap layout [4]. This method keeps the original order of the data set and tries to address the instability occurred in the dynamically data updating.

But most work is not suitable for displaying quantum-sized objects, such as images. Benjamin B. Bederson, Martin Wattenberg and Dow Jones introduced the quantum treemap to accommodate the items such as photos [6].

Moreover existing treemap layout algorithms suffer from poor mapping between data order and visual order to some extents. Jo Wood and Jason Dykes generalized the existing squarified algorithm so as to exploit nodes more effectively to display geographical statistics data [7].

However, quite a small proportion of the space results in awfully small size of the rectangles due to the lack of details, which may become difficult to be recognized [3]. Therefore, this motives the interaction for treemap.

1.2   Interaction for Treemap

The interaction for treemap explores the set of hierarchical data in-depth, including the basic operations and the distortion methods.

The basic interaction for treemap is drill-down and roll-up. Drill-down and roll-up navigate the further or former level of the node which gives the detail about its children or father [12].

Compared to the basic interaction, Liqun Jin and David C. Banks extended See-Through interface proposed by Bier and Stone's [7] and introduced an interactive system called TennisViewer. It is used for visualizing the dynamic and tree-structured tennis match data [8]. They adopted Magic Lenses to explore the information at lower layers which can be laid atop each other easily to produce deep zooming.

Keahey and Visual Insights, Inc. described how focus+context techniques can be integrated into other high-level visualization paradigms [9].

Furthermore, a distortion algorithm based on fisheye and continuous zooming techniques is introduced to browse the data in treemap representation by Shi, Iranni and Li [10]. Their distortion algorithm increases the size of the interested node while shrinking its neighbors.

Ying Tu and Han-Wei Shen presented a seamless multi-focus and context technique, called Balloon Focus. It allows users to smoothly enlarge multiple treemap items as the focus, while maintaining a stable treemap layout as the context [11].

In this article, a novel context-based hierarchical-layout algorithm is introduced to represent the hierarchical information on mobile devices more effectively. Furthermore, a focus+context distortion algorithm is proposed to help users understand the items.

2   Materials and Methods

In this section, a novel context-based hierarchical layout algorithm which extends the ordered layout algorithm [5] is presented in detail. The algorithm explores better aspect ratio of the rectangles by splitting the total value into one or two parts. Meanwhile, a novel focus+context distortion algorithm imitating fisheye is proposed in the way of increasing the interest and shrinking the others.

2.1 Data Structures

Each item in treemap data sets represented hierarchically as father and children like tree. Each node must contain enough information such as its size and label in order to represent the details of the item.

A node is defined by the following information:

- **Label (name):** it represents the name of the node, such as the menswear of a dress.
- **Size (weight):** it represents the size or the weight of the node in data set. It may be the size of the file for a data file or the value of a certain product sale.
- **Parent:** it points to the parent node.
- **Children:** this field contains an array of pointers to each of its children.
- **Width, Height:** the width and height of the rectangle influence the aspect ratio as it is drawn on the display area. These values are computed according to its size and the width and height of the display area.

In addition, this article also introduces several important data items for the distortion algorithm. The constant MIN_SIZE represents the smallest size that the node should increase to maintain enough information. The variable—sign will denote the number (one or two) of rectangles to be drawn, and is determined by the layout algorithm and the node size. A variable flag is employed to represent the orientation of the rectangle.

2.2 Hierarchical-Layout Treemap for Context-Based

The following layout algorithm extends the work by Shneiderman and Wattenberg [4]. It adopted the constant DIFF to determine the number of the rectangles drawn at the same time. Through this method, the algorithm gives the advantageous block aspect ratio for representing hierarchical information on mobile devices. The procedure of layout algorithm (see Fig. 1) will be described below.

Step 1: Sort the nodes
Sort the nodes in decreasing order according to the size (value or proportion) of each item in data set at the same level.

Step 2: Divide the nodes into two arrays
The function getPerfectSplitNumber is defined to search the advantageous split number of the blocks drawn at the same time. Since the nodes have already been sorted in Step 1, the nodes are further divided into two partitions: ArrayA and ArrayB, which contain the biggest node and the remaining notes respectively.

Step 3: Get the advantageous split number
The ratio denotes the division of the value in ArrayA by the total value at the same level. Then HEIGHT and WIDTH are used to set to the width and height of the ArrayA according to the following criteria.

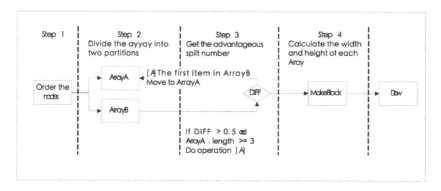

Fig. 1. The procedure of the proposed layout algorithm

$$\begin{cases} width = WIDTH, height = HEIGHT * ratio \\ when\ WIDTH < = HEIGHT \\ width = WIDTH * ratio, height = HEIGHT \\ when\ WIDTH > HEIGHT \end{cases}$$

The algorithm assists the division of width by height to the variable of ratioWH and the division of height by width. Then DIFF is calculated as follows.

$$\begin{cases} DIFF = 1 - ratioWH\ when\ width < height \\ DIFF = 1 - ratioHW\ when\ height > = width \end{cases}$$

If DIFF >0.5 and the length of the array ArrayA >= 3 then the advantageous split number is set to 2; otherwise 1. This means that the number of the rectangles which are drawn at the same time is 2 or 1.

Step 4: Set the height and the width for both arrays (rectangles)
If DIFF is more than 0.5, move the first node of ArrayB to ArrayA and calculate the width and height for ArrayA and ArrayB. Then Step 3 is performed recursively to calculate the advantageous split number.

Step 5: Draw rectangles
When the split number of the rectangles is 1, draw the rectangle with the width and height assigned by the method in Step 3 until all rectangles are finished.

2.3   Focus+Context Distortion

The distortion algorithm increases the size of the interest node and decreases the size of the others. To keep the original position of the node when distorted, the variable flag is introduced to represent the orientation of the rectangle and is combined with the advantageous split number. When flag equals 0 (or 1), it means the orientation of the rectangle is horizontal (or vertical). The constant MIN_SIZE donates the minimum size of the interested node to be increased when the size is less than MIN_SIZE. Otherwise, the size will be increased to three times of the original size.

The distortion algorithm gives the focus+context view of the interested nodes. This interaction is activated when the finger moves on the focus and is deactivated when the finger moves away the touch screen. The algorithm will efficiently find the corresponding node as the finger moves on the region. The procedure is described as follows.

Step 1: achieve the orientation of the rectangles

The orientation of the rectangles is determined in the process of the width and the height setting. Setting the width of the rectangle to WIDTH and the height to HEIGHT*ratio when WIDTH is less than HEIGHT means the orientation of the rectangle is determined by the value of the flag. The value of flag is 1 represents the vertical orientation when WIDTH is bigger than HEIGHT.

Step 2: catch the split number of the nodes at the level

The split number and the orientation determine the layout of all nodes at the same level. They guarantee the order and layout of all nodes when distorted.

Step 3: calculate the size of the interest node and the others

The default size that the interested node will be increased is three times the original size. But the distortion size must be at least the MIN_SIZE.

At last, the focus+context fisheye distortion works.

3   Experimental Results

The layout algorithm and the focus+context fisheye distortion algorithm are applied on the Android platform. The data set is constructed according to the hierarchical data storing in JSON document which is known as a lightweight data interchange format based on JavaScript. Some experiments are implemented as follows.

Experiment 1 shown in Fig. 2 was designed to display the weight of each part which makes up the visualization such as util, query and animate. The JSON document constructs the data set as the hierarchical data with multi-level of father and children. The labels including name and weight of the rectangle are displayed to give the details about the nodes.

The data set about composition of visualization methods is represented by the familiar hierarchical visualization—Tree, which has the drawback of low space usage in Fig. 2(a). Compared to the Tree, treemap describes the nodes with the attributes of name and proportion in Fig. 2(b). It shows the full-usage of screen rather than Tree. In Fig. 2(b), some rectangles may be too small to understand the details for the reason of the smaller proportion especially in the bottom right corner surrounding the red box. When the focus moves to that rectangle, the focus+context fisheye distortion algorithm will work, as shown in Fig. 2(c). The size of the rectangle increases to three times the original size as presented by the red box in Fig. 2(c). So users can quickly catch the details of the interested node including the name and the weight.

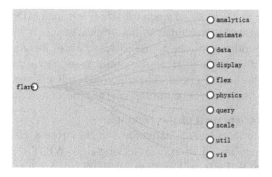

(a) data set at the first level

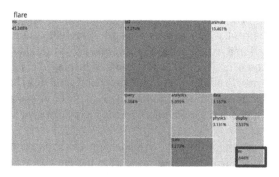

(b) normal view of the treemap

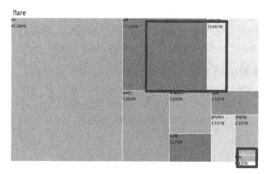

(c) distortion view of the treemap

Fig. 2. Treemap layout and focus+context distortion (Color figure online)

Drilling-down by finger touching on the region of the rectangle is also implemented.

The second experiment is also aimed to represent the actual sales data from taobao. com by layout method and focus+context distortion algorithm on mobile devices. Part of the data set is described in Fig. 4(a) by Tree. Figure 4(b) and (d) demonstrate the data with red circle and blue circle respectively. These two charts have the same

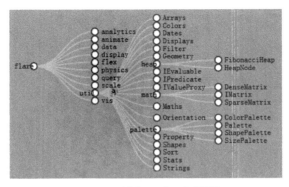

(a) children of node UTIL

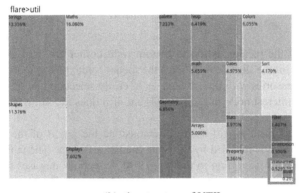

(b) the structure of UTIL

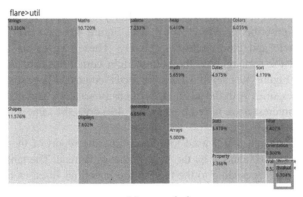

(c) normal view

Fig. 3. Visualization and distortion of node UTIL (Color figure online)

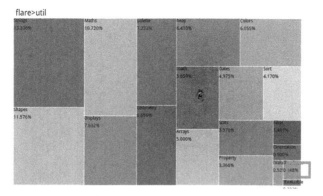

(d) distortion of node PREDICATE

Fig. 3. (*continued*)

characteristic that the rectangles in the bottom right corner are hard to select, understand and divide. Figure 4(c) demonstrates the focus+context fisheye distortion of node photographic accessories with the advantages of easily selecting and understanding the details about the interest node in red box. Figure 4(e) does the same work as Fig. 4(c) in blue box.

The third experiment is still used to demonstrate the report of the infectious diseases in China, which is released by the State Statistics Bureau. The table of data set is divided into two parts according to the type of the infectious diseases that contain the Class (A and B) infectious diseases and infectious disease C. The construct of the data is represented by Tree in Fig. 5(a).

The second experiment is also aimed to represent the actual sales data from taobao. com by layout method and focus+context distortion algorithm on mobile devices. Part of the data set is described in Fig. 4(a) by Tree. Figure 4(b) and (d) demonstrate the data with red circle and blue circle respectively. These two charts have the same characteristic that the rectangles in the bottom right corner are hard to select, understand and divide. Figure 4(c) demonstrates the focus+context fisheye distortion of node photographic accessories with the advantages of easily selecting and understanding the details about the interest node in red box. Figure 4(e) does the same work as Fig. 4(c) in blue box.

The third experiment is still used to demonstrate the report of the infectious diseases in China, which is released by the State Statistics Bureau. The table of data set is divided into two parts according to the type of the infectious diseases that contain the Class (A and B) infectious diseases and infectious disease C. The construct of the data is represented by Tree in Fig. 5(a).

The experiment with hierarchical-layout algorithm is presented in Fig. 5(b) and (d). This layout sorts the number of the death and sets the advantageous aspect of the

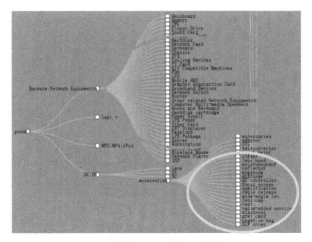

(a) composition of Tree

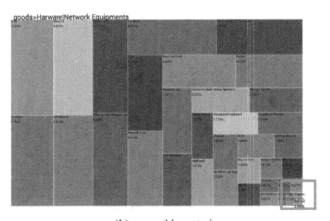

(b) normal layout view

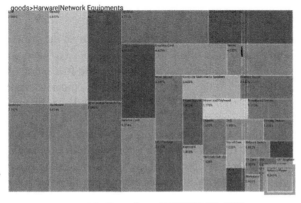

(c) distortion of PHOTOGRAPH

Fig. 4. Visualization and distortion presentation (Color figure online)

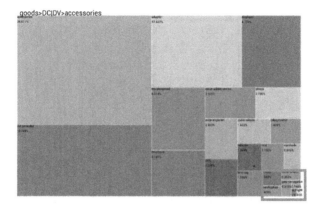

(d) normal view of LIGHT

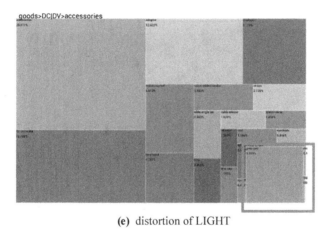

(e) distortion of LIGHT

Fig. 4. (*continued*)

rectangles for the nodes. In Fig. 5(b), users can easily discover the drawback caused by the layout: the bottom right corner of the display area looks crowded and it is hard to select the red box. Figure 5(c) solves this problem by the focus+context fisheye distortion algorithm. The size of the interested node of epidemic encephalitis B is increased to three times the original size in Fig. 3(c) with red box. Figure 5(e) also does the same work as described in Fig. 5(c).

The three experiments on Android platform are designed to evaluate the effectiveness and aspect ratio of rectangles by the novel methods on mobile devices. The results suggest that the subjects are faster at browsing and locating objects of interests in the layout. The effect will not be influenced even when there are a large number of nodes at the same level.

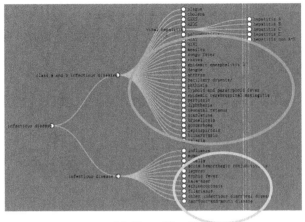

(a) Tree of the disease

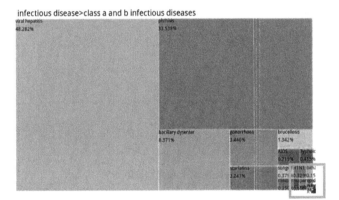

(b) unclear layout view

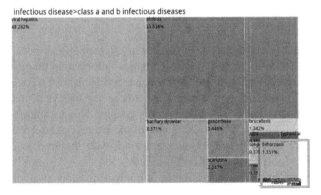

(c) distortion of BILHARZIASIS

Fig. 5. Comparison between tree and treemap and distortion of interest (Color figure online)

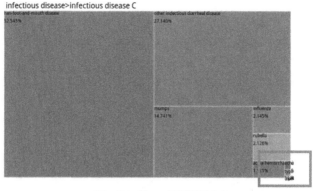

(d) distortion of RUBELLA

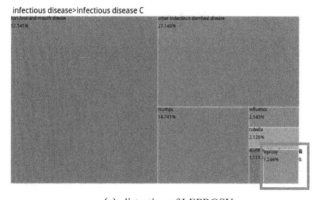

(e) distortion of LEPROSY

Fig. 5. (*continued*)

4 Conclusions and Future Work

The novel dynamic hierarchical-layout algorithm of treemap has been introduced to efficiently and aesthetically represent the hierarchical information on mobile devices as on PCs. This method has better layout performance with balanced aspect ratio which is closely related to the ascetics of treemap. Furthermore, the fisheye distortion algorithm helps users understand the details of the items deeply. This technique simulates the fisheye distortion in the way of increasing size of the interest and decreasing the other. This method gives a real-time focus+context view with the smooth transformation between the normal view and the distortion view.

Additional work under consideration is to improve the layout algorithm to better suit different data set which may cause the disadvantageous aspect ratio. The layout algorithm should enhance the adaptive ability to the distinct pieces of data.

In addition, another variation of the distortion is to consider more than one node distortion at the same time. The further work can be organized as the nodes in the circular region with certain radius increase. In this paper, only the linear distortion is considered, the nonlinear distortion of the fisheye will be investigated.

Acknowledgement. This work was supported in part by the National Key Technology Research and Development Program of the Ministry of Science and Technology of China (No. 2014BAK14B01), National Natural Science Foundation of China (No. 61379075), Zhoushan Municipal Science and Technology Plan Project (No.142014C21035). The authors are grateful for the anonymous reviewers who made constructive comments.

References

1. Shneiderman, B.: Tree visualization with treemaps: a 2D space-filling approach. ACM Trans. Graph. **11**, 92–99 (1992)
2. Jungmeister, W.A., Turo, D.: Adapting treemaps to stock portfolio visualization. Technical Report CS-TR-2996. University of Maryland, College Park, USA (1996)
3. Bruls, M., Huizing, K., van Wijk, J.: Squarified treemaps. In: Proceedings of the Joint Eurographics and IEEE TCVG Symposium on Visualization, 29–30 May 2000, Amsterdam, Netherlands, pp. 33–42 (2000)
4. Shneiderman, B., Wattenberg, M.: Ordered treemap layouts. In: Proceedings of the IEEE Symposium on Information Visualization, 22–23 October 2001, San Diego, CA, USA, pp. 73–78 (2001)
5. Wood, J., Dykes, J.: Spatially ordered treemaps. IEEE Trans. Visual. Comput. Graphics **14**, 1348–1355 (2008)
6. Bederson, B.B., Shneiderman, B., Wattenberg, M.: Ordered and quantum treemaps: making effective use of 2D space to display hierarchies. ACM Trans. Graphics **21**, 833–854 (2002)
7. Bier, E.A., Stone, M.C., Pier, K., Buxton, W., DeRose, T.D.: Toolglass and magic lenses: The see-through interface. In: Proceedings of the 20th Annual Conference on Computer Graphics and Interactive Techniques, 2–6 August 1993, Anaheim, CA, USA, pp. 73–80 (1993)
8. Jin, L., Banks, D.C.: TennisViewer: a browser for competition trees. IEEE Comput. Graphics Appl. **7**, 63–65 (1997)
9. Keahey, T.A.: Getting along: composition of visualization paradigms. In: Proceedings of the IEEE Symposium on Information Visualization, 22–23 October 2001, San Diego, CA, USA, pp. 37–40 (2001)
10. Shi, K., Irani, P., Li, B.: An evaluation of content browsing techniques for hierarchical space-filling visualizations. In: Proceedings of the IEEE Symposium on Information Visualization, 23–25 October 2005, Minneapolis, MN, USA, pp. 81–88 (2005)
11. Tu, Y., Shen, H.W.: Balloon focus: A seamless multi-focus+context method for treemaps. IEEE Trans. Vis. Comput. Graphics **14**, 1157–1164 (2008)
12. Turo, D., Johnson, B.: Improving the visualization of hierarchies with treemaps: design issues and experimentation. In: Proceedings of the IEEE 3rd Annual Conference on Visualization, October 19–23, 1992, Boston, MA, USA, pp. 124–131 (1992)

3D Indoor Environment Modeling and Detection of Moving Object and Scene Understanding

Bin Shao[1,2(✉)] and Zhimin Yan[3]

[1] School of Information Engineering,
Huzhou University, Huzhou 313000, China
shaobin@zjhu.edu.cn
[2] State Key Laboratory of CAD&CG,
Zhejiang University, Hangzhou 310027, China
[3] School of Teachers' Education,
Huzhou University, Huzhou 313000, Zhejiang, China
yzml211@zjhu.edu.cn

Abstract. Obtaining large-scale outdoor city environment is a mature technique, supporting many applications, such as search, navigation, etc. The indoor environment with same complexity often contains high density duplicate objects (e.g. table, chair, display, etc.). In this paper, special structure of indoor environment was applied to accelerate home video camera to conduct 3D collection and identification of indoor environment. There are two stages of this method: (i) Learning stage, gain three-dimensional model of objects which occurs frequently and variation pattern with only few scanning capture, (ii) identification stage, determine the objects which had been seen before but in different gestures and positions from the single scanning of a new field, which greatly accelerate identification process.

In addition, under indoor environment, detection of moving objects, such as lighting change, is also arduous task. Basic histons and histons roughness index (HRI) related to it have been reported by literature. It has impressive achievement for the segmentation of still image. We expand histons definition to 3D histons and consider the combined mode of the whole color plane, but not to consider single color plane. Besides, bring fuzziness into 3D HRI measurement. Move the object in accordance with the concept of rough set theory, change background gradually or set dynamic background as background, and pixel labeled at the same time won't let the objects that move slowly bring into background model.

Common home video camera was used to obtain typical area of a university construction, including classroom and laboratory, to prove result of the method we adopted, by qualitative and quantitative analysis, was satisfying.

Keywords: Image processing · Indoor environment modeling
Scene understanding · 3D histons · Rough set

© Springer-Verlag GmbH Germany, part of Springer Nature 2018
Z. Pan et al. (Eds.): Transactions on Edutainment XIV, LNCS 10790, pp. 40–55, 2018.
https://doi.org/10.1007/978-3-662-56689-3_4

1 Introduction

At present, the research of video surveillance has been developing greatly, for example, the investigative monitoring technology of safety demand in sensitive area (airport, office, railway station, etc.), and the detection of moving objects is one of basic steps of video surveillance. Acquisition of outdoor environment has obtained significant progress currently. However, capture of indoor 3D environment of private and public office building is still challenging. Further challenge is the change of building interior objects: e.g. open and close of doors and windows, around movement of chairs, rearrangement of plank-partitioned rooms, etc.

At the same time, low-cost camera is convenient for use and so it is widely used. This will be possible to carry out large indoor environment collection. Yet high frame speed and increase of portability are often on the cost of resolution ratio and data quality, and the scanning result usually is noisy in suitable schemes. Therefore, although we can acquire plenty of data very quickly, there is no general algorithm to abstract high level scene understanding. Furthermore, outer door of building is basically flat and has sufficient gap for scanning, while generally there are complex shapes, many connections and environment is crowded in indoor. Consequently, the traditional acquisition method that carries out different angles and multi semi-automatic scanning in a typical setting and establishes a 3D model finally, is not suitable.

But there are the following three assumptions to process corresponding problems for indoor environment 3D data acquisition:

(i) The basic elements of most offices or public building indoor composition, such as wall, door, window, furniture (table, chair, desk, desk lamp, computer, cabinet, etc.), are repeated a number of times by a few prototypes.

(ii) These building components are usually rigid parts and their geometries are often locally simple, namely they are common shapes, e.g. cylinder, cone, sphere, etc. Additionally, changes and connections are dominant (movement of chair or its base rotation, door's rotation, light's fold, etc.), and these changes are limited and low dimensionality (e.g. translation, connection, flexible, etc.).

(iii) Correlations of basic objects meet strong apriority (e.g. chair standing on the floor, display on the table, etc.).

Based on the above assumptions, a simple and effective method is proposed to acquire the models of indoor objects, e.g. furniture, combined with their change model and repeat of objects, and accelerate the high level scene understanding for large indoor acquisition by the use of it.

Detection of moving objects relies on background deduction method of establishing background model to detect the moving objects that deviate background model. But these methods are sensitive, for example, shadow change and lighting change have very large challenge for detection. Though there are several methods of background deduction method [1, 2], the problems still are not be effectively solved.

Background deduction method is roughly divided into methods pixel-based and block-based method. For pixel-based methods [3–5], each pixel is believed to be independent. Background interference will affect the characteristics of pixels, also their background models. Hence, these methods can't be used effectively under the environment with rapid background change.

In block-based methods, block level attribute of each frame is divided into overlapped block and non overlapped block [6–10]. In these two methods, the robustness of block-based background modeling for background change is strong due to background interference influence of only a few pixel blocks. For non overlapped block-based method, carry out detection at block level for model and foreground. Detection of moving objects in these methods is too rough for overlapped block method.

For method based on overlapped block, each pixel imitates block attribute and carry out foreground detection at pixel level. Because this method is detected under pixel level, its shape precision is superior to non overlapped block. Therefore, overlapped block-based method is preferred.

Overlapped block-based method adopts histogram—RGB histogram [6], local duality mode histogram [7, 8], local kernel histogram [9], local dependent histogram [10] in many forms, and there is no spatial information function for these method, very sensitive for background interference. Hence, properties of these algorithms based on histogram decrease rapidly in complex background, such as camera shake, shadow, disguise, illumination change, etc.

Consequently, on the enlightening of segmentation performance of still image used by Mushrif and Ray [11], histons concept is introduced. This concept was put forward by Mohabey and Ray [12, 13] and was carried out background modeling under rough set theoretical frame. Histons is a new concept, calculating number of pixel similar to color sphere range for each strength value in base histogram and calculate histons value of this strength by adding this value into histogram. Histogram and histons distribution shows its color and spatial information in comprehensive use. The same distribution of histogram and a block histons indicates that this block is short of similar space. Value of this block is used for simulating existing regional center pixel, and formulate the histons concept associated to rough set theory—histons flatness index (HRI). Advantages of HRI lie in that it uses color and spatial information.

In original histons [12, 13], each color channel is taken into consideration separately, calculating the histons of this color channel independently. However, the value of each pixel and its three color component determine a 3D spatial distribution together, providing spatial distribution detained information of three independent color plane.

Considering on this point, an integrated 3D histons concept is proposed to consider color values of three channels together. HRI 3D distribution of one block concentrates on one pixel for calculating and using 3D histons and 3D histogram.

2   Relevant Works

2.1   3D Indoor Environments

The method that Dey carries out surface reconstruction from scattered points has been widely studied [14] in the fields of computer graphics, computation geometry, computer vision, etc. However, main goals of us are different. We focus on acquiring and understanding large 3D indoor environment.

In the aspect of scanning technique, due to development of recent real time scanning, common user can easily get high frame speed 3D data, though some frame quality is poor. Hence, researcher Henry and Izadi put forward the algorithm that obtains better quality from several scanning [15, 16]. Unfortunately, this method may cause ghosting if camera or site moves suddenly during scanning process.

In the aspect of scanning processing, Rusinkiewicz et al. [17] firstly proposed the possibility of real time lightweight 3D scanning. In their frame, users held camera by hand, while system would update models to provide real time visual feedback to guide the next scanning for users. In other relevant studies, researcher Allen adopted formwork mode to know human space [18], Li used non rigid alignment for adapting many times scanning [19], and Zheng applied non local repeat to consolidate point cloud of city appearance [20]. Nonetheless, these methods don't abstract reasonable high level scene understanding appropriately from sparse and messy deformation input model.

In the aspect of shape analysis, objects of artificial filling indoor scene generally have low degree of freedom, and often arrange simply. Schnabel et al. [21] introduced an algorithm that abstracted basic shapes (e.g. plane, cylinder, sphere, etc.) of scattered point cloud automatically. Subsequently, Lee et al. abstracted a set consistent relation (e.g. coplane, coaxial, equal length, etc.) from GlobFit [22] and conformed to recover relation of reverse engineering. Moreover, Chang and Zwicker used space-time information of many frames to trace combination information, to recover deformation model [23].

In the aspect of image understanding, Lee et al. [24] established an indoor scene reconstruction on the basis of measuring volume, while Gupta et al. [25] obtained block-based 3D scene model by the use of geometric constraint and machinery factor. Under the condition of 3D scanning, some studies were on scene understanding of large data set. Boyko et al. [26] abstracted high level information from the noisy outdoor street. We'll abstract rapid and effective scene to understand high level information of indoor environment.

2.2 Detection and Understanding of Moving Objects in Indoor Environment

Definition of 3D histons: on the basis of original histons definition, for derivation histons [12, 13] of each color channel, single 3D histons and bin index was used to calculate values of three color components, and thus achieved complete color information. Actually, there were many information of color distribution, while three independent white-and-black distribution only existed in very few tonal colors. Additionally, didn't consider the mutually dependent fact of three channels, but considered distribution of each color channel respectively. This prompted us to formulate 3D histons, which is set of all points within radius range of one regional 3D histogram top sphere of one surface drawing method.

Definitions of 3D histogram (h) and 3D histons (H) are as follows:

$$h(i,j,k) = \sum_{m=1}^{M} \sum_{n=1}^{N} \delta(I(m,n) - (i,j,k)) \tag{1}$$

$$\text{for } 0 \leq i \leq l_1 - 1, \, 0 \leq j \leq l_2 - 1, \, 0 \leq k \leq l_3 - 1$$

$$H(i,j,k) = \sum_{m=1}^{M} \sum_{n=1}^{N} (1 + X(m,n))\delta(I(m,n) - (i,j,k)) \tag{2}$$

$$\text{for } 0 \leq i \leq l_1 - 1, \, 0 \leq j \leq l_2 - 1, \, 0 \leq k \leq l_3 - 1$$

Where:

$$X(m,n) = \begin{cases} 1, & d_T(m,n) < \text{Default threshold value} \\ 0, & otherwise \end{cases} \tag{3}$$

$$d_T(m,n) = \sum_{p=m-\lfloor R_S/2 \rfloor}^{m+\lfloor R_S/2 \rfloor} \sum_{q=n-\lfloor R_S/2 \rfloor}^{n+\lfloor R_S/2 \rfloor} \sqrt{\sum_{c\in(R,G,B)} (I(m,n,c) - I(p,q,c))^2} \tag{4}$$

I(m, n) represents the RGB value of one pixel (m, n) in M * N region, and (i, j, k) is bin index. $\delta(\bullet)$ is impulse function. $d_T(m, n)$ is sum of color distance between one pixel (m, n) and adjacent block with $R_S * R_S$ size. Quantity each color channel $L_i (L_i \ll 256 \text{ AND } i \in \{1,2,3\})$ to reduce calculation amount.

3D histons roughness index: histogram and histons can link concept of similar space and rough set theory [27]. Histogram can use lower approximate relevance to give the number of pixel I ($I \in (0, \Box l–1)$) with same strength, and can contact with infimum. Histons gives the number of pixel I with approximate strength, and it can contact with supremum. Calculate strength value of each basic histogram in accordance with the pixel number of color approximate field, and add this value into histogram to obtain histons strength. In one pixel point-centered block, similarity of each bin value shows that this block is totally anisotropic, namely, no space correlation existed in this block. This attribute can be defined by 3D histons roughness index (3D HRI) (refer to formula 5). Numerical value of 3D HRI is greater in homogenic region than in anisotropic region. Similarity of space and color information can be embedded into 3D HRI, while histogram only owns only color information. This is advantage of 3D HRI.

Definitions of 3D roughness index (3D HRI) are:

$$\text{3D HRI} = \rho(i,j,k) = 1 - \frac{h(i,j,k)}{H(i,j,k)} \tag{5}$$

3D fuzzy histons: when calculating histons, whether pixel (m, n) belongs to same color space relies on threshold value. Selection of threshold value is heuristic, having considerable influence on segment output. The degree of similarity (formula 6) of its same neighborhood is determined by Gaussian membership function but by clear classification, one 3D fuzzy histons, and this is expanded from basic fuzzy histons proposed by Mushrif and Ray [11].

$$X(m,n) = e^{-\frac{1}{2}\left(\frac{d_T}{\sigma}\right)^2} \tag{6}$$

It's distance of standard deviation. Low D_T means higher similarity, vice versa.

Definitions of 3D fuzzy histons (H_F) and 3D fuzzy histons roughness index ($\rho_F\Box$) are as follows:

$$H_F(i,j,k) = \sum_{m=1}^{M}\sum_{n=1}^{N}(1+X(m,n))\delta(I(m,n)-(i,j,k))$$

$$\text{for } 0 \le i \le l_1 - 1, 0 \le j \le l_2 - 1, 0 \le k \le l_3 - 1 \tag{7}$$

$$\text{3D FHRI} = \rho_F(i,j,k) = 1 - \frac{h(i,j,k)}{H_F(i,j,k)}$$

3 Modeling of Indoor Environment

Modeling method of indoor environment is mainly two stages: learning and identification.

In learning stage, scan (often scan 5–10 times from different angles) several times for the each interested object. The target of us is to fixedly divide scanned scene into some parts and connection of identification parts, to recover respective border attributes. Two characteristics of scene are used: (I) approximate the object (e.g. surface, box, round, etc.) by one simple element set; (II) connection between elements is limited (e.g. connection, translation, etc.) and with low complexity. Recover each scanned element set firstly. For each object, process all scanning together to abstract representative based on one element. Consequently, we obtain models M_1, M_2 ...

In identification stage, abstract the dominating plane—usually refers to ground, wall, desk, etc., on site start from the single on-site scanning S. Identify ground plane first, desk plane parallel with ground as label. Delete points of ground plane and optional desk plane and implement the other points (neighbor joining chart) connection component analysis to abstract point set S_1, S_2 ...

Test whether each point set S_i can give satisfying interpretation for object model M_j. However, this step is challenging, because data is unreliable and angle change may cause very big geometric change. A new type markov random field (MRF) is used and simple two-point prior scene is combined to solve this problem: (i) positional relationship (e.g. display on the desk, chair on the ground, etc.), (ii) there is allowable repeat mode for each model (e.g. display usually horizontal repeat, repeat of chair on the ground, etc.).

3.1 Learning Stage

Input of learning stage is a group of point cloud P_1, P_2, ..., P_n, and is the same object in different scenes. The target is to establish model M composed of joint connection parts. Please note that although scanning of this stage is seldom unstable, once there is sufficient data for establishing model M, subsequent identification stage will be simple and reliable. In learning stage, segment each point set P_i to set of element P_i^j. Then, establish corresponding relation of the entire scanning part and establish model M from the matched part. Please note that the conversion information t_i^j between parts of model and measured corresponding part can also be stored and abstracted, namely $T_j^i(p_j^i) \approx m_j$. Improve element by the use of conversion information t_i^j through the commonly matched parts in different measurements.

In this work, the selection of rigid, flexibility and rotation of round, square and connection type in element are confined. Finally, model M contains individual part element information and the deformation between them. In addition, necessary powerful matching can also be maintained. Height distribution of ground plane is prior to table, or objects can have preferred repeat direction, display or hall chair usually side repeat, etc. In identification stage, these attributes and relations can be as reliable rules when data is very sparse or noisy.

3.1.1 Single Original Matching

Original matching can believe to be alternate segmentation problem. For a set measurement, data is classified and each classification is composed of element set. Not to apply matched element to point directly, but segment point into a set patch points (x_1, x_2, ..., x_n). We obtain initial surface through repeat sampling seed point and repair of local plane patch. Such patch is enough to approximate surface and reduces complexity of problem. After confluence, ensure eigenvalue of each patch x_i to be $s_1(x_i) >= s_2(x_i) >= s_3(x_i)$, and its corresponding eigenvectors are respectively $e_1(x_i)$, $e_2(x_i)$ and $e_3(x_i)$.

Afterwards, begin from the larger patch as seed, and increase surrounding patches gradually. Carry out iteration between seeking candidate patch and seeking parameter, and keep these with sufficient proof, namely inlayer patch, to group the larger initial patches effectively. Initializations of patches are different from different elements. Algorithm is as follows:

Algorithm 1: complete a coherent model M step by step

For each i, when $\left| P_M^i \right| \rangle 0$, cyclic:

If $P_j^i \in P_M^i$, then cyclic: find a connection part $P_k^i \in P_M^i$, if such P_k^i exists, then

calculation the number of points at all measurement points and explain p_j^i by T_k^i,

Keeping the part with maximum count.

Added best candidate p_j^i to M and convert corresponding T_k^i to T^i

Add rotation or zooming if any measurement can't be explained by non deformation part

Delete the overlapped part P_M^i by new part.

End of cyclic;

End of algorithm.

Box: there are three mutually orthogonal directions $D_1, D_2, D_3 \in R^3$ of box parameter, offset $P_1, P_2, P_3 \in R$ and length along with respective direction $L_1, L_2, L_3 \in R$. If one of the following circumstances occurs, initialize one box parameter: (1) one patch has small normal change $\sigma_3(x_i) > \delta$ ($\delta = 0.01$), or (2) a pair of patches are nearly orthogonal, namely $e_1(x_i)^T e_1(x_j) \approx 0$. Under (1) circumstance, initialize one direction D_1 and offset P_1. When right angle adjacent patch (also applicable to initialization of circumstance (2)) is detected, then exchange two directions D_1 and D_2 as well as corresponding offsets P_1 and P_2 by actual value of new patch. Calculate the rest direction by formula $D_3 = D_1 \times D_2$. Otherwise, direction and length have attributes of main components, namely $e_1(x_i)$ approximates to e_2.

Cylinder: when one patch may be not plane, we'll match it to one cylinder, namely $\sigma_3(x_i) > \delta$ and is dreich, that is, $\sigma_2(x_i)/\sigma_1(x_i) < \rho$ ($\rho = 0.5$). Initialization of cylinder axle uses $E_1(x_i)$ and patch size, and the rest direction provides one initial radius.

3.1.2 Matching

When P^i was matching with $\left\{P_j^i\right\}$ one by one, work load war very large, so we compared adjacent elements and calculate how they overlapped, and selected the one with most overlapping. Consequently, bigger part shall be given priority, because smaller element may produce unstable matching, which was not unreliable in this stage. It was also observed that, a pair of elements and their relative positions formed local reference system. Added this pair of elements to current model M and aligned element measurement through adjusting parameters of connection fittings. And then exchanged matched element through converting model element $T_j^i \in T^i$. Note: measurement of P_i can be many conversions, because each part can deform with another parts.

3.1.3 Complete One Coherent Model

Measurement element $P_j^i \in P^i$ can map to current model P_M^i and can also map to $\overline{P_M^i}$ with unknown reasons. When matching step of a pair of parts is found in former step, begin from $\left|P_M^i\right| = 2$. Matched parts as seed parts carry out further matching and add to matched parts step by step (refer to Algorithm 1) for the remaining candidates.

Artificial structures are always layered. Therefore, it's believed that there are mirror symmetry and rotation symmetry in frame for each part of internal P_j^i cyclic test. Now describe how to consider such regularity in test phase.

Mirror symmetry: Test and measure each configuration of aspect. If there are n measurement objects, 2n parts that can be configured in the same element under mirror symmetry can be labeled and candidate as mirror symmetry. Symmetrical parts can also accept possible deformation. Optimum allocation is used to be in the place of all the detected symmetry conditions.

Rotation symmetry: Under rotation symmetry circumstance, not only seek reflection plane, but seek rotation axle. For any adjacent but not parallel mutually patches, find out approximate point or possible axle position. Then detect candidate axle position among all adjacent patches. If there is one position connecting all measurement axles, it may be rotation symmetry. Hence, coordinate rotation structure jointly after test. Fix the position of axle, but allow axle direction equal proportion or rotation deformation.

3.2   Identification Stage

In identification stage, acquire and understand environment quickly through a group of models (together with its deformation) M = {M₁, M₂, ..., Mₖ} understood in certain environment. Scene S includes acquired learning model by the use of code set within several seconds. As preprocessing, abstract big plane firstly, actually ground, desk table board and big plane of wall. The most dominant plane (ground plane) and plane significantly parallel with dominant plane (desktop) are kept. The rest points are divided into grouped connection adjacent points (use distance is 1 cm threshold value and neighborhood diagram). The generated cluster S = {S₁, S₂, ..., Sₙ} is as input of identification method.

Each single view point cloud S_i is tried to be matched with learned model M_j, how identification method returning S_i matched with model M_j except for relative conversion and deformation. If it succeeds, only converting corresponding point cloud and matching model with correct conversion and deformation parameters can establish a rapid lightweight level environment 3D model.

3.2.1   Initial Matching

M is an element set and model composed of their connections. Similar to learning step, create patch of input cluster s and generated initial section and candidate connection between adjacent sections. Take consideration of deformation parameters and connection comparison of each pair adjacent part in model together by markov random field (MRF) formula. That is, segment $s_1, s_2 \in S$, sub-model $m_1, m_2 \in M$. Then find optimum matching between them through solving the minimal value of the following energy function.

$$E = \underbrace{\sum_I D(s_i = m_i)}_{} + \eta \underbrace{\sum_{i,j} V(s_i = m_i, s_j = m_j)}_{}$$

(8)

unary element   binary element

Use energy function with distance d $(f_s, f_m) \in [0, 1]$ in accordance with features of $s \in S$, $m \in M$. For example, one variable can be sum of all possible feature distances:

$$D(s = m) = \sum_i d^i/n$$
$$d^{length}(f_s, f_m) = \min(|f_s - f_m|/f_m, 1)$$
$$d^{angle}(f_s, f_m) = |f_s - f_m|/\pi$$
$$d^{height}(f_s, f_m) = 1 - \sum_i \min(f_s(i), f_m(i))$$

(9)

$$V(s_1 = m_1, s_2 = m_2) = \begin{cases} \sum_i b^i/n & \text{If there is contour} \\ \psi & \text{If there is no contour} \end{cases}$$

(10)

Relative length and height distributions are used in many possible feature set. Height distribution condition is given by the histogram of the distance from ground plane, and distance is given by intersection distance histogram. Please note that it is easy to substitute shape characteristics, color or any other useful information, to strengthen identification ability. However, only geometric shapes are considered among all tests, ignoring texture information.

In our frame, low quality scanning can be powerfully and reliably processed, because it's conducted in binary element. Define binary element through comparison of feature distance of adjacent patch pairs in connections of model (refer to formula 10).

Not all connections can be observed due to data restraints of single view. The non existed connection distribution of $\psi > 1$ (select 5) is wrong, for the connection it captured may not be observed or wrongly distributed. Consider binary element for feature b^i, including relative positions of contact, angles between parts, lengths (maximum dimension from contact point) and widths (minimum dimension from contact point). Our self-adapting no change features are only compared to be deformed because possibility of spatial model joint deformation is known from model M. For example, angle of rotation joint and corresponding direction length of expansion joint are ignored by us.

Message passing algorithm is applied to solve minimum value problem of energy function by us. Minimization is rapid because space possibility of discrete distribution is very small. Result depends on the use of independent element certainly. Carry out initial conversion of S and M by matching of minimum binary element V connection.

3.2.2   Seek Transition and Deformation Parameters

After abstracting initial matching and conversion, increase matching gradually and find out the rest unknown local minimum number. Begin from the initial transition, finding out best deformation parameters to establish relations of S and M. Find out best conversion and then carry out iteration until convergence in accordance with given relations. If there is at least 80% point can be explained after convergence, substitute optimum matching model points.

4   Detection and Scene Understanding of Histons-Based Moving Objects

Three different roughness measurements are used by us after establishment of indoor environment model—Basic HRI, 3D HRI and 3D FHRI; and establish three algorithms of different versions and same background model, and there are three basic steps—background modeling, foreground detection and background updating.

4.1   Background Modeling

Calculate histons center histogram of M * N pixel area from the first frame of video sequence, and calculate roughness index (HRI, or 3D HRI or 3D FHRI) of this area by the use of histogram and histons, used for initializing model of this pixel.

4.2   Foreground Detection

Calculate its HRI from the next frame in corresponding pixel, similar to the process described in background modeling step. Calculate background model roughness index of each pixel and current roughness index distribution along each color channel by formula (11) algorithm.

$$\rho_F(i) = \frac{\rho_c(i)}{\sum\limits_{i=0}^{l_c-1} \rho_c(i)} \tag{11}$$

$\rho(i)$ is the i th roughness index of the C th color channel.

Color channel is considered to be algorithm integrated mode of an integral normalization histons in 3D version, as shown in the following formula:

$$\rho_F(i,j,k) = \frac{\rho(i,j,k)}{\sum\limits_{i=0}^{l_1-1}\sum\limits_{j=0}^{l_2-1}\sum\limits_{k=0}^{l_3-1} \rho(i,j,k)} \tag{12}$$

Use Bhattacharyya distance (d_B) to calculate similarity between normal background model roughness distribution and current roughness distribution:

$$d_B = \sqrt{1 - q(\overset{-cu}{\rho}, \overset{-bg}{\rho})} \tag{13}$$

If d_B is less than distance threshold value, color distribution background model is similar to current, namely, pixel is background pixel, otherwise foreground pixel. bg and cu in the above formula represents background model and current roughness index respectively.

In the version of histons basic algorithm, three color channels are considered to be independent and histons are derived from each color channel respectively.

$$q(\overset{-cu}{\rho}, \overset{-bg}{\rho}) = \sum\limits_{i=0}^{l_1-1}\sqrt{\overset{-cu}{\rho_r}(i)\,\overset{-bg}{\rho_r}(i)} \times \sum\limits_{i=0}^{l_2-1}\sqrt{\overset{-cu}{\rho_g}(i)\,\overset{-bg}{\rho_g}(i)} \times \sum\limits_{i=0}^{l_3-1}\sqrt{\overset{-cu}{\rho_b}(i)\,\overset{-bg}{\rho_b}(i)} \tag{14}$$

Use algorithm of histons 3D version to calculate whole cooperation efficiency of Bhattacharyya distance, as follows:

$$q(\overset{-cu}{\rho}, \overset{-bg}{\rho}) = \sum\limits_{i=0}^{l_1-1}\sum\limits_{j=0}^{l_2-1}\sum\limits_{k=0}^{l_3-1}\sqrt{\overset{-cu}{\rho}(i,j,k)\,\overset{-bg}{\rho}(i,j,k)} \tag{15}$$

Foreground detection step of 3D fuzzy histons is basically the same, except is substituted by $\rho_F\square$.

4.3   Background Model Updating

The first frame of video is used for background model initialization. Generally, the time of any moving object to be one pixel is short. That is, one pixel is the strength probability less than background probability for moving objects. Suppose one object exists in one area in the first frame and suppose the object leaves that position after n frames. Application of background reduction algorithm will lead to occurrence of ghost at (n + 1)th frame. To relieve this problem, if pixel strength value on this ghost position in one pixel model is updated, a real background approximation can be obtained by us after several frames, and thus identify correct moving objects. However, this method needs real background of several frames model convergence. Such foreground learning rate must be low, or the foreground objects that move slowly will also be absorbed into background model, establishing false negative. Common updating equation is described as follows.

$$\rho_{x,y}^{-bg}(t) = \begin{matrix} (1-\alpha)\,\bar{\rho}_{x,y}^{-bg}(t-1) + \alpha\,\bar{\rho}_{x,y}^{-cu}(t), & (x,y) \text{ is background pixel} \\ (1-\beta)\,\bar{\rho}_{x,y}^{-bg}(t-1) + \beta\rho_{x,y}^{-cu}(t), & (x,y) \text{ is not background pixel} \end{matrix} \qquad (16)$$

where $\beta \ll \alpha$, t is time index.

5   Experimental Analysis

The method has been tested in various scenes by us and the test scope is arranged at large space real world composed of many objects. Identification result is satisfying, e.g. in Fig. 1, most monitor and tables are found. Nevertheless, air-condition is not in the learning model, so it is not detected. 21 monitor are found among 24 monitor, and three monitor are not detected due to serious occlusion. Tables and part of tables and chairs in Fig. 2 are also not detected due to serious occlusion. Indoor environment model has been established basically.

Fig. 1. Detection result of laboratory

Basic HRI, 3D HRI and 3D FHRI methods are tested after establishing of indoor environment model, to detect moving objects, and carry out qualitative and quantitative analysis under various challenging conditions. There is no post processing technique, e.g. algorithms of median filtering, morphology operation, shadow removal, etc., so it is fair.

Fig. 2. Detection result of classroom

Figure 3 describes performance comparison of basic (BHRI) of HRI, 3D HRI and 3D FHRI under different circumstances.

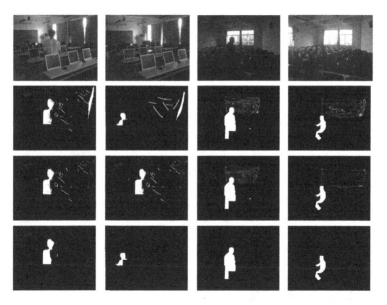

Fig. 3. Qualitative comparison of three types of HRI. a: original frame; b: effect of BHRI; c: effect of 3D HRI; d: effect of 3D FHRI.

Figure 4 describes quantitative evaluation by the use of matching index: 3D FHRI's matching index is the highest, followed by 3D HRI.

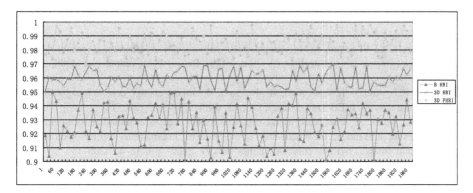

Fig. 4. Quantitative performance comparison of BHRI, 3D HRI and 3D FHRI

6   Conclusions

A rapid identification model system under 3D indoor environment was proposed by us. This method could be expanded and enlarged into more complex environments, mainly need reliable acquisition additional object model (and their change model) and good prior relation between objects. But it couldn't capture the features beyond function of sensor, especially small/thin prominent structure (e.g. wheel of chair) or reflective objects, it couldn't detect the component of very thin chair leg correctly.

A new background model updated process was proposed in the detection aspect of moving object, to achieve strong segmentation. Comparison of BHRI, 3D HRI and 3D FHRI showed that 3D FHRI had optimum performance, followed by 3D HRI. This method was to abstract shapes of moving objects, though there was area distribution for them. In dynamic background distribution, under the circumstance with linkage of multi- backgrounds, the method of us is still effective, even though don't use multi models of each pixel. The first frame of the frame series was used simply to initialize background model, not like the traditional methods which need a segment of ideal background frame for initialization.

The further studies need to be continued: (1) With more and more object proto- types, more complex search data structure is needed. But we believe that, many can be completed in small scene after simple setting. (2) In this work, we focused on one sensor input, i.e. confined by sparse data. We set color and texture on purpose, which will be very useful for future consideration, especially for appearance change.

Acknowledgement. This research is based upon work supported in part by National Natural Science Foundation of China (61370173), in part by Science and Technology Project of Zhejiang Province (2014C31084), and in part by Science and Technology Project of Huzhou City (2013GZ02).

References

1. Elhabian, S.Y., El-Sayed, K.M., Ahmed, S.H.: Moving object detection in spatial domain using background removal techniques—state-of-art. Recent Pat. Comput. Sci. **2008**, 32–54 (2008)
2. Radke, R.J., Andra, S., Al-Kofahi, O., Roysam, B.: Image change detection algorithms: a systematic survey. IEEE Trans. Image Process. **14**(3), 294–307 (2005)
3. Tang, Z., Miao, Z.: Fast background subtraction and shadow elimination using improve Gaussian mixture model. In: Proceedings of the 6th IEEE International Workshop on Haptic, Audio and Visual Environments and Games (HAVE 2007), pp. 38–41 (2007)
4. Kim, K., Chalidabhongse, T.H., Harwood, D., Davis, L.S.: Real-time foreground-background segmentation using codebook model. Real-Time Imaging **11**, 172–185 (2005)
5. Maddalena, L., Petrosino, A.: A self-organizing approach to background subtraction for visual surveillance applications. IEEE Trans. Image Process. **17**(7), 1168–1177 (2008)
6. Sobral, A., Vacavant, A.: A comprehensive review of background subtraction algorithms evaluated with synthetic and real videos. Comput. Vis. Image Underst. **122**, 4–21 (2014)
7. Kushwaha, A.K.S., Srivastava, R.: Performance evaluation of various moving object·segmentation techniques for intelligent video surveillance system. In: International Conference on IEEE Signal Processing·and Integrated Networks (SPIN), pp. 196–201 (2014)
8. Satpathy, A., Eng, H.-L., Jiang, X.: Difference of Gaussian edge-texture based background modeling for dynamic traffic conditions. In: Bebis, G., et al. (eds.) ISVC 2008. LNCS, vol. 5358, pp. 406–417. Springer, Heidelberg (2008). https://doi.org/10.1007/978-3-540-89639-5_39
9. Noriega, P., Bascle, B., Bernie, O.: Local kernel color histograms for background subtraction. In: VISAPP, vol. 1, pp. 213–219 (2006)
10. Zhang, S., Yao, H., Liu, S.: Dynamic background subtraction based on local dependency histogram. Int. J. Pattern Recognit. Artif. Intell. **23**(7), 1397–1419 (2009)
11. Mushrif, M., Ray, A.K.: Color image segmentation: rough-set theoretic approach. Pattern Recognit. Lett. **29**, 483–493 (2008)
12. Mohabey, A., Ray, A.K.: Rough set theory based segmentation of color images. In: Proceedings of the 19th International Conferences of the North America Fuzzy Information Processing Society (NAFIPS), pp. 338–342 (2000)
13. Mohabey, A., Ray, A.K.: Fusion of rough set theoretic approximations and FCM for color image segmentation. In: IEEE International Conference on Systems, Man, and Cybernetics, vol. 2, pp. 1529–1534 (2000)
14. Dey, T.K.: Curve and Surface Reconstruction: Algorithms with Mathematical Analysis. Cambridge University Press, Cambridge (2007)
15. Peter, H., Michael, K., Evan, H., Xiaofeng, R., Dieter, F.: RGB-D mapping: using kinect-style depth cameras for dense 3D modeling of indoor environments. Int. J. Robot. Res. **31**(5), 647–663 (2012)
16. Izadi, S., Kim, D., Hilliges, O., Molyneaux, D., Newcombe, R., Kohli, P., Shotton, J., Hodges, S., Freeman, D., Davison, A., Fitzgibbon, A.: KinectFusion: real-time 3D reconstruction and interaction using a moving depth camera. In: Proceedings of the 24th Annual ACM Symposium on User Interface Software and Technology (UIST 2011), pp. 559–568 (2011)
17. Rusinkiewicz, S., Hall-Holt, O., Levoy, M.: Real-time 3D model acquisition. In: Proceedings of the 29th Annual Conference on Computer Graphics and Interactive Techniques (SIGGRAPH 2002), pp. 438–446 (2002)

18. Allen, B., Curless, B., Popović, Z.: The space of human body shapes: reconstruction and parameterization from range scans. In: ACM SIGGRAPH 2003 Papers (SIGGRAPH 2003), pp. 587–594 (2003)

19. Li, H., Adams, B., Guibas, L.J., Pauly, M.: Robust single-view geometry and motion reconstruction. ACM Trans. Graph. **28**(5), 1–10 (2009). Proceedings of the ACM SIGGRAPH Asia 2009 (SIGGRAPH Asia 2009)

20. Zheng, Q., Sharf, A., Wan, G., Li, Y., Mitra, N.J., Cohenor, D., Chen, B.: Non-local scan consolidation for 3D urban scenes. ACM TOG (SIGGRAPH) **29**, 1–9 (2010)

21. Schnabel, R., Wahl, R., Klein, R.: Efficient RANSAC for point-cloud shape detection. CGF (EUROGRAPHICS) **26**(2), 214–226 (2007)

22. Li, Y., Wu, X., Chrysathou, Y., Sharf, A., Cohen-Or, D., Mitra, N.J.: GlobFit: consistently fitting primitives by discovering global relations. ACM TOG (SIGGRAPH) **30**(4), 1–12 (2011)

23. Chang, W., Zwicker, M.: Global registration of dynamic range scans for articulated model reconstruction. ACM TOG (SIGGRAPH) **30**, 1–15 (2011)

24. Lee, D.C., Gupta, A., Hebert, M., Kanade, T.: Estimating spatial layout of rooms using volumetric reasoning about objects and surfaces. In: Advances in Neural Information Processing Systems 23: 24th Annual Conference on Neural Information Processing Systems (NIPS 2010) (2010)

25. Gupta, A., Efros, A.A., Hebert, M.: Blocks world revisited: image understanding using qualitative geometry and mechanics. In: Daniilidis, K., Maragos, P., Paragios, N. (eds.) ECCV 2010. LNCS, vol. 6314, pp. 482–496. Springer, Heidelberg (2010). https://doi.org/10.1007/978-3-642-15561-1_35

26. Boyko, A., Funkhouser, T.: Extracting roads from dense point clouds in large scale urban environment. ISPRS J. Photogramm. Remote Sens. **66**(6), S2–S12 (2011)

27. Pawlak, Z.: Rough sets: Theoretical Aspects of Reasoning About Data. Kluwer Academic Publishers, Dordrecht (1991)

28. Engelhard, N., Endres, F., Hess, J., Sturm, J., Burgard, W.: Real-time 3D visual slam with a hand-held RGB-D camera. In: Proceedings of the RGB-D Workshop on 3D Perception in Robotics at the European Robotics Forum (2011)

29. Fisher, M., Savva, M., Hanrahan, P.: Characterizing structural relationships in scenes using graph kernels. ACM Trans. Graph. **30**(4), 34 (2011). SIGGRAPH 2011

30. Davison, A., Fitzgibbon, A.: KinectFusion: real-time 3D reconstruction and interaction using a moving depth camera. In: Proceedings of the 24th Annual ACM Symposium on User Interface Software and Technology (UIST 2011), pp. 559–568 (2011)

31. Herrero, S., Bescós, J.: Background subtraction techniques: systematic evaluation and comparative analysis. In: Blanc-Talon, J., Philips, W., Popescu, D., Scheunders, P. (eds.) ACIVS 2009. LNCS, vol. 5807, pp. 33–42. Springer, Heidelberg (2009). https://doi.org/10.1007/978-3-642-04697-1_4

A Watermarking Algorithm for 3D Point Cloud Models Using Ring Distribution

Jing Liu[1], Yajie Yang[1], Douli Ma[1], Yinghui Wang[1],
and Zhigeng Pan[2(✉)]

[1] Faculty of Computer Science and Engineering,
Xi'an University of Technology, No. 5 South Jinhua Road, Xi'an 710048, China
[2] Hangzhou Normal University, Hangzhou, China
zgpan@cad.zju.edu.cn

Abstract. A robust watermarking algorithm for 3D point cloud models based on feature vertices is proposed in this paper. Vertices with mean curvature less than zero are selected as feature vertices for watermark embedding. These feature vertices lying in the deeper surface can guarantee better imperceptibility for the watermarking information. The invariant space is established to resist geometric attacks by using the rest vertices, in which the 3D model are divided several ball rings according to the number of watermark bits. Scheme to embed watermarking information is to modify the radial distances of the feature vertices within the different ball rings. Experimental results show the proposed algorithm is robust against geometric attacks. It outperforms other methods in terms of imperceptibility and robustness.

Keywords: 3D point cloud · Mean curvature · Invariant space
Ball ring · Geometric attack

1 Introduction

With the development of multimedia technology, the application of three-dimensional (3D) digital media is more and more extensive, and accompanied by these applications, digital products theft, tampering and other infringement problems also appeared [1, 2]. As a technical means, digital watermark can effectively protect the copyright of 3D digital products. Generally, watermarking algorithms are categorized as blind or non-blind depending whether the original 3D object is required for authentication. The designing of blind algorithm is comparatively difficult when robustness is a major issue [3]. And according to the use of 3D model, it can be divided into mesh models and point cloud models.

So far, many types of 3D mesh watermarking algorithm have been proposed [4–7]. For example, Basyoni [5] used model's prominent feature points to divide the model into separate segments, and made feature segments projected from 3D representation to the 3 main 2D-Planes; Tao [6] presented a semi fragile watermarking algorithm based on the 3D mesh model calibrated by using principal component analysis, and built the structure of spherical coordinate mapping matrix to achieve 2D parameterization for geometric vertex data; Garg [7] proposed a robust watermarking algorithm having less

© Springer-Verlag GmbH Germany, part of Springer Nature 2018
Z. Pan et al. (Eds.): Transactions on Edutainment XIV, LNCS 10790, pp. 56–68, 2018.
https://doi.org/10.1007/978-3-662-56689-3_5

perceivable distortion for 3D polygon mesh objects based on geometrical properties. Now there are many algorithms for the 3D mesh watermarking, but many of the 3D models are represented by point cloud, and the point cloud watermarking algorithms are very few.

The current research on point cloud algorithms are as follows: Luo [8] proposed a non-blind reversible data hiding scheme for 3D point cloud model. The disadvantage is that if the original model is destroyed, this will not be able to extract the complete watermark bits. Ke [9] presented a robust spatial watermarking scheme for 3D point cloud models using self-similarity partition. This algorithm performs block preprocessing using octree structure and PCA preprocessing. Feng [10] presented a new method to embed watermark into a 3D point cloud model using distance normalization modulation, this scheme embeds the watermark by modulating the mean of the distance normalization in each bin, but its ability to resist against high strength of noise and large-scale cropping is not good.

Based on the existing problems in the above proposed method, we propose a robust watermarking scheme for 3D point cloud models using ball ring distribution in this manuscript. The proposed scheme include: (1) we use the vertices with mean curvature less than zero as the feature vertices to embed watermark, which can increase the imperceptibility of watermark; (2) the invariant space is established by using the mean curvature greater than zero, and the radial distances of less than zero vertices are used to adjust the embedding position for defense of geometric attacks such as rotation and shear, thus enhancing robustness of the watermark; (3) the multiple times embedding of watermark bits according to the partition area of the ring can improve the integrity of watermark extraction. So compared with other articles, the proposed method has stronger imperceptibility, robustness and integrity [11, 12].

The rest of this paper has following organization: In Sect. 2, we describe the proposed 3D watermarking scheme in detail. The experimental results are presented and analyzed in Sect. 3. Finally, we state the conclusion and discuss future work in Sect. 4.

2 The Proposed Algorithm

2.1 Vertex Classification

All the vertices of the 3D point cloud model are computed and categorized into two mutually exclusive groups. The first group is composed of those vertices whose mean curvatures are less than zero, and the second group contains the remaining vertices. Mean curvatures of the vertices are calculated using method suggested by Meyer [11]. All the vertices in the first group, called feature vertices, are selected to embed the watermark. These feature vertices lie in the deeper surface and they should have less perceivable distortion to human vision when embedded into the watermark. An example of the two groups of the point is shown in Fig. 1. The vertices marked with red are selected to carry the watermark, and the black vertices are used for establishing the invariant space.

| bunny | cattle | horse | human head |

Fig. 1. Vertex classification: the vertices marked with red forming the first group and the retained vertices model forming the second group. (color figure online)

2.2 Establishing the Invariant Space

In this study, we improve robustness against common attacks by establishing the invariant space. In order to avoid the impact of the embedded watermark on the invariant space, all the vertices of the 3D point cloud model are divided into two groups. The one used to establish the invariant space and the other used to embed the watermark. The watermark is embedded into those vertices whose mean curvatures are less than zero. Thus, the embedded watermark information neither cause visual effect on the surface of the 3D model, nor produce influence on the invariant space.

The steps in establishing the invariant space are described below:

- The origin of the invariant space: The mass center v_c of the vertices of the second group is the origin of the new coordinate system, and is calculated by using Eq. (1).

$$v_c = \frac{1}{N}\sum_{i}^{N} v_i \tag{1}$$

where the vertices $v_i(i = 1, 2, \cdots, N)$ belong to the second group.

- The axes of the new coordinate system: The covariance matrix Cov of the vertices belonging to the second group is calculated by using Eq. (2).

$$Cov = \begin{bmatrix} \sum\limits_{i=0}^{N} x_i^2 & \sum\limits_{i=0}^{N} x_i y_i & \sum\limits_{i=0}^{N} x_i z_i \\ \sum\limits_{i=0}^{N} y_i x_i & \sum\limits_{i=0}^{N} y_i^2 & \sum\limits_{i=0}^{N} y_i z_i \\ \sum\limits_{i=0}^{N} z_i x_i & \sum\limits_{i=0}^{N} z_i y_i & \sum\limits_{i=0}^{N} z_i^2 \end{bmatrix} \tag{2}$$

The u, v, and n axes of the invariant space are determined by the eigenvectors that correspond to the three largest eigenvalues λ_1, λ_2, and $\lambda_3(\lambda_1 > \lambda_2 > \lambda_3)$ of the covariance matrix Cov. Suppose the original coordinate system is O_{xyz}, and the new coordinate system is $\overline{O}_{uvn}$; then, the orthogonal transformation $M_{O_{xyz} \to \overline{O}_{uvn}}$ is represented as Eq. (3).

$$M_{O_{xyz} \to \overline{O}_{uvn}} = \begin{bmatrix} u_x & u_y & u_z & 0 \\ v_x & v_y & v_z & 0 \\ n_x & n_y & n_z & 0 \\ 0 & 0 & 0 & 1 \end{bmatrix} \bullet \begin{bmatrix} 1 & 0 & 0 & -v_{cx} \\ 0 & 1 & 0 & -v_{cy} \\ 0 & 0 & 1 & -v_{cz} \\ 0 & 0 & 0 & 1 \end{bmatrix} \tag{3}$$

Each vertex of the model is multiplied by the matrix $M_{O_{xyz} \to \overline{O}_{uvn}}$ to obtain the corresponding coordinates of the vertex in the new coordinate system $\overline{O}_{uvn}$. The watermark information is inserted in the coordinate system $\overline{O}_{uvn}$.

- Coordinate transformation

The Cartesian coordinates of each vertex $V_i = (u_i, v_i, n_i)$ on the 3D point cloud model are converted into spherical coordinates $S_i = (r_i, \theta_i, \varphi_i)$ by using Eq. (4).

$$r_i = \sqrt{(u_i - u_c)^2 + (v_i - v_c)^2 + (n_i - n_c)^2}$$
$$\theta_i = \arctan \frac{(v_i - v_c)}{(u_i - u_c)} \tag{4}$$
$$\varphi_i = \arccos \frac{(n_i - n_c)}{r_i}$$

Where $V_c = (u_c, v_c, n_c)$ is mass center of all the vertices of the second group. During embedding method the watermark, only radial distances r_i of the vertices are modified while keeping θ_i and φ_i unchanged.

2.3   Watermark Embedding

- Dividing ball ring

The 3D point cloud model is regarded as a sphere whose center is the mass center of all the vertices belonging to the second group, and sphere radius is the largest radial distance of the 3D model. The sphere is divided into N ball rings between the radial minimum distance r_{min} and radial maximum distance r_{max}, N is the number of the bits of embedded watermark. All feature vertices within each ball ring are embedded the same watermark bit. This is done to enhance the robustness of the method against the geometrical attack. The range of sphere radius R_n of the nth ball ring is defined as Eq. (5).

$$R_n = \{r_{n,j} | r_{min} + \frac{r_{max} - r_{min}}{N} \cdot (n-1) < r_i < r_{min} + \frac{r_{max} - r_{min}}{N} \cdot n\} \tag{5}$$

where n is less than or equal to N, $r_{n,j}$ represents the sphere radius of the jth feature vertex lying the nth ball ring. Figure 2(a) shows the plane projection of the feature vertices. All the feature vertices are projected onto the horizontal plane where they are represented by the green. Figure 2 (b) shows all the vertices falling within each ball ring. The red points correspond to the feature vertices and the black points correspond to vertices which are used to establish the invariant space. Figure 2(b) indicates that the

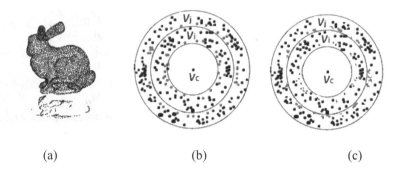

Fig. 2. The feature vertices within the ring area (Color figure online)

feature vertices in the model not only are less but distribute unevenly. However, for all the feature vertices, there is a clear character, that is, they are close to the area with the minimum radius in all ball rings.

- Normalization the vertices

In order to achieve robustness against scaling attacks, all the vertices are mapped into the normalized range of [0,1], by using Eq. (6).

$$\hat{r}_{n,j} = \frac{r_{n,j} - r^n_{min}}{r^n_{max} - r^n_{min}} \tag{6}$$

where $\hat{r}_{n,j}$ represents the normalized value of the jth feature vertex in the nth ball ring, r^n_{min} and r^n_{max} represent the minimum and maximum radium of the nth ball ring, respectively.

- Histogram adjustment to embed watermark

The watermark is embedded into the 3D point cloud model by modifying the radial distances r_i of the feature vertices. In order to make the modified radial distance be still in the normalized range [0,1], we utilize histogram mapping to adjust the radial distances of the feature vertices. The mapping function is defined as Eq. (7).

$$\hat{r}'_{n,j} = \left(\hat{r}_{n,j}\right)^\alpha \qquad 0 < \alpha < \infty \tag{7}$$

where $\hat{r}'_{n,j}$ is the radial distance of the watermarked vertex and the parameter α represents the modulation amplitude. When the watermark bit is 1, we raise the radial distances of the feature vertices and put them away from the minimum radius in the ball ring. So, the parameter α should be less than 1 (see Fig. 2(c), the pink points carrying the watermark bit 1 are a little away from the minimum radius). When the watermark bit is 0, we reduce the radial distances of the feature vertices and put them closer to the minimum radius in the ball ring (see Fig. 2(c), the green points carrying the watermark bit 0 are closer to the minimum radius). So, the parameter α should be more than 1. In

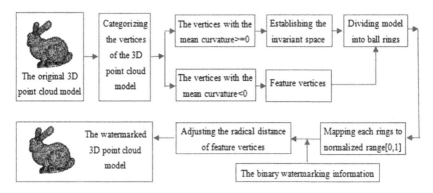

Fig. 3. Flow chart for watermark embedding of the proposed method

the two cases, the parameter value α depends on that the changing feature vertices should not cause perceptible degradation of the model. Figure 3 shows the steps of embedding the watermark.

2.4 Watermark Extraction

The watermark extraction process is the reverse process of the embedding. In the process of the embedding, we raise the radial distances of the feature vertices in the case that the embedded watermark bit is 1. That is, the average radial distance of the ball ring become larger, and vice versa. The mean value m'_n of the radial distances of all the vertices in each ring is calculated by using Eq. (8).

$$m'_n = \left(\sum_{j=1}^{T_n-t} \hat{r}_{n,j} + \sum_{j=1}^{t} \hat{r}'_{n,j} \right) \Big/ T_n \tag{8}$$

Where t is the total number of the feature vertices within the nth ring while T_n represents the total number of all the vertices in the nth ring. The watermark bits are embedded according to Eq. (9).

$$\begin{cases} w_n = 1 & if \quad m_n > m'_n \\ w_n = 0 & if \quad m_n < m'_n \end{cases} \tag{9}$$

Where, m_n represents the average distance of each ball ring in the original 3D model. The detail process of extracting watermark is illustrated in Fig. 4.

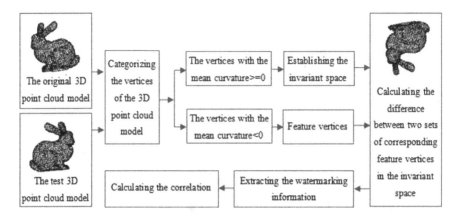

Fig. 4. Flow chart for watermark extraction of the proposed method

3 Experimental Results

For evaluating the performance of the proposed algorithm in this paper, four 3D models are used: bunny (5326 vertices), horse (712 vertices), cattle (2903 vertices) and human head (1884 vertices), as shown in Fig. 5. Invisibility and robustness are two main factors in assessing watermarking. Consequently, we will verify the invisibility and robustness of the proposed algorithm.

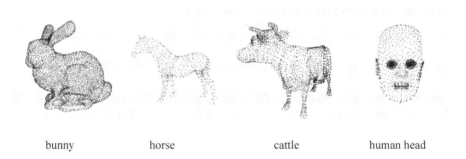

bunny   horse   cattle   human head

Fig. 5. Original 3D point cloud models

3.1 Watermark Invisibility

Invisibility is one of the most critical requirements for 3D watermarking. The most common method to measure watermark invisibility is the Root Mean Square Error (RMSE). RMSE refers to the root mean square of the distance which the corresponding vertices between the watermarked model and the original model [12]. The smaller the RMSE is, the better the transparency of the watermark is, and the smaller the model distortion is. The watermarked point cloud models are shown in Fig. 6. During the process of embedding the watermarking information, we only modify the radial

bunny   horse   cattle   human head

Fig. 6. Watermarked 3D point cloud models

distances of the feature vertices. Owing to these feature vertices having mean curvature less than zero and lying deeper in the surface, they have a better visual masking effect. This mechanism helps achieve good imperceptibility for the watermark. Figure 6 shows that the watermarking information embedded into each model is invisible and does not produce perceptible effects on the models. This observation is also confirmed by the objective metrics. In Table 1, the objective RMSE values obtained from our method are smaller than the corresponding values from the methods in [9, 16].

Table 1. Invisibility comparison of the watermarking methods in terms of RMSE(10^{-3}) when embedding 50,100 and 150 watermark bits

Methods	Models	The number of watermark bits		
		N = 50	N = 100	N = 150
Method in [9]	Bunny	0.26	0.21	0.16
	Horse	0.29	0.24	0.20
	Cattle	0.26	0.22	0.18
	Human head	0.28	0.25	0.21
Method in [16]	Bunny	0.29	0.23	0.19
	Horse	0.32	0.27	0.23
	Cattle	0.30	0.25	0.21
	Human head	0.35	0.26	0.23
Our method	Bunny	0.22	0.18	0.12
	Horse	0.24	0.20	0.16
	Cattle	0.21	0.17	0.14
	Human head	0.26	0.23	0.18

3.2   Watermark Robustness

The robustness of the embedded watermark is verified by geometric attacks such as cropping, rotation, noise, smoothing. The correlation coefficient *Corr* is used to measure the robustness of watermark [13], is calculated by:

$$Corr = \frac{\sum_n (w_n - m_n).(w'_n - m'_n)}{\sqrt{\sum_n (w_n - m_n)^2 \sum_n (w'_n - m'_n)^2}} \qquad (10)$$

Where m_n and m'_n are the mean of the embedded watermark sequence, w_n and w'_n are the mean of the extracted sequence, respectively.

3.2.1   Cropping Attack

The watermarking algorithm only embeds the watermark information in the feature vertices, thus it also shows the obvious advantage in resisting the cropping attack. In the proposed method, the watermarked model with fewer vertices unable to extract the complete watermark information when it suffered a cropping attack. So the effect of resisting cropping attack for the models of having more vertices is well. Figure 7(a) shows the results of cropping 10% to 50%. Notice that the *Corr* of our method is still over 0.5 even if the original models have been cut 50%. The reason is that the watermarking information is repeatedly embedded into the model; further, it is embedded throughout the model instead of being concentrated in only one region. If the vertices are removed from one direction of the watermarked model, the watermark can still be extracted from the other parts of the model. So the method of multiple embedding watermark bits in the ball ring greatly reduces the impact of shear attacks and ensures the proposed method has strong shearing resistance.

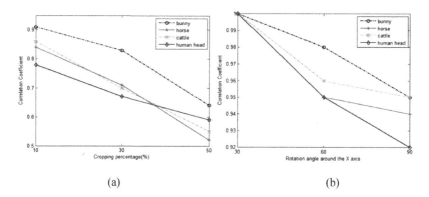

(a)   (b)

Fig. 7. Comparison of the correlation coefficients: (a) cropping and (b) rotation

3.2.2   Rotation Attack

As the vertices coordinates may be changed during the rotation, the invariant space is established to resist the rotation attack, to ensure which has a reference when the vertices coordinates changed. In this experiment, contrasting with the original 3D point cloud models, the embedded 3D watermarked models mainly rotate along the x-axis. Figure 7(b) shows the results of rotating 30° to 90° along the x-axis. In this comparison range, the *Corr* is not less than 0.9, and we notice that the models of bunny and cattle have bigger correlation value. The reason is that the two 3D point cloud models have more vertices to establish the invariant space. The existence of invariant space makes it possible for the vertices to find the corresponding position in the rotation model. The result shows that the watermarking information is robustness at different rotation angles, and the proposed method has better performance against rotation attack.

3.2.3   Noise Attack

Noise attack is a common attack way to detect watermark robustness. We use random additive noise with variances (σ) to attack each watermarked model, the amplitude of the noise is, 0.15%, 0.3%, respectively [14]. Figure 8(a) shows the experimental results of adding noise amplitude 0.05% to 0.3%. We have compared the correlation coefficients of the different noise amplitude in the figure, it can be observed that the increase of amplitude cause the decrease of the *Corr*. The greater the noisy amplitude is, the larger the distortion of the model is, and the lower of the *Corr* is. Vertices which have mean curvatures being less than zero are almost in the concave of the model. The added noise has little influence on them. So the proposed method has fairly good performance in terms of watermark detection for noise attack.

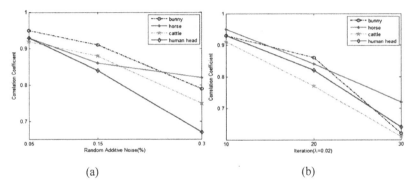

Fig. 8. Comparison of the correlation coefficients: (a) noise and (b) smoothing

3.2.4   Smoothing Attack

We use the Laplacian smoothing algorithm proposed [15] with the deformation factor $\lambda = 0.02$ to carry on experiment, and we apply to the marked models 10, 20, and 30 iterations of Laplacian smoothing to evaluate robustness. The directions of their vertices normal vector of the models will be changed after suffering from the smoothing attack. However, the positions of the vertices remain unchanged. When the watermarked models are attacked by smoothing operations, the watermarked positions can still be found, thus improving the robustness of the watermark against the smoothing attack greatly. Figure 8(b) shows the results of Laplacian smoothing with different number of iteration ranging from 10 to 30. The correlation coefficients for the four 3D models are still above 0.75 after 20 iterations. It indicates that our proposed method has very good performance when subjected to a weak smoothing attack.

3.3   Comparison of Watermarking Algorithms

We compare the performance of the proposed method with the well-known methods in [9, 16] to further validate the robustness against various attacks. Use the bunny, horse, cattle and human head 3D point cloud models as experimental models. The BER (bit error rate) is adopted to test the robustness, respectively. The BER represents the bit error percentage in the bit stream of the extracted watermark. The smaller BER value indicates better robustness.

As shown in Table 2, for the four 3D point cloud models, we test the BER of the extracted watermark under additive noise attack and simplification attack. From the results we observe that the proposed method shows much lower BER when compared with the method proposed [9] in resisting additive noise attack and simplification attack, however, it has almost equivalent BER to method [16]. We choose the imperceptible vertices as the watermark embedding feature vertices. All the vertices for watermark embedded belong to curvature region of the model, which helps to retrieve the watermark vertices even after such attacks. In order to further enhance the robustness of proposed watermarking method, we establish the invariant space, which is established by using the non-feature vertices in the model, to reduce the effect of simplification and noise attacks to a great extent. Therefore, our method is more resistant against noise and simplification attack.

Table 2. Comparison of the BER between additive noise attack and simplification attack than other methods

Models	Methods	Additive noise attack (%)					Simplification attack (%)			
		0.1	0.2	0.3	0.4	0.5	0	20	40	60
Bunny	Method in [9]	0.03	0.14	0.23	0.34	0.40	0.00	0.04	0.13	0.24
	Method in [16]	0.00	0.03	0.08	0.10	0.15	0.00	0.00	0.01	0.03
	Our method	0.00	0.02	0.05	0.09	0.17	0.00	0.01	0.04	0.10
Horse	Method in [9]	0.02	0.10	0.21	0.33	0.39	0.00	0.05	0.09	0.16
	Method in [16]	0.00	0.02	0.06	0.16	0.23	0.00	0.00	0.02	0.04
	Our method	0.00	0.01	0.04	0.08	0.19	0.00	0.01	0.03	0.08
Cattle	Method in [9]	0.05	0.13	0.20	0.31	0.36	0.00	0.03	0.10	0.21
	Method in [16]	0.00	0.02	0.05	0.11	0.17	0.00	0.01	0.03	0.06
	Our method	0.00	0.01	0.04	0.10	0.18	0.00	0.00	0.02	0.05
Human head	Method in [9]	0.03	0.09	0.17	0.30	0.40	0.00	0.06	0.15	0.27
	Method in [16]	0.00	0.04	0.08	0.12	0.20	0.00	0.02	0.07	0.10
	Our method	0.00	0.02	0.06	0.11	0.15	0.00	0.01	0.05	0.12

4   Conclusion

In this paper, a robust 3D point cloud models watermarking algorithm is proposed in spatial domain. The feature vertices are picked out by calculating their mean curvatures, and the rest vertices are used to establish the invariant space. The watermark information is embedded into the 3D point cloud model by modifying the radial distances of the feature vertices. Based on the analysis and extensive experiments above, the proposed method can obtain the better invisibility and robustness. In the future, we will combine the proposed framework with the geometric properties of the surface [16] to further improve robustness. We would also like to focus on watermark scheme against local deformations.

Acknowledgments. This work is supported in part by the National Natural Science Foundation of China (No. 61472319), by Natural Foundation of Shanxi Province Key Project (No. 2015JZ015), and by Xi'an Science and Technology Project (No. XALG025).

References

1. Zeki, A.M., Abubakar, A.: 3D digital watermarking: issues and challenges. In: International Conference on Artificial Intelligence and Computer Science, pp. 344–351 (2013)
2. Li, X.-W., Kim, S.-T., Lee, I.-K.: 3D image copyright protection based on cellular automata transform and direct smart pixel mapping. Opt. Commun. **329**, 92–102 (2014)
3. Liu, J., Wang, Y., Li, Y., Liu, R., Chen, J.: A robust and blind 3D watermarking algorithm using multi-resolution adaptive parameterization of surface. Neurocomputing **237**, 304–315 (2017)
4. Cho, J.-W., Prost, R., Jung, H.-Y.: An oblivious watermarking for 3-D polygonal meshes using distribution of vertex norms. IEEE Trans. Signal Process. **55**, 142–155 (2007)
5. Basyoni, L., Saleh, H.I., Abdelhalim, M.B.: Enhanced watermarking method for 3D mesh models. In: International Conference on Information Technology, pp. 612–619 (2015)
6. Tao, X., Cai, Z.: Semi-fragile watermarking algorithm of 3D mesh models based on content certification. In: Computer Applications & Software (2014)
7. Garg, H., Arora, G., Bhatia, K.: Watermarking for 3-D polygon mesh using mean curvature feature. In: Computational Intelligence and Communication Networks(CICN), International Conference, pp. 903–908 (2014)
8. Luo, H., Lu, Z., Pan, J.: A reversible data hiding method for 3D point cloud model. In: International Symposium on Signal Processing and Information Technology, pp. 863–867 (2006)
9. Ke, Q.,Xie, D., Zhang, D.: A robust watermarking scheme for 3D point cloud models using self-similarity partition. In: Wireless Communications, Networking and Information Security (WCNIS), pp. 287–291 (2010)
10. Feng, X.: A watermarking for 3D point cloud model using distance normalization modulation. In: International Conference on Computer Science and Network Technology (ICCSNT), pp. 1282–1286 (2015)
11. Meyer, M., Desbrun, M., Schröder, P., Barr, A.H.: Discrete differential-geometry operators for triangulated 2-manifolds. In: Hege, H.C., Polthier, K. (eds.) Visualization and Mathematics III. Mathematics and Visualization, pp. 35–57. Springer, Heidelberg (2003). https://doi.org/10.1007/978-3-662-05105-4_2
12. Yang, Y., Pintus, R., Rushmeier, H., Ivrissimtzis, I.: A 3D steganalytic algorithm and steg analysis-resistant watermarking. IEEE Trans. Visual Comput. Graphics **2**, 1002–1013 (2017)
13. Urvoy, M., Goudia, D., Autrusseau, F.: Perceptual DFT watermarking with improved detection and robustness to geometrical distortions. IEEE Trans. Inf. Forensics Secur. **9**, 1108–1119 (2014)

14. Li, C., Zhang, Z., Wang, Y., Ma, B., Huang, D.: Dither modulation of significant amplitude difference for wavelet based robust watermarking. Neurocomputing **166**, 404–415 (2015)
15. Taubin, G.: Geometric signal processing on polygonal meshes. In: Eurographic State of the Art Report, pp. 81–96 (2000)
16. Bors, A.G., Luo, M.: Optimized 3D watermarking for minimal surface distortion. IEEE Trans. Image Process. **22**, 1822–1835 (2013)

A Novel Algorithm Related with Customers Based on Image Gradient Orientation

Xiaofen Li$^{(\boxtimes)}$ and Defa Zhang

School of Electrical Engineering and Information, Taizhou Vocational
and Technical College, Taizhou 318000, Zhejiang, China
2636369@qq.com

Abstract. Based on the study of image gradient orientation and relevant technique about customers, this paper has proposed a algorithm related with customers based on image gradient orientation (CS-IGO-LDA). Face images are vulnerable to illumination changes, resulting in most of the traditional subspace learning algorithms which rely on image representation information are robust. In order to alleviate this problem, we represent the original samples by using image gradient orientation rather than the pixel intensity. And, in order to better describe the differences between different categories, we use methods related with customers to extract sample feature vector of each individual. The proposed CS-IGO-LDA method has made full use of the advantage of image gradient orientation and methods related with customers in face recognition. Experiments in face databases of Yale, JAFFE and XM2VTS have proved the validity of the new algorithm in face recognition and face verification.

Keywords: Image gradient orientation · Face recognition · Face verification

1 Introduction

Face recognition has always been one of the most worth studying topics in the fields of computer vision, machine learning and biometric identification. Face representation plays an important role in the process of recognition. As the most commonly used feature extraction algorithm, subspace learning method has been widely studied by many scholars in face recognition. Principal component analysis (PCA) and linear discriminant analysis (LDA) are the two most typical feature extraction methods based on subspace. In real life, due to the influence of changes of illumination, expressions, poses and other external conditions, face images are prone to have high light, shadows, occlusion and dark light etc. All these factors will affect the robustness and accuracy of algorithm. Traditional subspace learning methods mostly rely on image pixel intensities to represent the linear correlation between pixels. So when the facial images change

Fund Project: general project fund from education department of Zhejiang province (Y201738405).
Authors' Information: X. Li (1981)—female, lecturer, majoring in and researching art design. D. Zhang (1962)—male, professor, machine learning is his main researching area.

© Springer-Verlag GmbH Germany, part of Springer Nature 2018
Z. Pan et al. (Eds.): Transactions on Edutainment XIV, LNCS 10790, pp. 71–81, 2018.
https://doi.org/10.1007/978-3-662-56689-3_6

much, feature space extracted by subspace learning method is hard to accurately describe the original image, and affect the final recognition results. Recent studies have shown that the image gradient orientation can not only reflect the variation amplitude of the image. And due to its characteristics of being sensitive to the edge, and not being sensitive to the changes of illumination, it has been widely used in face recognition, image processing and other fields. By using gradient direction of the image instead of intensity information of pixels, the original sample information can be better described, the effects of the changes of illumination and other conditions on the recognition results can be alleviated, and the robustness of the algorithm is improved. Recently, Georgios and others have proposed a face recognition algorithm based on image gradient direction [1]. Different from the traditional PCA and LDA methods, which use pixel intensity to show the correlation between pixels, Georgios and others have adopted the image gradient orientation to represent the original samples, and proved the advantages of the new algorithm by experiments.

For the traditional subspace learning and related algorithms, mostly are dependent on all of the input training sample data to extract common feature projection vectors. Therefore in the process of classification, they can not reflect the differences between different individuals. Kittler and others has proposed subspace method related with customer (CSLDA) [2]. Through this method, each individual sample can get a corresponding feature vector, which fully reflects the differences between the individuals of different samples. In order to solve the complex calculation of discriminant criterion in traditional Fisher of CSLDA, Wu and Kittler has introduced an equivalent Fisher criterion on the basis of that and proposed an improved CSLDA method [3], which can reduce computational complexity and improve performance of verification [4]. Following up them, Sun, Yin and others have also studied algorithm of subspace related with customers, and have applied it in the fields of face verification and face recognition [5, 6].

In order to get more effective face representation space and better distinguish the differences between different individuals, this paper has proposed a algorithm related with customers based on image gradient orientation, and has respectively proved its validity in face recognition and face through the experiments in face database of Yale, Jaffe and XM2VTS.

2   The Main Principles of the Algorithm

Most of the traditional feature extraction algorithms extract the common projection space based on all the training samples. While the Fisher faces based on relevant customers can get the corresponding projection vector for each category. In order to make full use of the advantages of the subspace algorithm of relevant customers, the paper has further integrated the gradient orientation information of the image so as to overcome the influence of illumination changes on the face image, and improve the recognition result. The improved algorithm mainly contains the following steps, as shown in Fig. 1:

   i. transform the original sample into a gradient direction matrix;
   ii. reduce the dimension of the transformed samples;

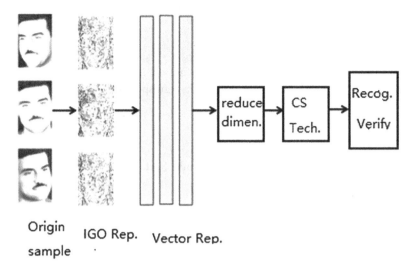

Origin sample   IGO Rep.   Vector Rep.

Fig. 1. The main thoughts of CS-IGO-LDA algorithm

iii. adopt the subspace algorithm of relevant customers for feature extraction, to get the projection vector of each category respectively;

iv. face recognition or face verification.

2.1 IGO-Methods

If the matrix of face image sample set is marked as Z, that is, $Z = [z_1, z_2, \cdots, z_N]$. The size of each sample image is $m \times n$, that is $z_i \in R^{m \times n}$. N is for the total samples. Supposed that these samples points has categories of C: $\omega_1, \omega_2, \ldots, \omega_C$, the number of samples in class i is N_i.

Assumed that $I(x, y)$ represents the intensity and gray scale of an arbitrary point (x, y) in any sample z_i, the gradient of the horizontal and vertical direction of the point can be expressed as respectively:

$$G_{i,x} = h_x * I(x, y)$$
$$G_{i,y} = h_y * I(x, y)$$
(1)

Where * represents the convolution, h_x and h_y respectively presents the bias in the horizontal and vertical direction of any point of the image.

Therefore, the gradient direction of point (x, y) is:

$$\Phi_i(x, y) = \arctan \frac{G_{i,y}}{G_{i,x}} (i = 1, 2 \ldots, N)$$
(2)

Then transform the gradient direction matrix Φ_i into a column vector φ_i, after that transform the sample into a complex matrix according to the formula (3):

$$x_i(\phi_i) = e^{j\phi_i} \tag{3}$$

where $e^{j\phi_i} = [e^{j\phi_i(1)}, e^{j\phi_i(2)}, \ldots, e^{j\phi_i(K)}]^T$, $e^{j\theta} = \cos\theta + j\sin\theta$, and K is the number of dimensions of sample image vectors, name $K = m \times n$.

We adopt the LDA transformation to get the corresponding projection vector UL for the changed sample vector xi.

2.2   CS-IGO-Methods

Assumed that it represents the vector of the xi in the Sect. 2.1, then the overall average of the sample is:

$$m' = \frac{1}{N} \sum_{i=1}^{N} t_i \tag{4}$$

Defined the orthogonal basis obtained by the IGO-LDA as UL, then all the samples are normalized to meet:

$$p_i = U_L^H (t_i - m') \tag{5}$$

As a result, the total scatter matrix of the projection vector is expressed as:

$$S = \frac{1}{N} \sum_{i=1}^{N} p_i p_i^H \tag{6}$$

All samples are divided into two parts: the customers and the jactitators: the sample of class i is defined as the customer model, the sample which is different from the sample of class i is defined as the jactitator model.

$$\mu_i = \frac{1}{N_i} \sum_{i=1}^{N_i} p_i, p_i \in \omega_i \tag{7}$$

Of which ω_i represents the class i.

Then the mean vector of the jactitators different from class i is

$$\mu_\Omega = -\frac{N_i}{N - N_i} \mu_i \tag{8}$$

In order to avoid the complex calculation of the traditional Fisher criterion, we can use the equivalent identification criterion proposed by Wu in the literature [3]:

$$J(v) = \frac{v^H B_i v}{v^H S v} \tag{9}$$

Of which, B_i is the inter class scatter matrix of the two classes:

$$B_i = \frac{N_i}{N - N_i} \mu_i \mu_i^T \tag{10}$$

The optimal solution of the formula (10) is:

$$v_i = S^{-1} \mu_i \tag{11}$$

Then get the feature projection vector of class i is

$$a_i = U_L v_i \tag{12}$$

3 Experimental Design and Analysis

In order to test the effectiveness of the improved algorithm in face recognition and face verification, we have respectively carried out experiments in common face recognition database of Yale, JAFFE and common face recognition database of XM2VTS at the same time.

3.1 Face Recognition Experiment

Yale face database contains a total of 15 normalized gray scale image with the size of 160×112. Each person has collected 11 samples in different illumination, poses and expressions. In the experiment, we each has randomly selected 5 samples as training samples, the remaining samples as testing set. It should be pointed out that the maximum dimension of the projection space in LDA algorithm during the experiment can not exceed C-1. The recognition results of different algorithms are shown in Table 1.

Table 1. The recognition accuracy of different algorithms in Yale face database

Dim	3	7	11	14	29	40
PCA	61.24	73.67	78.56	78.89	85.00	85.00
LDA	69.26	80.83	83.33	89.56	N/A	N/A
IGO- PCA	62.96	76.33	80.43	80.44	86.44	90.67
IGO- LDA	79.26	86.90	90.67	92.78	N/A	N/A
CSLDA	60.89	83.11	88.89	92.00	N/A	N/A
CS-IGO-LDA	**77.56**	**88.00**	**94.44**	**96.44**	**N/A**	**N/A**

In order to test the feasibility and effectiveness of the improved algorithm in the field of facial expression recognition, we have done experiments in the classic facial expression database of JAFFE. JAFFE database contains a total of 213 expression images of Japanese adult women. The size of each image is 256×256. Each of us has

Table 2. The recognition accuracy of different algorithms in JAFFE face database

Dim	5	10	13	15	19	35
PCA	62.94	86.01	86.71	88.81	89.51	88.81
LDA	88.81	89.61	N/A	N/A	N/A	N/A
IGO- PCA	77.62	83.92	86.71	88.81	90.91	91.61
IGO- LDA	92.31	93.01	N/A	N/A	N/A	N/A
CSLDA	89.33	91.80	N/A	N/A	N/A	N/A
CS-IGO-LDA	**93.31**	**95.71**	**N/A**	**N/A**	**N/A**	**N/A**

collected respectively the $2 \sim 4$ images of the basic expressions of anger, disgust, fear, happiness, neutral, sadness and surprise. In the JAFFE facial expression database, we have planned to divide all the sample images into two parts: training set and testing set. A training set consists of 70 images, each of which is randomly selected from one sample of every expression of the 10 individuals, the other 143 contains as testing set. In the experiment, all the images are normalized and cut into a sample image of 80×80.

From the recognition results of the above two face databases, we can find out:

(A) The recognition result of algorithm based on the image gradient direction is better than that of the traditional PCA and LDA algorithm. In the process of feature extraction, the correlation between the pixels of the original sample, which is represented by the gradient direction of the image, can preserve original sample information to a greater extent, alleviate the effects of the shadow, occlusion etc. caused by the changes of light and other conditions on the face image, so as to obtain more effective feature projection space and improve the recognition accuracy of the algorithm.

(B) The recognition effectiveness of CSLDA algorithm is almost as that of IGO-LDA algorithm. It shows that the two algorithms have their own advantage in facial expression recognition, and the recognition accuracy of which is slightly higher than that of the LDA algorithm. But in most cases, the recognition accuracy of CS-IGO-LDA algorithm is the highest. For in the improved algorithm, the image gradient direction information is used to reduce the dimension of samples; then select more effective feature space; after that extract the projection vector of each category through the algorithm of customers relevant, so as to improve the final recognition result.

3.2   Face verification experiment

3.2.1   Experimental preparation

We have done experiments in XM2VTS face database to test the performance of verification in the proposed algorithm. Minimum distance classifier is used in the experiment. Assumed that the sample to be tested is b, we have designed two kinds of classification models, namely, the customer model and the jactitator model.

The classification based on the customer model is defined as follows: the distance between the sample to be tested and the center of class i is, if dc does not exceed a certain threshold value t_c, then the sample to be measured belongs to the class i, otherwise it does not belong to class i.

The classification based on the jactitator model is defined as: the distance between the sample to be tested and the center of class i is, if td_i does not exceed a certain threshold value t_i, then the sample to be tested is the pseudo class of class i, otherwise it is class i.

XM2VTS face database is one of the commonly used database in face verification. It contains a total face images of 295 people in 8 different cases. In order to prove the validity of the algorithm, we have followed the Lausanne protocol [2] in the database experiment. We firstly divide the 295 samples of database into two categories: the customer category and the jactitator category, of which, 200 is customers, 95 is jactitators. In order to test the performance of verification of different algorithms comprehensively, the experiments have adopted two evaluation criteria of the error rejection rate (FRR) and the false acceptance rate (FAR) at the same time.

The results of FAR and FRR will be affected by different thresholds in the experiment. In general, the greater the threshold thter is, the greater the FAR is, the smaller the FRR is. Therefore, before testing, we need an evaluation process to adjust the threshold, and to find the appropriate thter value by adjusting the relationship between FAR and FRR. When the FAR is equal to FRR, the threshold value of thter can be determined, so that the wrong decision is minimized, and the reliable verification rate is obtained. Then the threshold value of thter got he evaluation phase is used to test, so as to judge the performance of verification of different algorithms in face verification. Therefore, all the samples in the XM2VTS database need to be divided into three sets of training set, evaluation set and testing set:

  i. Training set: the training set use all the customer model samples, that is, a total of 200 people, take each person's first to forth sample images, a total of 800 samples consisting of the training face collection.
 ii. Evaluation set: the assessment set is mainly used to determine the threshold value of thter, therefore, it contains both samples of the customer model and the jactitator model. In the experiment, the 5th and 6th samples of 200 people as well as all the 8 samples of the former 25 in jactitator model consist of evaluation set.
iii. Testing set: the testing set is composed of two kinds of samples, which are the customer model and the jactitator model. Of which part of the customer model contains 7th and 8th samples of 200 people, part of jactitator model consists of all 8 samples of the remaining 70 jactitators.

3.2.2   Experimental Results and analysis

In order to fully explain the advantages of the improved algorithm in face verification, the experiment has compared and analyzed it with CSLDA, CSLPP and CSKDA several methods. And the experimental results are shown in Table 3.

Table 3 shows the verification results of the different algorithms in the two models of customer and jactitator. The On C represents customer model, On I denotes the impostor model, TER in Table 2 indicates a general recognition error rate, result of which is false acceptance rate (FAR) and the false refuse rate (FRR). From the verification results in Table 1, we can find that, compared with other methods, the

Table 3. Comparison of verification results of different algorithms in XM2VTS face database

Methods	Evaluation			Test		
	Model	FAR	FRR	FAR	FRR	TER
CSLDA	On C	3.03	3.00	2.78	3.00	5.79
	On I	4.50	4.50	5.28	4.50	9.78
CSLPP	On C	2.58	2.50	2.64	2.50	5.14
	On I	1.69	1.75	1.91	1.75	3.66
CSKDA	On C	2.50	2.50	2.42	2.50	4.92
	On I	1.75	1.75	1.92	1.75	3.67
CS-IGO-LDA	On C	**1.05**	**1.00**	**1.00**	**1.00**	**2.00**
	On I	**1.13**	**1.25**	**1.15**	**1.25**	**2.40**

CS-IGO-LDA method has the lowest error rate, and the effects of CSKDA and CSLPP are equivalent. Because the CS-IGO-LDA method has taken into consideration of the advantage of the image gradient direction being not sensitive to the illumination changes, and adopted the gradient direction of the image to replace the traditional pixel information during the process of feature extraction, so as to get more effective feature vectors. Therefore the overall error rate of verification on the two models is significantly lower than that of the other algorithms. The CSKDA method is the kernel extension of the CSLDA method, taking into account of nonlinear information of the samples, so the verification result is much better than that of CSLDA. CSLPP method considers the part of the samples information, so the verification result is more ideal.

Figs. 2, 3, 4 and 5 has respectively in turn given the ROC diagram based on customer model and jactitator model of CSLDA, CSLPP, CSKDA and CS-IGO-LDA

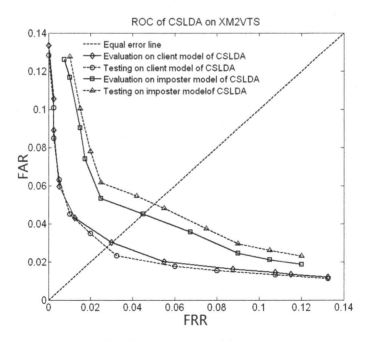

Fig. 2. ROC diagram of CSLDA

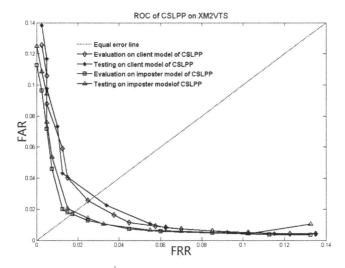

Fig. 3. ROC diagram of CSLPP

four methods in the XM2VTS face database. By comparison, we can find that of the four algorithms, the stability of CS-IGO-LDA method is best, that of CSKDA and CSLPP is equivalent. While compared with CSLDA method, whether in customer model or jactitator model, the error rate of recognition decreases a lot and stability improves a lot. Because the CSKDA method is the kernel extension of the CSLDA method, the nonlinear information of the sample is taken into consideration, so the verification result is obviously better than that of the CSLDA method. CSLPP method

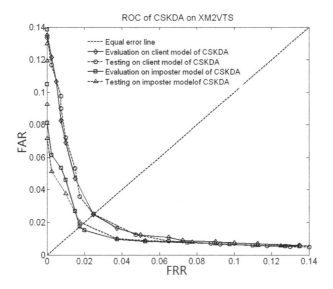

Fig. 4. ROC diagram of CSKDA

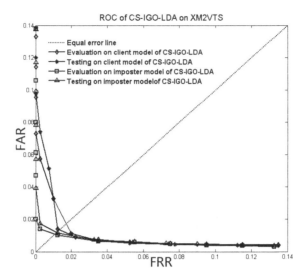

Fig. 5. ROC diagram of CS-IGO-LDA

has taken into account of part of the sample information during the process of features extraction, so it can alleviate the impact of illumination changes on the sample image from a certain extent, and the stability is also respectively ideal. But CS-IGO-LDA method not only takes advantage of the customer related method in face identification, uses the image gradient direction to replace the traditional pixel information, and extracts more accurate feature vector when reducing dimension, so it has higher stability, lowest error rate of recognition compared with other three algorithms.

4   Conclusions

The improved algorithm proposed in this paper, has been based on the full use of customer related technologies, but also further integrated the information of image gradient direction. It not only can alleviate the influence of illumination, poses and facial expression changes on the traditional feature extraction algorithm, but also can provide more effective classification information for face recognition. Through the experimental results on different typical face database, the advantages of the improved algorithm in face recognition and face verification has been fully proved.

Acknowledgements. This work was supported in part by the Humanities and Social Science Foundation of Ministry of Education of China under Grant No. 16YJCZH112, by Zhejiang Provincial Natural Science Foundation of China under Grant No. LY16F030012, LY14F020009, and LY16F030016, and by Scientific Research Fund of Zhejiang Provincial Education Department with Grant No. Y201534788.

References

1. Tzimiropoulos, G., Zafeiriou, S.: PAntic., M.: Subspace learning from image gradient orientations. IEEE Trans. Pattern Anal. Mach. Intell. **34**(2), 2454–2466 (2012)
2. Kittler, J.: Face authentication using client specific fisherfaces. In: Proceedings of Center for Vision Speech and Signal Processing. University of Surrey (2001)
3. Wu, X., Josef, K., Yang, J., Kieron, M., Wang, S., Lu, J.: On dimensionality reduction for client specific discriminant analysis with application to face verification. In: Li, S.Z., Lai, J., Tan, T., Feng, G., Wang, Y. (eds.) SINOBIOMETRICS 2004. LNCS, vol. 3338, pp. 305–312. Springer, Heidelberg (2004). https://doi.org/10.1007/978-3-540-30548-4_35
4. Su, X.: Face Recognition Algorithms and its Application. Chinese Thesis, Jiangnan University, Wuxi, China (2013)
5. Yin, H.-F., Wu, X.-J., Sun, X.-Q.: Client specific image gradient orientation for unimodal and multimodal face representation. In: Schwenker, F., Scherer, S., Morency, L.-P. (eds.) MPRSS 2014. LNCS (LNAI), vol. 8869, pp. 15–25. Springer, Cham (2015). https://doi.org/10.1007/978-3-319-14899-1_2
6. Sun, X.Q., Wu, X.J., Sun, J., Montesinos, P.: Hybrid client specific discriminant analysis and its application to face verification. In: Hatzilygeroudis, I., Palade, V. (eds.) Combinations of Intelligent Methods and Applications. Smart Innovation, Systems and Technologies, vol. 23. Springer, Heidelberg (2013). https://doi.org/10.1007/978-3-642-36651-2_8
7. Jian, C., Chen, X.: Unsupervised feature Selection based on locality preserving projection and sparse representation. Pattern Recogn. Artif. Intell. **28**(3), 247–252 (2015)
8. Yao, L., Deng, K., Xu, Y.: Face recognition based on gradient information. Comput. Eng. Appl. **46**(35), 170–172 (2010)
9. Tzimiropoulos, G., Zafeiriou, S., Pantic, M.: Principal component analysis of image gradient orientations for face recognition. In: Proceedings of International Conference on Automatic Face & Gesture Recognition and Workshops, pp. 553–558 (2011)
10. Chen, X., Yang, J., Zhang, D., Liang, J.: Complete large margin linear discriminant analysis using mathematical programming approach. Pattern Recogn. **46**(6), 1579–1594 (2013)
11. Yao, C., Lu, Z., Li, J., Xu, Y., Han, J.: A subset method for improving linear discriminant analysis. Neurocomputing **138**, 310–315 (2014)

Automatic Recognition of Pavement Crack via Convolutional Neural Network

Shangbing Gao[1,2](✉), Zheng Jie[1], Zhigeng Pan[2], Fangzhe Qin[1], and Rui Li[1]

[1] The Key Laboratory for Traffic and Transportation Security
of Jiangsu Province, Faculty of Computer and Software Engineering,
Huaiyin Institute of Technology, Huai'an 223003, People's Republic of China
luxiaofen_2002@126.com
[2] Virtual Reality and Human-Computer Interaction Research Center,
Hangzhou Normal University, Hangzhou 311121, China

Abstract. Conventional visual and manual road crack detection method is labor-consuming, non-precise, dangerous, costly and also it can affect transportation. With crack being the main distress in the actual pavement surface, digital image processing has been widely applied to cracking recognition recently. This paper presents the preprocessing method, segmentation method, the locating method, and a novel convolutional neural network based pavement cracking recognition method in the area of image processing. This paper trains and tests aforementioned 5-layer convolutional neural network on the pavement crack dataset. The experimental result shows that this 5-layer convolutional neural network performs better than that classical conventional machine learning method. Actual pavement images are used to verify the performance of this method, and the results show that the surface crack could be identified correctly and automatically. The convolutional neural network can learn the features of crack well and sort these aircraft with a high classification accuracy.

Keywords: Active contour · Convolutional neural network · Pavement crack

1 Introduction

Pavement distress detection [1] plays a key role in highway maintenance and rehabilitation due to the fact that surface crack is the most common distress of all pavement distress. Therefore, the detection of crack is necessary for the highway especially high-grade highway maintenance. Traditionally, pavement crack detections are accomplished by manual approaches, which are not only time-consuming, labor-consuming, and dangerous, but costly. More importantly, besides the fact that ongoing detections affect traffic, the quality of detection is determined subjectively. Thus, the automatic pavement crack detection methods should be applied to overcome the shortcoming of conventional visual and manual method.

There have been many thoughtful studies on cracking auto-recognition [2, 3]. In general form, crack image detection is composed of preprocessing, description and identification. Pavement surface image has two characteristics: small scale of gray

© Springer-Verlag GmbH Germany, part of Springer Nature 2018
Z. Pan et al. (Eds.): Transactions on Edutainment XIV, LNCS 10790, pp. 82–89, 2018.
https://doi.org/10.1007/978-3-662-56689-3_7

values, and small difference between background and objective within original image. In addition, there could be many noises in the image due to the diversity of image acquisition and the difference of surface materials. Many researchers have paid great attention to crack image processing in recent years, and the study centralized on the image enhancement and segmentation [4, 5].

In recent years, the advanced convolutional neural networks can automatically learn feature and generalized, which was applied to the pattern recognition tasks, and received a good response, such as image classifications [6], target detection [7], vehicle detection [8], and so on. But now crack classification is rare using convolutional neural networks.

The remainder of this paper is organized as follows. Section 2 presents the crack detection method. Section 3 describes the crack reorganization using convolutional neural networks. Section 4 demonstrates extensive experimental comparison results. Section 5 finally draws the conclusions.

2   The Detection of the Crack

2.1   Preprocessing

Gamma correction is an important nonlinear transformation. It is actually a transformation of the input image gray value, and then correct the brightness deviation, which usually is applied to expand the details of the dark light. In general, when Gamma correction value is greater than 1, the image highlights parts will be compressed and dark color will be expanding. When Gamma correction value is less than 1, highlights part is expanding and dark part of the image is compressed. By definition the following formula:

$$V_{out} = AV_{in}^{\gamma} \tag{1}$$

where A is constant, V_{in} is the input image before correction, V_{out} the rectified image, γ is gamma correction parameter. In this experiment, after repeated tests, when $\gamma = 0.75$ for crack images, the results will be the best. Gamma can be used to enhance the crack fractures.

Gaussian filter is a linear smoothing filtering, which is applicable to eliminate the Gaussian noise. It is widely used in image processing of the noise reduction. Popular speaking, Gaussian filtering is a process to the weighted average of the whole image, each pixel values, all by itself and other neighborhood pixels after the weighted average (Fig. 1).

2.2   The Segmentation of the Crack

In [9], Lankton et al. proposed a natural framework that allows any region-based segmentation energy to be re-formulated in a local way. For example, we choose the

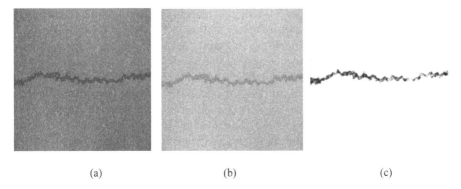

(a)   (b)   (c)

Fig. 1. Image preprocessing result: (a) original image, (b) Gamma correction and (c) filtering result

global region-based energy that uses mean intensities is the one proposed by Yezzi et al. [10] which we refer to as mean separation energy:

$$E_{MS} = \int_{\Omega_y} (u - v)^2 \tag{2}$$

where u and v represents the global mean intensities of the interior and exterior regions, respectively. Optimizing this energy causes that the interior and exterior means have the largest difference possible (Fig. 2).

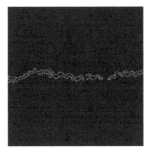

Fig. 2. The segmentation result

$B(x, y)$ is introduced to mask local regions. This function $B(x, y)$ will be 1 when the point y is within a ball of radius r centered at x, and 0 otherwise.

Accordingly, the corresponding F is formed by localizing the global energy with local mean equivalents as shown:

$$F_{MS} = (u_x - v_x)^2 \tag{3}$$

We can get the following local region-based flow:

$$\frac{\partial \phi}{\partial t} = \delta\phi(x) \int_{\Omega_y} B(x,y)\delta\phi(y) \cdot \left(\frac{(I(y)-u_x))^2}{A_u} - \frac{(I(y)-v_x))^2}{A_v}\right)dy$$
$$+ \lambda\delta\phi(x)div\left(\frac{\nabla\phi(x)}{|\phi(x)|}\right) \tag{4}$$

where A_u and A_v are the areas of the local interior and local exterior regions respectively given by

$$A_u = \int_{\Omega_y} B(x,y) \cdot H\phi(y)dy \tag{5}$$

$$A_v = \int_{\Omega_y} B(x,y) \cdot H(1-\phi(y))dy \tag{6}$$

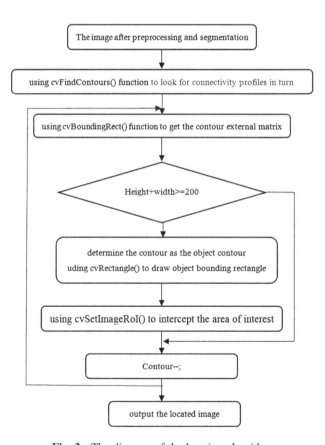

Fig. 3. The diagram of the locating algorithm

2.3   The Location of the Crack Based on OpenCV

After the image preprocessing and segmentation module, we can locate the crack in the original image. The specific method is morphologic closing operation to enhance regional characteristics of crack. Due to the segmentation of pavement cracks is a certain connected components of the image, by image contour detection function, to search for each connected component contour matrix, to judge the size of the contour by scanning in turn, to select the largest contour matrix which is selected as the largest connected component. Also it is available through intercepting the area by Region of interest function (Fig. 3).

The results of the locating algorithm are shown in Fig. 4.

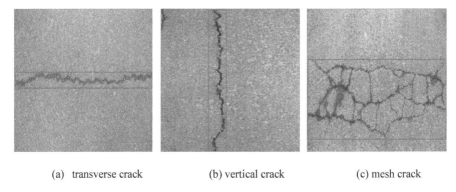

(a) transverse crack   (b) vertical crack   (c) mesh crack

Fig. 4. The running samples of locating algorithm of pavement cracks

3   The Recognition of the Crack

In recent years, deep convolutional neural network has been very popular. It can learn features by itself and shows excellent generalization ability. And it has been widely used in the areas of computer vision and pattern recognition. However, at present, it is rare to apply convolutional neural networks to this issue. This paper aims at solving aircraft classification problem in optical remote sensing images using convolutional neural networks.

For crack classification problems, this convolution neural network structure is shown in Fig. 5, the network has 5 layers, the first 4 are a convolution layer, the final layer is for all connections.

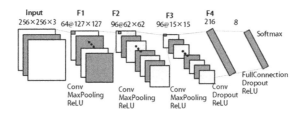

Fig. 5. The structure of convolutional neural network

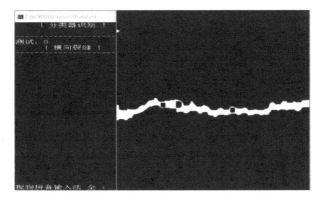

(a) The result of transverse crack image recognition

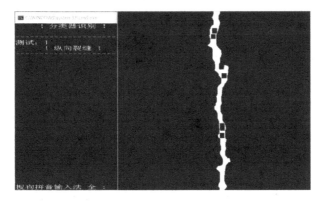

(b) The result of vertical crack image recognition

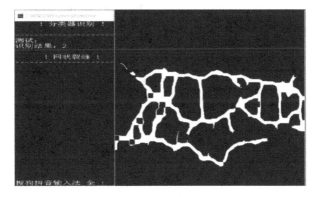

(c) The result of mesh crack image recognition

Fig. 6. The results of different fracture images recognition

The input of Network are the 256×256 size of the three channels (RGB) images. To ensure the network depth, to reduce the parameter, to improve network generalization, the convolution kernels using in the first three volumes of the network layer are smaller, they are 3×3. Finally a convolution kernel size is 15×15. All the convolution kernel effect simultaneously on all the features to the previous one, and the same different characteristics of convolution kernel to the former figure weight is not consistent. Four layers of convolution type of convolution kernel used is 64, 96, 96, 216, layer-by-layer abstraction to extract different features.

In the first three volumes are all connected to the pooling layer the pooling method is the largest pooling. Images are not expanded in the pooling, the window size of pooling are 2×2, 3×3, 4×4, sliding windows step are 2, 2, 4. After each pooling layer are nonlinear activation through the LeRU.

The final layer are all connection layer, a total of 8 nerve cells. The final convolution and all connection layer are added by random dropout layer to improve network generalization, the percentage is 0.5. Finally softmax function is used for output.

4 Experiments

The experiments are implemented with VC++ code run on a Dell Dimension 4600 PC, with Pentium 4 processor, 2.80 GHz, 1 GB RAM, on Windows XP.

They are downsampled as 8 * 8 images, which are composed of 128 dimensional vector as input layer, the hidden layer of 3 layers and 128 dimensions, the output layer of 10 dimensions. The images are classified to four categories (transverse crack, longitudinal crack, reticular crack sets, excess road information set), each type of 50 crack images are for training, and crack classifier is exported. After experiment and testing, and the crack can be accurately identified. Furthermore, high recognition rate.

The results of different crack images recognition are shown in Fig. 6. We further list the testing accuracy between the proposed method and the classic SVM (support vector machine) method (Table 1).

Table 1. Comparison with different methods

	The number of training samples	The testing accuracy
SVM	1024/class	81.3%
The convolutional neural network	1024/class	97.1%

5 Conclusions

In this paper we present a novel convolutional neural network based cracking identification method. Image preprocessing is introduced first as consisting of Gamma correction, spatial filtering, and binary processing. Then by segmenting pavement crack images using active contour model and locating crack, we locate the cracks efficiently, and use them to train our neural network. After convolutional neural network converges and identifies crack from pavement surface image. We finally revise convolutional network outputs to remove isolated crack points and connect crack for better identification accuracy. Our experiment indicates that crack could be identified by the convolutional network based identifier correctly and automatically.

Acknowledgment. This work is sponsored by the National Natural Science Foundation of China (NSFC) #61402192, six talent peaks project in Jiangsu Province (XYDXXJS-011, XYDXXJS-012), the Jiangsu Key Laboratory of Image and Video Understanding for Social Safety (Nanjing University of Science and Technology) Grant No. 30916014107, Jiangsu university students' innovative undertaking projects No. 201611049034Y.

References

1. Zhang, J., Huai, G., Sun, Z.: Based on digital image processing of pavement crack automatic identification and evaluation systems. Nat. Sci. Chang'an Univ. J. **2**, 18–22 (2004)
2. Sun, B., Qiu, Y.: Pavement cracks identification using image technology. J. Chongqing Jiaotong Univ. (Nat. Sci.) **27**(1), 61–64 (2008)
3. Yan, M., Bo, S., Li, X., He, Y.: An adaptive fuzzy image enhancement algorithm for local regions. In: Proceedings of the 26th Chinese Control Conference, China, pp. 308–311 (2007)
4. Lee, B.J., Lee, H.: A position-invariant neural network for digital pavement crack analysis. Comput. Aided Civ. Infrastruct. Eng. **19**, 105–118 (2004)
5. Sun, B., Qiu, Y.: Automatic identification of pavement cracks using mathematic morphology. In: International Conference on Transportation Engineering America, pp. 1783–1788. American Society of Civil Engineering Press (2007)
6. Szegedy, C., et al.: Going deeper with convolutions. In: Proceedings of IEEE Computer Vision and Pattern Recognition, Boston, MA, USA, 8–10 June 2015, pp. 1–9 (2015)
7. Girshick, R., Donahue, J., Darrell, T., et al.: Rich feature hierarchies for accurate object detection and semantic segmentation. In: Proceedings of IEEE Computer Vision and Pattern Recognition, pp. 580–587 (2014)
8. Chen, X., Xiang, S., Liu, C., et al.: Vehicle detection in satellite images by hybrid deep convolutional neural networks. IEEE Geosci. Remote Sens. Lett. **11**(10), 1797–1801 (2014)
9. Lankton, S., Tannenbaum, A.: Localizing region-based active contours. IEEE Trans. Image Process. **11**(17), 2029–2039 (2008)
10. Yezzi, J.A., Tsai, A., Willsky, A.: A fully global approach to image segmentation via coupled curve evolution equations. J. Vis. Commun. Image Representation **13**(1), 195–216 (2002)

Image Zooming Model Based on Image Decomposition

Yongguo Zheng[(✉)] and Songhe Gao

College of Computer Science and Technology,
Shandong University of Science and Technology, Qingdao 266510, China
zhengyg206@163.com, gsh208@163.com

Abstract. According to the different morphological characteristics between cartoons and textures in images, an image zooming model was proposed which based on image decomposition. The model decomposed the image into cartoons and textures by decomposition model; it analyzed the features of isotropic model and anisotropic model, the cartoon part was zoomed by isotropic model and the texture part was zoomed by anisotropic model. The using of shock filter eliminated the weak edge due to image zooming. At last, it achieved the amplification by combining the two zoomed parts. Simulation experiment results showed the model was good enough to zoom the image, strengthen the edge and guarantee the smoothness of the image. The model had better visual effects and the value of Peak Signal-to-Noise Ratio (PSNR) and Root-mean-square error (RMSE) was better than Bi-cubic and anisotropic model.

Keywords: Image zooming · Image decomposition · Isotropy
Anisotropy · Shock filter

1 Introduction

The traditional image zooming mainly adopts interpolation method, for example Nearest Neighbor Interpolation, Bilinear Interpolation, Bi-cubic Interpolation. The traditional Image zooming model is widely used, but with the increasing of zooming times, the traditional method will appear image edge serrated, light and dark areas migration and so on, these problems affect the quality of image. Recently, Image processing research based on partial differential equation proposes a new method. In 2008, Luhuili et al. proposed two models based on Isotropic and Anisotropic diffusion, it realized the image zooming by PDEs and image diffusion [1]. In 2013, Wang et al. proposed a image zoom based on thermal diffusion and TV model, according to the gradient characteristics of the pixel to carry out adaptive diffusion [2]. In 2013, Li provided two anisotropy of fourth order PDEs, considering the suppression of the edge serrated by the anisotropic diffusion, at the same time, considering the suppression of the block effect by the high order PDE, it obtained better result [3]. In 2015, Li et al. proposed a model based on sparse decomposition, extracting the cartoon and texture by RDWT and WAT model, self-snake and bi-cubic interpolation methods are used for

© Springer-Verlag GmbH Germany, part of Springer Nature 2018
Z. Pan et al. (Eds.): Transactions on Edutainment XIV, LNCS 10790, pp. 90–99, 2018.
https://doi.org/10.1007/978-3-662-56689-3_8

cartoons and textures, in this way, the model guaranteed the quality of zoomed image [4]. Research has shown that the method of PDE could eliminate image edge serrated and light and dark areas migration in a better way. At the same time, it could improve the quality of image.

This paper proposes a new image zooming based on the image decomposition, zooming the image by traditional interpolation model, using the decomposition model to decompose the image into cartoons and textures. Considering the difference between cartoon and texture part, the processing of image zoom can be divided into two steps— Isotropic zooming and anisotropic zooming. In the end, combining the two parts which have been zoomed.

2 Image Decomposition and Image Zooming Models

2.1 Image Decomposition

We decompose a given image into cartoon and texture parts. In 1992, Rudin et al. proposed an image decomposition model named ROF model [5],

$$f(x, y) = u(x, y) + v(x, y) \tag{1}$$

This model is posed a minimization problem in the space of functions of bounded variation BV $(\mathbb{R}2)$:

$$\inf_{u \in L^2} F(u) = \int |\nabla u| + \lambda \int |f - u|^2 dxdy \tag{2}$$

where f: $\mathbb{R} \rightarrow \mathbb{R}2$ is the given image, u is formed as cartoon image and v is formed as texture image.

Vese et al. defined v(texture image) where proposed in ROF model in a new way and proposed VO model, let $v = \mathrm{div}\, \vec{g}$, where $\vec{g} = (g_1, g_2)$, $g_1 = -\frac{1}{2\lambda} \frac{u_x}{|\nabla u|}$, $g_2 = -\frac{1}{2\lambda} \frac{u_y}{|\nabla u|}$, and $g_1^2(x, y) + g_2^2(x, y) = \frac{1}{2\lambda}$ [6], the energy function of the VO model can be expressed as:

$$\inf_{u, g_1, g_2} \{ G_p(u, g_1, g_2) = \int |\nabla u| + \lambda \int |f - u - \partial_x g_1 - \partial_y g_2| dxdy$$
$$+ \mu \left[\int \left(\sqrt{g_1^2 + g_2^2} \right)^p dxdy \right]^{\frac{1}{p}} \} \tag{3}$$

where the first term can make sure u belong to BV$(\mathbb{R}^2)$, the second term can make sure $f \approx u + \mathrm{div}\, \vec{g}$, the third is as punished term, it acts on $v = \mathrm{div}\, \vec{g}$.

The case p = 1 yields faster calculations per iteration, so the energy function (1–3) yields the following Euler-Lagrange equations:

$$u = f - \partial_x g_1 - \partial_y g_2 + \frac{1}{2\lambda} \text{div}\left(\frac{\nabla u}{|\nabla u|}\right)$$

$$\mu g_1 / \sqrt{g_1^2 + g_2^2} = 2\lambda \left[\frac{\partial}{\partial x}(u - f) + \partial_{xx}^2 g_1 + \partial_{xy}^2 g_2\right] \tag{4}$$

$$\mu g_2 / \sqrt{g_1^2 + g_2^2} = 2\lambda \left[\frac{\partial}{\partial y}(u - f) + \partial_{xy}^2 g_1 + \partial_{yy}^2 g_2\right]$$

The number of v and u decide the definition of cartoon and texture images in the above equations, when the μ value is relatively small or λ value is relatively large, the image of the texture part is clearer.

2.2   The Second - Order Zooming Models of the Image

The image can be represented by a binary function u (i, j), where i = 1: M and j = 1: N, image zooming can be considered as a reconstitution of a binary function. In 1998, Carmona proposed a second order PDE model [7].

$$\frac{\partial u}{\partial t} = au_{\eta\eta} + bu_{\xi\xi} \tag{5}$$

a and b represent diffusion coefficient, they control the smoothness of diffusion model in ξ and η two different directions. According to the values of a and b, the model can be divided into different model, isotropic and anisotropic model.

The Eq. (5) introduces the concept of local coordinate system (ξ, η), in which $\xi = \frac{\nabla^{\perp} u}{|\nabla u|}$ represents a unit tangent vector for the isophotes of an image and $\eta = \frac{\nabla u}{|\nabla u|}$ represents a unit tangent vector for the gradient of an image. Giving the following expression,

$$u_{\xi\xi} = \frac{u_{xx}u_y^2 - 2u_{xy}u_xu_y + u_{yy}u_x^2}{u_x^2 + u_y^2} \tag{6}$$

$$u_{\eta\eta} = \frac{u_{xx}u_x^2 + 2u_{xy}u_xu_y + u_{yy}u_y^2}{u_x^2 + u_y^2} \tag{7}$$

Isotropic Model. When a equals b, the model (5) is isotropic, which means the image uniformly diffuses in the direction of ξ and η. Lu et al. [1] thinks the gray value is viewed as temperature and the process of image zooming is viewed as the diffusion of temperature. The heat diffusion model can be written as.

$$\frac{\partial u}{\partial t} = \Delta u(x, y, t) \quad (x, y) \in \Omega, t > 0 \tag{8}$$

In line with the definition of local coordinate system, $\Delta u = u_{xx} + u_{yy} = u_{\eta\eta} + u_{\xi\xi}$, it satisfies the model (5) which a equals b, so the heat diffusion model is isotropic. At the same time, we assume it is adiabatic on the boundary.

$$\frac{\partial u(x, y)}{\partial n} = 0, (x, y \in \partial\Omega.) \tag{9}$$

In the heat diffusion model, we treat the gray value in the given image as diffusion source. Iterating the model for many times, in the end, the adjacent area's gray value is close to diffusion source. Isotropic model can guarantee the image homogeneously diffuse in the direction of normal and tangential on the boundary, in this way, the isotropic model shows a better way in the smoothness region, it is also simple in computation. But it can't protect the edge of given image, it can lead to blur on the edge of the image and cause serration phenomenon.

Anisotropic Model. In order to protect the edge of the image, eliminate the serration phenomenon which causes by the isotropic model, we can enlarge the conductivity coefficient in the smoothness region; reduce the conductivity coefficient on the edge of image, like that, the edge remains unaffected. Morse proposes the following model [8].

$$\frac{\partial u}{\partial t} = \begin{cases} 0 & \text{Anchor} \\ k|\nabla u| & \text{Others} \end{cases} \tag{10}$$

In this model, the anchor represents the gray value in the given image; it is viewed as diffusion source, $k = \text{div}\left(\frac{\nabla u}{|\nabla u|}\right)$ represents the curvature. Putting the curvature into model (10) yielded the following PDE.

$$\frac{\partial u}{\partial t} = u_{\xi\xi} \tag{11}$$

In the model (11), we can consider it is a transformation from model (5) where a equals 0 and b equals 1, which means the diffusion in the direction of tangent vector and normal vector on the isolux line is not consistent. Model (11) is anisotropic, it can protect the image from appearing light and dark areas; It can also eliminate the hackly phenomenon. Although the model can guarantee the smoothness on the edge of image, it cannot sharpen the edge, which would cause fuzzy edge.

3   Image Zooming Model Based on Image Decomposition

The process of zooming model can be divided into two steps, zooming of cartoon image and zooming of texture image. The cartoon image, contains most smoothness of a given image, can adopt isotropic zoom; the texture image, contains most texture details, can adopt anisotropic zoom. In order to sharpen the edge of image, in order to keep the edge and texture of image, Gilboa et al. proposed the following model combined shock filter and PDEs [9, 10].

$$u_t = -\frac{2}{\pi}\arctan\left(au_{\eta\eta}\right)|\nabla u| + \gamma u_{\xi\xi} \tag{12}$$

where a represents limiting figure.

3.1   Zooming Model

Combining the image decomposition, Isotropic model, Anisotropic model and the shock filters, we propose the new image zooming model.

$$f_t = RUP_1 u_t + RUP_2 v_t, \begin{cases} u_t = -\alpha\left(u_{\eta\eta} + u_{\xi\xi}\right), & u \subset \text{Cartoon} \\ v_t = -\beta\arctan\left(au_{\eta\eta}\right)|\nabla u| + \gamma c(\nabla u)u_{\xi\xi}, & v \subset \text{Texture} \end{cases}$$

$$\tag{13}$$

where RUP_1 and RUP_2 represent the iterations of the part of cartoon and texture, α, γ represent the diffusion coefficient, β represents the sharping coefficient, $c(\nabla u) = 1/(1 + \nabla u)$ represents diffusion function.

3.2   The Process of Image Zooming

The concrete steps of image zooming can be concluded as:

- First, zoom the given image by initial zooming model;
- Second, decompose the image which has been zoomed by step one. Using VO decomposed model;
- Third, zoom the cartoon part by Isotropic model, iterate until get the optimal solution;
- Fourth, zoom the texture part by Anisotropic model, combined with the shock filters, iterate until get the optimal solution;
- Finally, integrate the zoomed cartoon and texture part and get the final image. The specific zooming model of the flow chart is shown in Fig. 1.

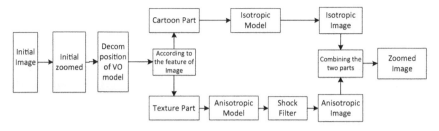

Fig. 1. The process of image zooming

3.3 Discretization

We set time step Δt and space interval h, usually, the space interval setting is 1. Contraposing the model (13), combining the following discretization models:

$$u_x = \frac{u_{i+1,j} - u_{i-1,j}}{2h} \; ; \quad u_y = \frac{u_{i,j+1} - u_{i,j-1}}{2h}$$

$$u_{xx} = \frac{u_{i+1,j} + u_{i-1,j} - 2u_{i,j}}{h^2} \; ; \quad u_{yy} = \frac{u_{i,j+1} + u_{i,j-1} - 2u_{i,j}}{h^2} \tag{14}$$

$$u_{xy} = \frac{u_{i+1,j+1} + u_{i-1,j-1} - u_{i-1,j+1} - u_{i+1,j-1}}{4h^2}$$

and

$$\left| \nabla u_{i,j} \right| = \sqrt{u_{x(i,j)}^2 + u_{y(i,j)}^2} \tag{15}$$

The model (6), (7) can be discretized.

$$u_{\xi\xi(i,j)} = \frac{u_{xx(i,j)}u_{y(i,j)}^2 - 2u_{xy(i,j)}u_{x(i,j)}u_{y(i,j)} + u_{yy(i,j)}u_{x(i,j)}^2}{u_{x(i,j)}^2 + u_{y(i,j)}^2} \tag{16}$$

$$u_{\eta\eta(i,j)} = \frac{u_{xx(i,j)}u_{x(i,j)}^2 + 2u_{xy(i,j)}u_{x(i,j)}u_{y(i,j)} + u_{yy(i,j)}u_{y(i,j)}^2}{u_{x(i,j)}^2 + u_{y(i,j)}^2} \tag{17}$$

The final discretization format of the new image zooming model is.

$$f_{i,j}^{n+1} = u_{i,j}^{n+1} + v_{i,j}^{n+1}$$

$$\begin{cases} u_{i,j}^{n+1} = u_{i,j}^n - \alpha\Delta t \left(u_{\eta\eta(i,j)}^n + u_{\xi\xi(i,j)}^n \right) \\ v_{i,j}^{n+1} = v_{i,j}^n - \beta\Delta t \left(\arctan\left(a u_{\eta\eta(i,j)}^n \right) \right) \left| \nabla u_{i,j}^n \right| + \gamma \left(\frac{1}{1 + \sqrt{u_{x(i,j)}^2 + u_{y(i,j)}^2}} \right) u_{\xi\xi(i,j)}^n \end{cases} \tag{18}$$

3.4 Result and Analysis

Our experimental environment is Windows 7 and Core i5. We use MATLAB 2014a as programming tool. To keep effectiveness of the new model, we adopt a few images as experimental subject. We set RUPD, RUP1, and RUP2 as limited iterations of Image decomposition, Isotropic model and anisotropic model. The experiment shows when $RUPD \leq 5, RUP1 \leq 15$ and $RUP2 \leq 5$, the new model gets optimal solution. We set $\lambda = 0.02, \mu = 0.1, \beta = \gamma = 10, \alpha = 1, \Delta t = 0.01$ as our experiment's parameters. In order to compare the new model with other models, adopt Peak signal to noise ratio (PSNR) and Root mean square error (RMSE) as experiment's standard.

$$PRNR = 20 \times lg\left(\frac{255}{RMSE}\right) \tag{19}$$

$$RMSE = \sqrt{\frac{\sum_{i,j}\left(u(i,j) - u(i,j)^0\right)^2}{M \times N}} \tag{20}$$

Where u represents zoomed image, u^0 represents initial image. According to the definition of PSNR and RMSE, the larger the PSNR, the smaller the RMSE, the zoomed image would be better. Firstly, we shrink the initial image Lena, Camera, Peppers twice. Then, we use the new model zoom the image twice. Compare the new model with other models on PSNR and RMSE. We get the result as shown in the Table 1.

Table 1. Comparison of PSNR, RMSE

Initial image	Multiple	Bi-cubic model		Anisotropic model [1]		The new model	
		PSNR	RMSE	PSNR	RMSE	PSNR	RMSE
Lena 256	2	30.45	7.65	30.40	7.69	**30.97**	**7.21**
Barbara 512	2	25.40	13.69	25.37	13.74	**25.75**	**13.16**
Camera 256	2	26.33	12.31	26.29	12.36	**26.74**	**11.73**
Peppers 512	2	31.98	6.41	31.96	6.43	**32.13**	**6.31**

Table 1 shows the new model has a better effect in the comparison of PSNR and RMSE among the three models. The paper proposes a new second order model based on the image decomposition. From the result shown in the Table 1, we find the new model can achieve the desired effect; the value of PSNR is increased by 0.5 dB. Give the Lena image as example, as shown in the Fig. 2.

The new model divides the given image into two parts; it reduces the degree of relevance between smooth area and texture area. In this way, the new model takes advantages of two parts' features and avoids the interference from one part to the other

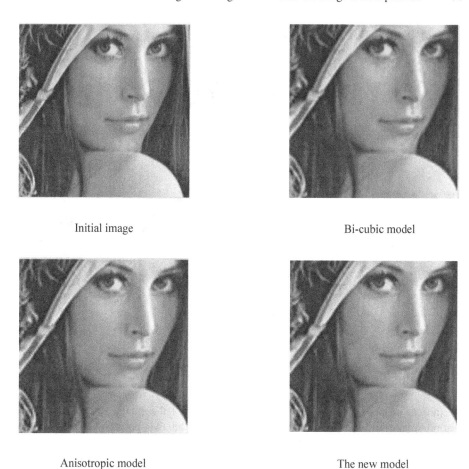

Initial image   Bi-cubic model

Anisotropic model   The new model

Fig. 2. Part of Lena image

part, so the new model has better effect in image zooming. In order to reflect the advantages of the new model, give the following figures (from left to right, respects the Initial image, the texture part, the Bi-cubic effect, the new model effect) (Figs. 3, 4 and 5).

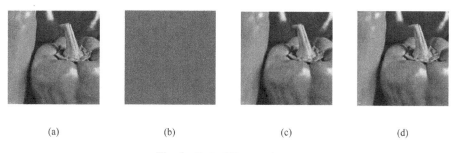

(a)   (b)   (c)   (d)

Fig. 3. Part of Pappers image

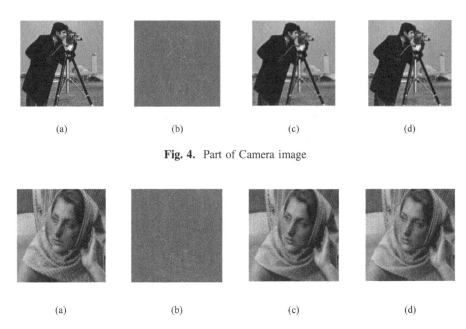

(a)   (b)   (c)   (d)

Fig. 4. Part of Camera image

(a)   (b)   (c)   (d)

Fig. 5. Part of Barbara image

4   Conclusions

The article proposes a new model which decomposes the image into two parts—cartoon image and texture image, then it zoomed the two parts specifying to the differences of two parts. About the cartoon image, the new model adopts isotropic model, it is easy to compute and it restrains the skewing of the light and dark areas and block phenomenon. To zoom the texture part, the new model uses anisotropic model, it eliminates the border jagged phenomenon, at the same time, adds the shock filters on the edge of the sharpening treatment, so that the boundary is clearer. Experiments show that the new model reaches the initial demands; it has a better effect than others. Because the different weights of each image between cartoon part and texture part, the iteration is different on each part, so how to find a standard to measure the different iteration will be an important task.

References

1. Lu, H.-L., Wang, Y.-D., Li, S.-Y.: Image enlargement based on isotropic and anisotropic diffusion. J. Shanghai Univ. Natural Sci. Edition **14**(4), 383–387 (2008)
2. Wang, X.-H., Ai, X.-N.: Image adjustment model of thermal adjustment and global variation model adaptive adjustment. J. Image Graph. **18**(11), 1398–1406 (2013)
3. Li, P., Zou, Y., Yao, Z.: Fourth-order anisotropic diffusion equations for image zooming. J. Image Graph. **18**(10), 1261–1269 (2013)

4. Li, Q.-J., Zhu, X., Zhang, X.-F., et al.: A new image amplification method based on sparse decomposition. Comput. Sci. **42**(3), 271–273 (2015)
5. Rudin, L.I., Osher, S., Fatemi, E.: Nonlinear total variation based noise removal algorithms. Phys. D **60**(1–4), 259–268 (1992)
6. Vese, L.A., Osher, S.J.: Modeling textures with total variation minimization and oscillating patterns in image processing. J. Sci. Comput. **19**(1), 553–572 (2003)
7. Zhong, S.: Adaptive smoothing respecting feature directions. IEEE Trans. Image Process. **7**(3), 353–358 (1998). A Publication of the IEEE Signal Processing Society
8. Morse, B.S., Schwartzwald, D.: Image magnification using level-set reconstruction, vol. 1, pp. I-333–I-340 (2001)
9. Osher, S., Rudin, L.I.: Feature-oriented image enhancement using shock filters. Siam J. Numer. Anal. **27**(4), 919–940 (1990)
10. Gilboa, G., Sochen, N.A., Zeevi, Y.Y.: Regularized shock filters and complex diffusion 2350, 399–413 (2002)

Salient Object Detection Based on the Fusion of Foreground Coarse Extraction and Background Prior

Lingkang Gu[1(✉)] and Zhigeng Pan[2]

[1] School of Computer and Information,
Anhui Polytechnic University, Wuhu 241000, Anhui, China
glk_81@163.com
[2] VR Research Institute, NINEDVR Corp., Guuangzhou 310036, China
zhigengpan@gmail.com

Abstract. In order to obtain more refined salient object detection results, firstly, the coarse salient regions are extracted from the bottom-up, the coarse saliency map contains local map, frequency prior map and global color distribution map, which are more in accord with the rules of biological psychology. Then, an algorithm is proposed to measure the background prior quality by using three indexes, namely, salient expectation, local contrast and global contrast. Finally, the weighted algorithm is designed according to the prior quality to improve the saliency, so that the saliency prior and the saliency detection results are more accurate. Compared with 9 state-of-the-art algorithms on the 2 benchmark datasets of ECSSD and MSRA 10k, the proposed algorithm highlights salient regions, reduces noise, and is more in line with human visual perception, and reflects the excellence.

Keywords: Salient object detection · Foreground coarse extraction
Local contrast · Global contrast · Prior fusion

1 Introduction

The research of visual selective attention mechanism, which is called "salient object detection", is one of the hotspots in the field of computer vision [1]. Image saliency detection has a wide range of applications, such as object detection and recognition [2], image and video compression [3], video saliency detection [4], image quality assessment [5], and image segmentation [6] and other fields.

In view of saliency driven and object independent saliency detection, many researchers have done relevant work. In the reference [7], based on the region of global contrast calculation, first of all, the image is segmented to obtain a number of super pixel regions, and then use the color distance and spatial distance weighted to calculate the saliency of the region. Achanta *et al.* [8] were calculated according to the frequency tuning theory, firstly by using Gauss filter of fuzzy image, and calculate the fuzzy image color mean; then by calculating the distance between each pixel in the original image and the color mean to get the saliency map. These methods do not make full use of the foreground, background and prior information of the image, leading to the detection effect is not very excellent.

© Springer-Verlag GmbH Germany, part of Springer Nature 2018
Z. Pan et al. (Eds.): Transactions on Edutainment XIV, LNCS 10790, pp. 100–114, 2018.
https://doi.org/10.1007/978-3-662-56689-3_9

Integrating bottom-up approach and top-down approach into a framework to improve the accuracy and efficiency of detection is the current research idea [9–12]. Liu *et al.* [9] use conditional random fields to integrate the local multi-scale contrast feature map, and the central-periphery histogram feature map and the color space distribution feature map based on global computation, and obtain the expected saliency map. Reference [13] considers the global and local cues, and proposes a saliency computation method based on encoding. Reference [14–16] try to distinguish between background and object, create a saliency fusion map based on foreground and background, and extended to other salient model detection. The detection accuracy is based on the appropriate selection of the background seed. Reference [17] uses an improved model, but it is not suitable for complex heterogeneous background scenarios. Most of these methods use single or similar linear weighting to combine salient features computed by bottom-up and top-down algorithms. When these algorithms are applied to different types of images, its universality will be poor, resulting in unstable performance and low operating efficiency.

2   The Framework of Our Method

In view of the above problems, this paper proposes a multi-feature linear weighted join method which is more in line with the rules of biological psychology than the traditional methods, *i.e.*, a saliency detection and optimization algorithm that can integrate the computation of bottom-up and top-down. Among them, the bottom-up saliency region coarse extraction algorithm is complementary to local and global computation, the global computation takes full advantage of the prior information of frequency and the prior information of color space distribution. The top-down computation is based on the background prior optimization to obtain the image background weight map. The framework of this algorithm is shown in Fig. 1.

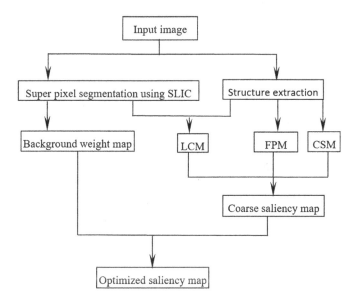

Fig. 1. The algorithm framework of this paper

3   Coarse Extraction of Saliency Regions

In this section, 3 main parts of image saliency region coarse extraction are introduced: local contrast map, frequency domain prior map and global color distribution map. Then the three parts are weighted to get the coarse extraction of salient regions. Before these operations, we need to use the structure extraction algorithm to preprocess the image. After the main structure of the image is extracted, the texture suppressed smooth image is obtained, and then the image is segmented of super pixel by SLIC method [18].

3.1   Local Contrast Map

On the basis of image super pixel segmentation, a local contrast map function is defined according to the following 3 properties:

(a) The greater the contrast between a super pixel and its neighborhood is, the greater the value of its saliency is;
(b) The closer a super pixel is to the center of the image, the more salient it is;
(c) If a super pixel region has a large number of pixels located on the boundary of the image, then the region is likely to belong to the background.

Firstly, a given image is divided into k super pixels, for a super pixel s_i and its corresponding neighborhood $\{n_i\}$, $i = 1, \ldots K_i$, where k_i represents the number of neighbors. Define the saliency of s_i, as shown in Eq. (1)

$$S(s_i) = \left(\sum_{j=1}^{K_i} \omega_{ij} f\left(d\left(s_i, n_j\right) \right) \right) \times t(x, y) \times h(u). \tag{1}$$

where $d\left(s_i, n_j\right)$ is the Eulerian distance of the histogram, $d\left(s_i, n_j\right) = max\left(D_{col}\left(s_i, n_j\right), D_{wld}\left(s_i, n_j\right)\right)$ represents the feature distance between super pixels s_i and n_j, $D_{col}\left(s_i, n_j\right)$ and $D_{wld}\left(s_i, n_j\right)$ represent the x^2 distance between the Lab color histogram and the WLD histogram respectively; ω_{ij} is the ratio of n_j and its total area of its neighborhood $\{n_j\}$; In order to highlight the salient area, suppose function $f(\emptyset) = -log(1 - \emptyset)$.
In Eq. (1) x and y are the average values of all super pixels location, and normalized to [0, 1]; $t(x, y)$ is the normalization of the distance between the super pixel central s_i and the center of the image (x_0, y_0), as shown in Eq. (2):

$$t(x, y) = \exp\left(-\frac{(x - x_0)^2}{2\sigma_x^2} - \frac{(y - y_0)^2}{2\sigma_y^2} \right). \tag{2}$$

Suppose σ_x as the image width value 1/3, σ_y as the image high value 1/3, so the closer the pixel is to the center of the image, the greater the weight. $h(u)$ is a function that represents the super pixel integrity of the boundary,as shown in Eq. (3).

$$h(u) = \begin{cases} \exp\left(-\frac{u}{\lambda \times E}\right), & \frac{u}{E} \leq \eta \\ 0, & otherwise \end{cases}. \tag{3}$$

In Eq. (3), u represents the pixel number on the boundary in the super pixel s_i, E is the total amount of all pixels on the edge of the image, λ is a parameter adjustment, η is a threshold value. Suppose $\lambda = 0.05$ and $\eta = 0.07$. The super pixel of the larger u means that it's unlikely to make a salient object, if $u = 0$ represents that the super pixel isn't on the boundary, and the $h(u) = 1$; otherwise, $h(u) \in [0, 1]$.

3.2 Frequency Prior Map

This paper detects salient objects using bandpass filter. The filter selected in this paper is based on Log-Gabor rather than the usual Gog [8], because that:

(a) it can construct Log-Gabor filters with arbitrary bandwidth and no DC component. When natural images are observed in the logarithmic-frequency range, the filters with Gauss transfer function can be encoded better; in the linear frequency range, the Log-Gabor function $g(t)(t = (x, y) \in R^2)$ of the transfer function as shown in Eq. (4):

$$G(f) = \exp\left(\frac{-\left(\log\left(\frac{f}{f_0}\right)\right)^2}{2\left(\log\left(\frac{\delta}{f_0}\right)\right)^2}\right). \tag{4}$$

where f_0 is the central frequency of the filter, $\delta/f0$ is the bandwidth of control filter. According to the definition, the Log-Gabor function does not contain the DC component and can construct arbitrary bandwidth Log-Gabor filtering.

(b) The transfer function of Log-Gabor filter has a long tail effect in the high frequency end, which makes it to more adapt to natural image encoding than other ordinary band pass filters. Due to the singularity at the origin of the log function, which leads to $g(t)$ not to analytical expression, only through the $G(f)$ digital inverse Fourier transform to get $g(t)$.

An image of RGB color space $\{f(x): | x \in \Omega, \Omega$ as image spatial domain$\}$, $f(x)$ is actually a vector containing 3 color component values R (red), G (green) and B (blue) in x position, similar to the reference [8], its saliency map can be got by band pass filtering modeled, $f(x)$ needs to be first converted to the CIELab color space, and its generated frequency domain prior graph, as shown in Eq. (5):

$$S_F(x) = \left((f_L * g)^2 + (f_a * g)^2 + (f_b * g)^2\right)^{\frac{1}{2}}(x). \tag{5}$$

where $*$ represents a convolution operation.

3.3 Color Spatial-Distribution Map

If a color types are widely distributed in the image, then the color is likely to belong to the background color, *i.e.* which is less likely to be included in the salient object. The smaller the spatial variance of the color component is, the more likely it is to be part of the salient object color. The purpose of using the variance distribution of color space is to consider the global color information of the image.

In general, each pixel in the Gauss mixture model can be represented as formula (6):

$$\frac{p\left(c|I_{(x,y)}\right)\left(\omega_c N\left(I_{(x,y)}|\mu_c,\Sigma_c\right)\right)}{\sum_c \omega_c N\left(I_{(x,y)}|\mu_c,\Sigma_c\right)}. \tag{6}$$

where ω_c, μ_c and $\sum_c$ are respectively the weight, mean and variance of c-th component; $N(\bullet)$ is the Gauss model; $I(x,y)$ is the pixel at the position (x, y). Unlike the solving method of probabilistic model in reference [9], the maximum likelihood estimator is used in this paper, such as Eq. (7):

$$c_{I_{(x,y)}}^* = \arg \max_{c \in C} p\left(c|I_{(x,y)}\right). \tag{7}$$

where c is the set of all components. So, the horizontal and vertical space positions of each color component-$v_h(c^*)$ and $v_v(c^*)$ can be further simplified to Eqs. (8) and (9):

$$v_h(c^*) = \frac{1}{N}\sum_{I(x,y)\in c^*} |x - \mu_x(c^*)|^2. \tag{8}$$

$$v_v(c^*) = \frac{1}{N}\sum_{I(x,y)\in c^*} |x - \mu_y(c^*)|^2. \tag{9}$$

where μ_x and μ_y are respectively the mean value of x coordinate and y coordinate. N is the pixel number of c^* maximum likelihood. Then the color space variance of the c^*-*th* component can be defined as the maximum variance of x and y coordinates, as shown in Eq. (10):

$$V(c^*) = \max(v_h(c^*), v_v(c^*)). \tag{10}$$

It should be noted that the color space variance of all components must be normalized to [0, 1], and finally the global color feature distribution map can be obtained, as shown in Eq. (11):

$$S_C\left(I_{(x,y)}\right) = V\left(c_{I_{(x,y)}}^*\right). \tag{11}$$

In our experiment, $c = 5$. When the image background is monotonous, the global features can have a high accuracy to detect salient object; but when the image contains complex background color, these features cannot distinguish the salient object in the image.

3.4   Saliency Map of Coarse Extraction

After the above 3 feature maps are obtained, local contrast map (LCM), frequency prior map (FPM) and color spatial-distribution map (CSM) are generated. Saliency map of coarse extraction (SMC) can be obtained by joint computation, as shown in Eq. (12):

$$SMC = \exp(FPM + CSM) \times LCM. \qquad (12)$$

where LCM, CSM and FPM are normalized to [0, 1], LCM is calculated from local perspective, and CSM and FPM are calculated from global view, which format the complementary relationship with LCM. The exponential function is used, mainly because LCM has the greatest impact on the final result.

4   Optimized Background Weight Map Computation

According to the distribution of salient objects in images, it is necessary to have three conditions for the reasonable estimation of the background saliency: (a) salient regions account for a relatively small proportion of the image; (b) salient regions are relatively concentrated, salient values of same regions close to; (c) the contrast between salient and non salient areas is obvious. According to the above conditions, three indexes are designed to judge the confidence of the saliency estimation.

4.1   Salient Expectation

Firstly, the salient expectation of background salient estimation is defined, as Eq. (13):

$$E = \frac{1}{n} \sum_{i=1}^{n} S(i). \qquad (13)$$

where n is the number of super pixel blocks. According to the condition (a), the proportion of salient regions is less in the image, therefore, the salient expectation E of a reasonably salient prior should be low. If the E is too high, it is shown that in the salient prior, the salient region is too large in the image, or the salient value in the region is too high.

4.2   Local Salient Contrast

Secondly, the definition of local salient contrast, as shown in Eq. (14):

$$C_{local} = \frac{1}{n} \sum_{i=1}^{n} \frac{1}{|k_i|} \sum_{t \in k_i} |S(i) - S(t)|^2. \qquad (14)$$

where i is a label of super pixel block, k_i is a set of all super pixel blocks adjacent to the *i-th* super pixel block. The local contrast reflects the difference between the super pixel block and adjacent areas. As salient prior, according to the condition (b), in addition to the boundary of the image and the boundary area of the object in the image, the difference between the super pixel block and the adjacent super pixel block should be smaller, so the C_{local} is smaller. C_{local} is too large to indicate that the salient regions are not concentrated, or the difference of salient value within the salient regions is too large.

4.3   Global Salient Contrast

Finally, the global salient contrast is defined, such as the formula (15):

$$C_{global} = \sum_{\delta} \delta(i,j)^2 P_{\delta}(i,j). \tag{15}$$

where i and j represent adjacent super pixel blocks, $\delta(i,j)$ represents the gray difference between adjacent super pixel blocks, $P_{\delta}(i,j)$ is the super pixel block distribution rate of the gray difference δ. According to the conditions (c), a reasonable prior is that salient region and non salient region should be obvious contrast, so C_{global} should be larger. If C_{global} is too small, the distinction between salient region and non salient region is not obvious, so it is not a reasonable salient prior.

4.4   Confidence

According to the above definition and analysis, salient expectation E should be smaller, local contrast C_{local} should be small, and global contrast C_{global} should be larger, so the definition of confidence is shown in Eq. (16):

$$p = \frac{C_{global}}{C_{local} \times E}. \tag{16}$$

The confidence p is larger, the salient prior more reasonable, whereas the more unreasonable. The confidence of 4 background salient estimation is calculated respectively, such as $p_{top}, p_{left}, p_{bottom}, p_{right}$; and the background salient estimations are fused through weighted addition, so background prior weight map is obtained, as shown in Eq. (17):

$$S_{BG} = \sum_{i} p_i S_i. \tag{17}$$

where $i \in \{top, left, bottom, right\}$. Compared with the previous algorithm, the weighted addition method can achieve higher recall rate under the same accuracy.

5   Improved Saliency Map

The foreground SMC and the background feature BG extracted from above are complementary and mutually reinforcing, but they are still coarse and have more noise. Therefore, the combination of two can be considered naturally, integrated into a regular algorithm framework, and further refined to obtain the final improved saliency map.

This algorithm combines with salient information which are obtained from the foreground and background, the saliency detection is formulated as an optimization problem of all super pixels salient values in an image. By minimizing the designed cost function, the object area is assigned to 1 as much as possible, and the background area is assigned to 0.

The cost function constructed in this paper consists of 3 constraint items, such as formula (18):

$$\sum_{i=1}^{N} \omega_i^{BG} s_i^2 + \sum_{i=1}^{N} \omega_i^{SMC} (s_j - 1)^2 + \sum_{i,j} \omega_{ij} (s_i - s_j)^2. \tag{18}$$

where $S_i (i = 1, \ldots, N)$ is the final saliency value of the super pixel p_i after the minimization of the cost function. The first item is to promote the super pixel p_i as much as possible with a large background probability ω_i^{BG} to get a value tending to 0. Accordingly, the second item ω_i^{SMC} represents foreground weight associated with super pixel p_i, the bigger which value that p_i can tend to 1. After optimization, the coarse salient map generated in the previous paper can be improved obviously. The last item is the smoothing term, which guarantees the stationarity and continuity of the adjacent super pixel saliency values. For any 2 adjacent super pixels p_i and p_j, the weight value ω_{ij} is defined as the formula (19):

$$\omega_{ij} = \exp - \left(\frac{d_{app}^2 (p_i, p_j)}{2\delta^2} \right) + \tau. \tag{19}$$

In the smooth region of image pixels, the value of ω_{ij} is larger, but there is a smaller ω_{ij} value at the edge of the region. In order to minimize the interference of the background noise and foreground noise, also add a regular item $\tau = 0.1$.

6   Simulation Experiments and Analysis

In order to fully verify the effectiveness of our algorithm, we test this algorithm on a PC with Intel i7 3.6 GHz and 32G RAM. The test datasets are ECSSD [19] and MSRA 10k [20]. MSRA 10k contains images which backgrounds are relatively simple, the images in ECSSD are rich colors, diversity texture and complex background. We compare our proposed algorithm with 9 state-of-the-art methods which are HS [19], CHM [20], HC [7], RPC [21], CTC [22], SCUL [23], HCCH [24], MDBL [25], ODSR [26].

6.1   Qualitative Analysis

Figure 2 contains some salient maps generated by our algorithm and the other 9 algorithms on MSRA10k and ECSSD. It can be seen from the Fig. 2a that, because the background of MSRA 10k is simple, our algorithm performs better than other algorithms. From the Fig. 2b, it can be seen that the performance of our algorithm is relatively best on the ECSSD dataset with more complex background or texture than MSRA 10k, and it can detect the salient objects in the image better.

A good algorithm for detecting salient object should be as uniform as possible complete highlight the salient goals, a clear target boundary, while suppressing the

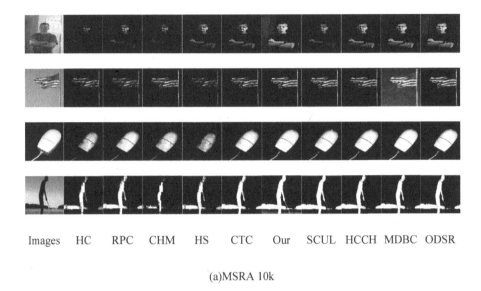

Images   HC   RPC   CHM   HS   CTC   Our   SCUL   HCCH   MDBC   ODSR

(a)MSRA 10k

Images   HC   RPC   CHM   HS   CTC   Our   SCUL   HCCH   MDBC   ODSR

(b)ECSSD

Fig. 2. Illustrations of the results generated by different methods on the two public datasets

background. In this paper, it is found that compared with other methods, MDBC, ODSR and the proposed algorithm can preserve the target boundary better than other methods based pixels or blocks; Although HC and RPC algorithms can detect the contour of object, there are some omissions in it; CHM algorithm sometimes mistakenly detects some background parts as salient object; HS algorithm is easy to lose small objects.

6.2   Quantitative Analysis

The commonly used indexes of evaluating algorithm effect are P-R curve, F-measure value (F_β) and mean absolute error (MAE).

Precision-Recall Curve (P-R). The P-R curve is the most commonly used means of evaluation algorithms, Precision P as shown in Eq. (20), and Recall R as shown in Eq. (21):

$$P = \frac{|B \cap G|}{|B|}. \tag{20}$$

$$R = \frac{|B \cap G|}{|G|}. \tag{21}$$

where G is saliency true value map of artificial labeled; B is 2-value mask map generated by thresholding the saliency map S; $|\cdot|$ is the area of the corresponding image region.

   If the saliency value of pixel is larger than the segmentation threshold, then the point is marked as salient foreground, otherwise marked as background. Then the obtained 2-valued map is compared with the true value map G, to calculate P and R. when the threshold changes from 0 to 255, you can draw the P-R curve, to evaluate the performance of the algorithm model under different conditions, such as Fig. 3a and b. From these 2 figures, we can see that the performance of our algorithm is outstanding, which is equivalent to the latest 2 excellent algorithms ODSR and MDBL, and far better than the other 7 algorithms. Experimental results show that the proposed algorithm has the best performance on MSRA10k, and is equivalent to ODSR on ECSSD.

F-measure (F_β). Generally, P-R can't be used alone to evaluate the quality of saliency map. Therefore, this paper uses F-measure value F_β to weight harmonic mean about Precision and Recall to judge the quality of the algorithm, F_β such as formula (22):

$$F_\beta = \frac{\left(1 + \beta^2\right) \times P \times R}{\beta^2 \times P + R}. \tag{22}$$

where $\beta^2 = 0.3$ is used to emphasize the importance of accuracy; the higher the F_β value the better algorithm. You can see from Fig. 4, this algorithm has the best F_β value on MSRA 10k, the ODSR method is slightly worse. On ECSSD, our algorithm has better F_β value, which is only inferior to MDBL method. These are further proved that our algorithm is effective and accurate.

Mean Absolute Error (MAE). In theory, the saliency map generated by an algorithm is more consistent with the truth map, which shows that the performance of the algorithm is better. But only using P-R curve and F_β to evaluate one algorithm still has

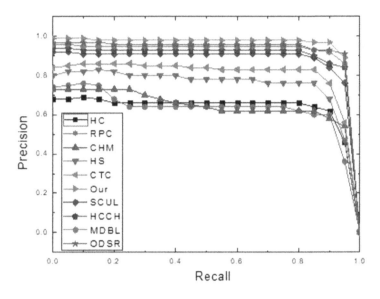

(a)P-R curves on MSRA 10k dataset

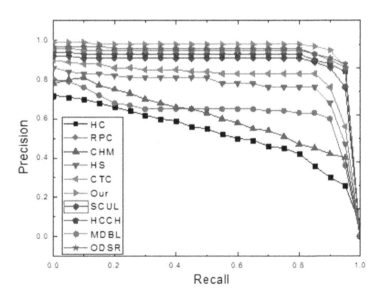

(b)P-R curves on ECSSD dataset

Fig. 3. Comparison of precision-recall curves of different methods on the two public datasets

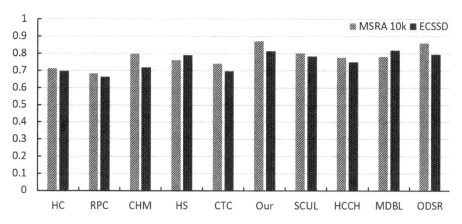

Fig. 4. Comparison of F-measure values

limitations, so this paper uses MAE as an additional measure of evaluation to calculate the error between the saliency map S and the saliency truth value map G of the artificial marker, such as formula (23):

$$\text{MAE} = \frac{1}{W \times H} \sum_{i=1}^{W} \sum_{j=1}^{H} |S(i,j) - G(i,j)|. \tag{23}$$

where $S(i, j)$ is saliency value at the pixel position (i, j); W and H denote the width and height of the image respectively. One good saliency detection algorithm should have a good P-R curve representation and a smaller MAE value. From Table 1, we can see that on MSRA 10k, the MAE of our algorithm is slightly larger than that of ODSR, but less than other algorithms; on RCSSD, the MAE of this algorithm is minimal. This shows that our algorithm is superior to many other algorithms on different indexes on two datasets, which shows the high accuracy of the proposed algorithm.

Table 1. Comparison of MAE and efficiency

Algorithms	Datasets		Time/s
	MSRA 10k	ECSSD	
HC	0.317	0.297	0.203
RPC	0.302	0.309	0.201
CHM	0.285	0.291	0.283
HS	0.273	0.269	0.216
CTC	0.281	0.274	0.317
Our	0.105	0.109	0.206
SCUL	0.218	0.211	0.241
HCCH	0.176	0.192	0.352
MDBL	0.107	0.113	0.479
ODSR	0.102	0.114	0.375

6.3   Running Time Analysis

The average running time of our proposed approach and other methods mentioned above is presented in Table 1. The implementation is taken on ECSSD dataset using Matlab or C, and most of the test images have resolution 300×400. The time consuming of our algorithm is mainly in the coarse extraction process of salient object, which accounts for about 57%. The average running time of our algorithm is moderate, and it consumes less time than most algorithms. Especially for the better effect MDBL algorithm and the newer ODSR algorithm, our algorithm speed is much faster than them. For fast algorithms, such as RPC, our approach works better.

7   Conclusion

In this paper, according to the characteristics of images, we propose an algorithm of salient object detection based on the fusion of foreground coarse extraction and background prior; which uses the prior information of the image boundary, local and global information to extract the saliency map to construct the coarse saliency map. Then according to the distribution of salient objects in the image, we design a background salient estimation index, with salient expectation, local contrast and global contrast three indexes to measure the quality of the prior algorithm. Lastly, in order to improve salience, using the prior quality to design weight addition, thereby the saliency prior and the saliency detection results are more accurate. On 2 open datasets, compared with related other algorithms, experimental results show that the performance of our proposed algorithm is excellent.

Acknowledgements. This work was supported by "National Natural Science Foundation of China (No. 61300170)" and "Anhui province higher education to enhance the general project plan of Provincial Natural Science Research (No. TSKJ2014B11)". The authors wish to thank the Education Department of Anhui Province for their help.

References

1. Wang, W., Zhang, Y., Li, J.: High-level background prior based salient object detection. J. Vis. Commun. Image Representation **48**, 432–441 (2017)
2. Ren, Z.X., Gao, S.H., Chia, L.T., et al.: Region-based saliency detection and its application in object recognition. IEEE Trans. Circ. Syst. Video Technol. **24**(5), 769–779 (2014)
3. Guo, C.L., Zhang, L.M.: A novel multiresolution spatiotemporal saliency detection model and its applications in image and video compression. IEEE Trans. Image Process. **19**(1), 185–198 (2010)
4. Chen, C., Wu, X., Wang, B., et al.: Video saliency detection using dynamic fusion of spatial-temporal features in complex background with disturbance. J. Comput. Aided Des. Comput. Graph. **28**(5), 802–812 (2016)
5. Li, A., She, X.C., Sun, Q.: Color image quality assessment combining saliency and FSIM. Proc. SPIE. Bellingham Soc. Photo Opt. Instrum. Eng. **8878**, 88780I–88780I-5 (2013)

6. Qin, C.C., Zhang, G.P., Zhou, Y.C., et al.: Integration of the saliency based seed extraction and random walks for image segmentation. Neurocomputing **129**, 378–391 (2014)
7. Cheng, M.M., Mitra, N.J., Huang, X.L., et al.: Global contrast based salient region detection. IEEE Trans. Pattern Anal. Mach. Intell. **37**(3), 569–582 (2015)
8. Achanta, R., Hemami, S.S., Estrada, F.V., et al.: Frequency-tuned salient region detection. In: Proceedings of the Computer Vision and Pattern Recognition, Los Alamitos, pp. 1597–1604. IEEE Computer Society Press (2009)
9. Liu, T., Yuan, Z.J., Sun, J., et al.: Learning to detect a salient object. IEEE Trans. Pattern Anal. Mach. Intell. **33**(2), 353–367 (2011)
10. Wei, Y., Wen, F., Zhu, W., Sun, J.: Geodesic saliency using background priors. In: Fitzgibbon, A., Lazebnik, S., Perona, P., Sato, Y., Schmid, C. (eds.) ECCV 2012. LNCS, vol. 7574, pp. 29–42. Springer, Heidelberg (2012). https://doi.org/10.1007/978-3-642-33712-3_3
11. Rasolzadeh, B., Tavakoli Targhi, A., Eklundh, J.-O.: An attentional system combining top-down and bottom-up influences. In: Paletta, L., Rome, E. (eds.) WAPCV 2007. LNCS (LNAI), vol. 4840, pp. 123–140. Springer, Heidelberg (2007). https://doi.org/10.1007/978-3-540-77343-6_8
12. Tian, H., Fang, Y., Zhao, Y., et al.: Salient region detection by fusing bottom-up and top-down features extracted from a single image. IEEE Trans. Image Process. **23**(10), 4389–4398 (2014)
13. Tong, N., Lu, H.C., Zhang, Y., et al.: Salient object detection via global and local cues. Pattern Recogn. **48**(10), 3258–3267 (2015)
14. Wang, J.P., Lu, H.C., Li, X.H., et al.: Saliency detection via background and foreground seed selection. Neurocomputing **152**, 359–368 (2015)
15. Li, S., Lu, H.C., Lin, Z., et al.: Adaptive metric learning for saliency detection. IEEE Trans. Image Process. **24**(11), 3321–3331 (2015)
16. Huo, L., Jiao, L.C., Wang, S., et al.: Saliency detection with color attributes. Pattern Recogn. **49**, 162–173 (2016)
17. Frintrop, S., Werner, T., Garcia, G.M.: Traditional saliency reloaded: a good old model in new shape. In: Proceedings of the IEEE Computer Society Conference on Computer Vision and Pattern Recognition, Piscataway, pp. 82–90. IEEE Computer Society (2015)
18. Achanta, R., Shaji, A., Smith, K., et al.: SLIC super pixels compared to state-of-the-art super pixel methods. IEEE Trans. Pattern Anal. Mach. Intell. **34**(11), 2274–2282 (2012)
19. Yan, Q., Xu, L., Shi, J., et al.: Hierarchical saliency detection. In: Proceedings of the IEEE Conference on Computer Vision and Pattern Recognition, Los Alamitos, pp. 1155–1162. IEEE Computer Society Press (2013)
20. Li, X., Li, Y., Shen, C.H., et al.: Contextual hypergraph modeling for salient object detection. In: Proceedings of the IEEE International Conference on Computer Vision, Los Alamitos, pp. 3328–3335. IEEE Computer Society Press (2013)
21. Lou, J., Ren, M.W., Wang, H.: Regional principal color based saliency detection. PloS One **9**(11), e112475 (2014)
22. Zhang, Q., Lin, J., Tao, Y., et al.: Salient object detection via color and texture cues. Neurocomputing **243**, 35–48 (2017)
23. Zhang, Q., Liu, Y., Zhu, S., Han, J.: Salient object detection based on super-pixel clustering and unified low-rank representation. Comput. Vis. Image Underst. **161**, 51–64 (2017)
24. Liu, Q., Hong, X., Zou, B., et al.: Hierarchical contour closure-based holistic salient object detection. IEEE Trans. Image Process. **26**(9), 4537–4552 (2017)

25. Song, H., Liu, Z., Du, H., et al.: Depth-aware salient object detection and segmentation via multiscale discriminative saliency fusion and bootstrap learning. IEEE Trans. Image Process. **26**(9), 4204–4216 (2017)
26. Yan, X., Wang, Y., Song, Q., Dai, K.: Salient object detection via boosting object-level distinctiveness and saliency refinement. J. Vis. Commun. Image Representation **48**, 224–237 (2017)

E-learning and Games

EasyCouplet: Automatic Generation of Chinese Traditional Couplets

Zhigeng Pan[1,2,3(✉)], Shicheng Zhang[3], and Yanhua Guo[4]

[1] Institute of Industrial VR, Foshan University, Foshan, China
[2] NINED Digital Technology Corp., Guangzhou, China
[3] DMI Research Center, Hangzhou Normal University, Hangzhou, China
zgpan@hznu.edu.cn
[4] College of Computer Science, Zhejiang University, Hangzhou, China

Abstract. In order to inherit and develop the Couplet culture, one of the most famous language culture in China, this paper implements a creation system of couplets. In this paper, a noval way to generate the customized couplet is discussed from the name-embedded couplet. The 2-gram word graph technology is used to generate the first sentence which contained the given word. Then, combined with language model which based on statistical method, grammar model and mutual information model, improved Viterbi Algorithm based on HMM is used to decode the second sentence. It turned out that the system can realize the automatic generation of the name embedded couplet. According to the contents involved in the given couplet, the system can generate pictures to match the couplet. This system is aimed for Spring Festival couplets and Birthday couplets, both are name-embedded couplet that generated with the name of people. Users can choose the templates and relative special elements freely to create a satisfactory multimedia couplet picture.

Keywords: Name-embedded couplet · 2-gram word graph technology
Interactive multimedia couplet picture · Computer aided couplets creation

1 Introduction

Chinese couplets known as "Duilian" or "contrapuntal couplets" may be painted on both sides of the doorframes of traditional Chinese construction. On the first morning of Chinese New Year, Chinese people change the old couplets to new one, which is called "Chunlian", presenting good wish for the coming year. Couplet is a kind of ancient poetry which consists of two sentences. Usually, each line of the couplet should have the same number of words, similar meaning and rhyme. In brief, we define the two sentences of a couplet as "first sentence" (FS) and the "paired sentence" (PS) [1] respectively, shown as Fig. 1.

(1) Classical poem generation

In the field of natural language research, from the very beginning of the first German poem generated by computer in 1959 [2], the development of the computer generation poetry go through the following several stages: the random words link,

© Springer-Verlag GmbH Germany, part of Springer Nature 2018
Z. Pan et al. (Eds.): Transactions on Edutainment XIV, LNCS 10790, pp. 117–132, 2018.
https://doi.org/10.1007/978-3-662-56689-3_10

Fig. 1. The couplet

poetry generation system based on template, generate and test method, based on evolutionary algorithm and based on case reasoning [3–7].

The domestic research on computer generating poetry began in the mid-1990s. A computer support environment for classical poetry study model, developed by the team from Beijing university and Yuan-ze university in the late 90 s [8], implemented the functions of reading, retrieval, statistics and assisted learning for the classical poetry. A statistic machine translation system was applied to generate new sentences under the situation that previous sentence was given [9].

Tones auxiliary machine system made by Fengzhu Luo, contained the inspection and rhyming word lookup rules [10]. Junfeng Hu extracted and accumulated the base of the elements of the classical poems [11], with the aid of statistical technical data information of the original poems. Genzel [12] do research on poetry machine translation based on statistical machine translation method.

(2) The PS Creation

There are a few research works on couplet creation. The automatic online couplet generating system [13], presented by Microsoft Research Asia, with the application of a phrase-based SMT approach, is very popular. While the FS is given by user, the system will automatically generate numerous PSs, and then the user can choose his/her favorite. The system is based on large-scale couplet corpus, works well in translating between the ancient text and modern words.

Fei [14] developed a system by using the neural network method to test the Spring Festival couplet corpus and constructed the image thinking level of the semantics. The system can present Spring Festival couplet which contains less than six words. Yi [15] applied machine learning model method which contains supervision sequence to establish the PS creating system based on error rate driven [16], hidden markov model (HMM) and probability language model [17]. Zhang [18] introduced the maximal matching algorithm into the word segmentation of the FS, and used the maximum entropy markov model to create the PS. Yu [19] designed an automatic couplet answering system.

For the time being, the effect of the creation of the PS under given FS (we called this form the PS Creation) is becoming nice gradually. In short, the related researches have two limits: either the FS (one sentence) should be given first, or the number of the words in a couplet is limited.

In our daily life, except PS Creation, which is only a small part of the couplet writing, there are many kinds of couplet writing such as name-embedded couplet writing, phrase-separated couplet writing. In this paper, our work focuses on the generation of Word-embedded Couplet (as known as Name-embedded Creation), in which only several words is needed instead of one sentence (the FS). Name-embedded Creation means that the system can generate the couplet automatically with only one or two words given, which is usually the given name of a Chinese person. Compared with the PS creation, name-embedded couplet has more refined constraints and difficulties in creation. It not only requires the same number of word in two sentences, but also focuses more on the meaning of the couplet.

Therefore, we propose a prototype system (EasyCouplet) satisfying the following demands:

a. Only several words are needed instead of one sentence (the FS).
b. The sentence could illustrate the special theme: spring festival or birthday.
c. The number of words in one sentence can be changed.

EasyCouplet can not only generate couplets, such as name-embedded couplets, but also design couplet picture to enrich the display interface and meet the user's individualized preference. Couplet is created based on natural language generation theory and statistical machine learning method. In this paper, we mainly describe the generation of couplet, the automatic generation of couplet image, and the app on iOS we developed.

2   The Framework of EasyCouplet System

The system (named EasyCouplet) mainly covers two aspects: the generation of couplets and the design of couplet image adapted to the pair of couplets. This section mainly introduces two typical couplets categories: Spring Festival couplet and Birthday couplet. For the characteristics of different categories, the system can generate the suitable picture interactively.

2.1   The Automatic Generation of Name-Embedded Couplet

EasyCouplet focuses on name-embedded and theme couplet, classified as Table 1. Theme couplet is described as that the content of the couplet should be consistent with the theme given. The creation of the theme couplet must meet the high requirement of expressing the relevant content around a given theme. The Spring Festival couplet and Birthday couplet are the typical theme couplets in this research.

Name-embedded couplet is that the word in the name is shown in the sentence. The EasyCouplet system could generate name-embedded couplet to match the special theme: spring festival or birthday.

Table 1. Name-embedded and theme couplet

Theme / Name-embedded	Spring festival	Birthday
NO	Spring festival couplet	Birthday couplet
YES	Spring festival couplet containing the given name	Birthday couplet containing the given name

Define 1: Couplet = {*FS, PS*}

$$FS = \{w_i \mid w_i \in R, 0 < i < m\} \; 1 \leq m \leq 20$$

$$PS = \{wp_i \mid wp_i \in R, 0 < i < m\}$$

Define 2: Name_embedded couplet = {*FS, PS*}, $A \in FS$, $B \in PS$.

Where R is word thesaurus, m is the word number in a couplet sentence, A and B (two single character) are given by user, and we called them embedded words. The example is shown as Fig. 2. In this case, 志 is A,庚 is B.

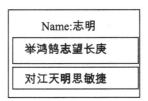

Fig. 2. Name-embedded couplet example

The flowchart of Name-embedded couplet generation is shown in Fig. 3.

Step 1: Input

(*A, B, n*) should be input, n is the character number of the sentence and A, B must not be null. The relation between n and the word segment sequence S is defined as follow:

$$S = \begin{cases} \left. \begin{array}{l} w_1..w_A...w_{k-1} + w_{tri} \\ w_1..w_A...w_k + w_{sin\,gle} \end{array} \right\} & n = 2k+1 \\ w_1...w_A...w_k & n = 2k \end{cases} \quad (1)$$

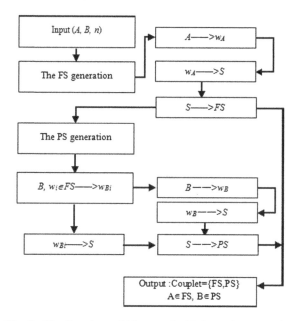

Fig. 3. The flowchart of Name-embedded couplet generation

$w_i (1 < i < k)$ is described as the word group which contain two characters, w_{tri} is a word group which contain three characters, $w_{\text{sin } gle}$ is a single character, w_B and w_A also contain two characters.

Step 2: The FS Generation

(1) From single character A to w_A:

GetWord (input: A; output: w_A), $w_A = \{A'A, AA''\}$, Both A' *and* A'' also are single character.

Define 3: 2-gram word graph model *wordGraph:*

$$\overrightarrow{w_{i-1}w_i} \in \ wordGraph,$$

$$\text{length } (\overrightarrow{w_{i-1}w_i}) = P(w_i w_{i-1}) = \frac{C(w_{i-1}w_i)}{\sum\limits_{w_i} C(w_{i-1}w_i)} \tag{2}$$

(2) Extend wA to phrase S by preferential breadth searching with step size constraint (shown as Fig. 4).

$$G_{et}S_{CORE}(S) \ = \lambda \times G(S) + \mu \times LM(S) + \eta \times MI(S) \tag{3}$$

```
1: GetSent(input : w_A ; output: S)
2:      shortSent.insert(S, G_etSCORE(S) ) //According to the formula (3) to calculate the
G_etSCORE(S) and inserted into the heap
3:      for   every lword of S in wordGraph do //extend the S on it's left side
4:          GetSent(input:lword +S, ,output: S)
5:      end for
6:      for every rword of S in wordGraph do //extend S on it's right side
7:          GetSent(input: rword+S, ,output: S)
8:      end for
9: end procedure
```

Fig. 4. Extend wA to phrase S

Where G is the statistics grammar model, LM is the 2-gram language model, MI is the mutual information model. All of these models are used in evaluation in the generation of the sentence FS. The parameters λ, μ and η can be adjusted by random hill climbing combined with BLEU score criteria.

Mutual information model refers to the rational evaluation of compatibility between two words (shown as formula (4)). $P(s_i, s_j)$ is the probability of the co-existence of the words at the place i and j in the sentence.

$$MI(S) = \sum_{i=1}^{n-1} \sum_{j=i+1}^{n} \log \frac{P(s_i, s_j)}{P(s_i)P(s_j)} \tag{4}$$

The grammar rule in this paper is rule extraction method based on statistics model. We adopt 4-gram model. For example, the part of speech sequence of a sentence is illustrated as $T = \{t_1 t_2 \ldots \ldots t_i\}$. According the grammar model, the formula is given as below.

$$G(S) = P(t_1)P(t_2|t_1)\ldots\ldots.P(t_i|t_{i-1}\ldots t_1.)$$
$$\approx \prod_{i-1}^{M} P(t_i|t_{i-1}\ldots t_1.) \tag{5}$$

$$P(t_i) = \frac{C(t_i)}{\sum_{j=1}^{n} C(t_j)} \tag{6}$$

$$P(t_i|t_1\ldots t_{i-1}) = \frac{C(t_1 t_2 \ldots t_i)}{C(t_1 \ldots t_{i-1})} \tag{7}$$

(3) Extend phrase S to FS

As in Eq. 1, in the case of $n = 2k$, S equals to FS.

For $n = 2k + 1$, there are two cases, one needs to add a word w_{tri}, the other case need to add a word w_{single}. For two cases, the extension should be based on the state transition table. State transition table is trained based on the HMM [20]. In this table there are all possible word groups which can match the given node w_i on the right side.

Corresponds to the case of $S = w_1 w_2 \ldots w_{k-1} + w_{tri}$: for each sentence which generated in the last step in the candidate set *shortSents*, we take w_{k-1} as the starting point, then extend a word group which contain 3 single characters as the word w_{tri} according to the trained HMM [20] state transition table, and then we put the sentence into the *FSs* as a candidate of the FS.

Corresponds to the case of $S = w_1 w_2 \ldots w_{k-1} w_k + w_{single}$: for each sentence which generated in the last step in the candidate set *shortSents*, we take w_{k-1} as the starting point, then extend a word group which contains only one character as the word w_{single} according to the trained HMM state transition table, and then we put the sentence into the *FSs* as a candidate of the FS.

Step 3: The PS Generation

In this paper, we use 2-gram word graph, combined with modified Viterbi to extend the *PS*. Before decoding, the system will make a judgment: For each word w_i in the FS ($i = 0 \ldots k-1$), we search its emit state table to find the word w_B which contain the character B.

If the result is not null, the position of the word w_B which we found in the *PS* is the same as w_i in the *FS*, and then we extend the w_B to generate a sentence as the corresponding *PS*, in this step, we should follow the rules:

(1) On the left side, we extend i words and each of them contains two single characters.
(2) On the right side, we extend $k-i-1$ words, and each word contains the same number character to the corresponding position of the *FS*, generating multiple matching *PS*.
(3) Every word is not only selected by the word graph, but also considered the emit table whether contains the word on the corresponding position word in the *FS*. The PS generating m. But in this process, the evaluation function is illustrated as the following:

$$G_{et}S_{CORE}(S) = \lambda \times G'(S) + \mu \times LM'(S) + \eta \times MI(S) \tag{8}$$

$$G'(S) = G(S) \bullet P(t_{w_j}, t_{wp_j}) \tag{9}$$

$$LM'(S) = LM(S) \bullet P(w_j, wp_j) \tag{10}$$

State emit table which trained based on the HMM, in this table there are all possible word groups which can match the given node w_i be wp_i at the correspond position in the *PS*, as well as the probability $P(w_i, wp_i)$ of co-occurrence at the same position in two sentences of a pair of couplet.

If there is no solution, then we apply the original decoding method in Step 2. And we will get a candidate set *PSs*.

(1) *GetWord (input: B; output: wB)*, $w_B \in wordGraph$ && $w_B = \{dA, Ad\}$, d also is a single character.

(2) *PS = GetSent (input: wB, wordGraph; output: S)*

$$+ \begin{cases} w_{\sin gle} & n = 2k + 1 \&\& \ s = w_1 \ldots w_k \\ w_{tri} & n = 2k + 1 \&\& \ s = w_1 \ldots w_{k-1} \\ null & n = 2k \end{cases}$$

In order to evaluate the matching degree between *PS* and *FS* candidate. We apply the evaluate function *GetScore(S)* (shown as in Eq. 8) to find the best one *PS* for the *FS* save as a pair of couplet.

Therefore, mutual information, statistic grammar model, statistic language model are applied in the evaluation of the original sentences set to automatically select the sentences which get the score over than the standard we set.

2.2 Interactive Creation of Couplet Image

If the display page of the couplet is only composed of text, it appears very monotonous. Therefore, in order to stimulate the users' enthusiasm and allow the users to create couplet initiatively, EasyCouplet can combine the couplets with many kinds of medias such as the pictures, music, animations and video elements to accomplish the goal for extending couplet to multimedia couplet.

In order to enhance the artistic and interactivity of the display interface, the system automatically creates a picture to match the couplet. If the user is not satisfied with the output, he/she can freely choose and modify the elements in the picture. The system provides three sets of templates, a variety of fonts and different relevant background elements, and other functions such as scene preservation, transparency regulating, picture moving and zooming. At the same time, the users can design the display page by themselves to create individualized multimedia couplet image.

(1) Classical elements

Classical elements of Spring Festival couplet include: many kinds of handwriting Chinese character "福" (as shown in Fig. 5), pictures of lanterns, firecrackers and zodiac. Background elements of birthday couplet include: numerous kinds of handwriting Chinese character "寿" (as shown in Fig. 6), pictures of peaches, congratulating words. The users can explore the couplet interface freely with which had been automatically created, and design the personalized elements。

(2) Interactive operation

EasyCouplet can also create the display page to meet the user's own preference. The entire page is divided into three blocks. One block is used to show a menubar, which includes three menu items: template selection, font selection and elements matching. A floating menu is applied to select the relevant background elements. On the left of the page, there is another block showing the output of couplet, background pictures, and couplet elements from top to bottom. Couplet picture display area is on the right block (as shown in Fig. 7).

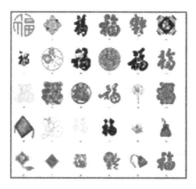

Fig. 5. The classical element "福"

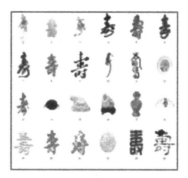

Fig. 6. The classical element "寿"

Fig. 7. Interactive couplet picture design window

3 Experimental Results and User Study

(1) Prototype design based on iOS

As we all know, Apple mobile terminal products are taking the lead in the sales and industrial technologies, therefore the development of the application based on the iOS System [21] in Apple terminals can bring more perfect experience to the users. The proposal system provides users with three kinds of couplet generation methods: name-embedded couplet, name-embedded Spring Festival couplet and profession Spring Festival couplet. Mobile terminal users can input required name, occupation and other attributes in the corresponding interface. The system will return dozens of the eligible couplets, and the results will be automatically stored in the memory of the mobile terminal. Meanwhile, the user can choose a pair of couplet she or he likes to generate beautiful couplet image, and share it with friends through the Microblog, Qzone, MMS, etc.

3.1 The Architecture of Couplet Creation Application

As the performance and memory of mobile device cannot reach for that of desktop computers and notebook, the running speed of the program should be improved avoiding feedback delay problem caused by large amounts of data communication. Couplet creation system needs a large number of corpus and complex computation. Based on the system requirements, corpus database is stored in the server. The client employs parameters user input through the network to invoke the WebService interface. After the server receives parameters, it will generate a certain number of couplets. Then couplet data will return to the user's mobile terminal. The client simply sends HTTP POST or GET request, and then parses the XML data returned [22]. System architecture is shown in Fig. 8.

3.2 Client Program of the Couplet Creation System

UI design is an important part of the iOS application. Ease of use, versatility and compatibility of the interface become the key of whether APP software enables the user to quickly get started. The design principle that this system mainly adopted is simple, meeting the user's habits. For pages switching control we use the mixture of two approaches: (1) UITabBarController for providing three main interfaces of the system: "Generation", "History" and "Setting"; (2) UI Navigation Controller to control the switching from the main interface to the sub-interface. "Generation", "History" and "Setting" modules have an equal level of relationship, using tabbar as rootViewController makes the three modules in the size limited screen clearly, makes it possible to know the system's function easily. There are several subfunctions in the three modules, they have the relationship between the upper and lower levels. The design of simple operation guide and fresh list are best for meeting the needs of the public.

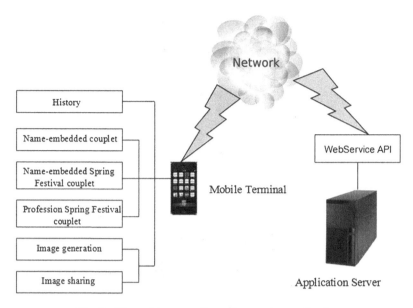

Fig. 8. The architecture of couplet creation application

Button "Generate" provides three types of name embedded couplet generation mode. As couplet is a classic Chinese literary form, the hollow door frame style design of buttons reflects the traditional Chinese culture characteristics. Well-designed table items of "History" clearly shows previously generated couplets.

We not only use pure text to show generated couplet, but also provide couplet image. The system can generate beautiful couplet image for any user-made couplet, providing 17 optional background pictures (shown as Fig. 9).

Using the software's sharing function, users can share couplet image to Microblog, Kaixin and other four major social networking platform. At the same time, users can also share couplet image with their friends through the E-mail and MMS (shown as Fig. 10).

(2) Couplet evaluation

In our system, we conducted user study evaluation from the following three aspects: the *FS* generation, the *PS* generation and A pair of couplet.

Experiment 1: the *FS* evaluation. Evaluating the *FS* generated with a given embedded word.
Experiment 2: the *PS* evaluation. Evaluating the *PS* generated with the given *FS*.
Experiment 3: Couplet evaluation. Evaluating a pair of couplet after using Human-Computer Interaction.

When implementing experiment, 50 names (A_iB_i) $1 = <i< = 50$ are chosen randomly, with fist word used in experiment 1, and the other word used in experiment 2.

Fig. 9. Couplet picture matching

Fig. 10. Sharing interface

(1) The *FS* evaluation.

For each A_i, 20 *FSs* will be generalized by our system, the best one should be chosen manually. we take four rules with different weight to evaluate it: Fluency degree of representation, Grammar matchability, Content richness and Appropriation for being *FS*. Table 2 shows the different weights and scores.

Table 2. The *FS* evaluating rules

Rule	Weight (%)	Unaccept	Accept	Fine
Fluency degree of expression	30	0	50	100
Grammar matchability	30	0	50	100
Content richness	20	0	50	100
Appropriation for being FS	20	0	50	100

In this experiment, we get an average score of 79.5, with 50 embedded words, which shows that the application of 2-gram word graph can work well in the FS generation and the expanding strategy is consisting with the language custom, so the result is satisfactory.

(2) The *PS* evaluation.

We chose the top 10 *FS* in experiment 1, and generalize the *PS* in order, with the embedded character B_i in accordance with A_i in *FS*. After evaluating, we get the results shown in Table 3. Therefore, we can acquire average score, and classify the *PS* into two scale according to Table 4.

Table 3. The PS evaluating rules

Rule	Weight (%)	Unacceptable	Acceptable	Fine
Fluent degree of expression	24	0	50	100
Grammar matchability	24	0	50	100
Content richness	16	0	50	100
Appropriation for being PS	16	0	50	100
Rhythm Matchability with FS	20	0	50	100

Table 4. The acceptable level of PS candidates

Level	Fine	Acceptable
Score	=100	>= 50

For a given *FS*, the case will pass test when at least a fine or acceptable PS occurs in the N candidates. And then the ratio of cases pasting test is shown in the Table 5.

Table 5. Result of the ratio of candidates of PS which can meet users' favor

Item/Level	Fine (%)				Acceptable (%)			
	First 1	First 5	First 10	First 20	First 1	First 5	First 10	First 20
PSs	12	28	56	64	62	84	92	96

It shows that the first *PS* candidate of 60% *FS* samples is acceptable. While the ratio of samples have acceptable *PSs* in top 5/10/20 candidates grows gradually.

However, we can find the proportion of fine level PS for the sample is small. The result shows our system can generate *PS* confirm to the Chinese oral custom, language model and grammar rule; but seldom express colorful emotion or specific context and background, which shows that emotion tag can be used to improve the weakness of our system.

(3) Couplet evaluation.

10 pairs couplets are judged by 10 domain experts according to Table 6, which contains normal couplet, computer generated embedded couplet and embedded couplet generated by HCI method, Table 7 shows the result.

Table 6. Rules of couplet evaluation

Rule	Weight	Worse	Well	Better
Fluent degree of expression	7/20	0	50	100
Custom satisfactory	7/20	0	50	100
Rhythm matchability	3/20	0	50	100
Theme relevance	3/20	0	50	100

Table 7. Evaluation result

	Normal couplet without special name	Name-embedded couplet generated automatical method	Name-embedded couplet generated by HCI method
Fluent degree of expression	73.2	53.6	71.6
Custom satisfactory	50.3	81.5	87.6
Rhythm matchability	62.5	42.2	59.4
Theme relevance	51.8	76.4	8.03
Avg. score	60.4	65.1	76.7

It suggests that the idea of embedded couplet generation system is better than normal one in the aspect of UE. Normal couplet gets higher score in Fluent degree of expression and Rhythm matchability because of the less constraint of the generation, while users are more satisfied with embedded couplet in satisfactory level and theme relevance, which coincidence with the personalized customization motivation. Judging from Avg. score, HCI method have the highest score, which shows that HCI method makes up the shortage of the automatical method, and improved the quality of the couplet in its generation. We get a satisfactory result considering the limitation about nature language generation research and difficulty in name-embedded couplet writing.

4 Conclusion

We creatively proposed an automatical method composed with 2-gram word graph tech and statistic translation model method, it expands the embedded word given by customer to get more relative phases, and generated the *FS* by applying HMM model. Strict evaluation rules are formated to assess the *FS, PS* and {*FS, PS*}. The experiments show a satisfactory result and provided a new way to personalized name-embedded couplet generation.

Future work can include:

(1) In our study, we will focus on emotion tag to improve the context matchability and background relevance.
(2) We consider improve the optimization algorithm from locally optimal to global optimization to add the diversity of the result.
(3) Comprehensive rules of grammar should be format, and grammar tree should be built to raise the generation quality. In current grammar model, grammar rules are not comprehensively extract, and there are a lot of limitations which lead to simple language model and unappropriate grammar tree.

Acknowledgements. This work was finished with the kind support of my formal students, they are Ruiying Jiang, Shunting Wang, Jing Guo and Wenda Fang.

References

1. http://baike.baidu.com/subview/2925/4924756.htm?fr=aladdin
2. Lutz, T.: Stochastische texte. Augenblick **4**(1), 3–9 (1959)
3. Gervás, P.: Wasp: evaluation of different strategies for the automatic generation of Spanish verse. In: Proceedings of the AISB-00 Symposium on Creative & Cultural Aspects of AI, pp. 93–100 (2000)
4. Oliveira, H.R.G., Cardoso, F.A., Perreira, F.C.: Tra-La Lyrics: an approach to generate text based on rhythm. In: Proceedings of the Fourth International Joint Workshop on Computational Creativity (IJWCC 2007), pp. 47–54 (2007)
5. Wang, H.: Based on the examples of the machine translation-method and issue. Terminol. Stand. Inf. Technol. **3**(2), 33–36 (2003)

6. Somers, H.: Review article: example-based machine translation. Mach. Transl. **14**(2), 113–157 (1999)

7. Wu, Y., Zhao, J., Xu, B.: Chinese named entity recognition combining a statistical model with human knowledge. In: The Workshop on Multilingual and Mixed-language Named Entity Recognition: Combining Statistical and Symbolic Models (ACL 2003), Sapporo, Japan, pp. 65–72 (2003)

8. Liu, Y., Yu, S., Sun, Q.: The realization of computer support poetry research. J. Chin. Inf. **11**(1), 27–35 (1996)

9. He, J., Zhou, M., Jiang, L.: Generating Chinese classical poems with statistical machine translation models. In: Proceedings of the Twenty-Sixth AAAI Conference on Artificial Intelligence, pp. 1650–1656. EB/OL. http://cls.hs.yzu.edu.tw/tang/PoemTone/index.asp

10. Zhang, Y., Jin, R., Zhou, Z.: Understanding bag-of-words model: a statistical framework. Int. J. Mach. Learn. Cybernet. **1**(1–4), 43–52 (2010)

11. Hu, J.: The computer aided research work of Chinese ancient poems. Acta Sci. Nat. Univ. Pekin. **37**(5), 727–733 (2001)

12. Genzel, D., Uszkoreit, J., Och, F.J.: "Poetic" statistical machine translation: rhyme and meter. In: Proceedings of the 2010 Conference on Empirical Methods in Natural Language Processing, pp. 158–166 (2010)

13. Jiang, L., Zhou, M.: Generating Chinese couplets using a statistical MT approach. In: Proceedings of the 22nd International Conference on Computational Linguistics (Colin 2008), vol. 1, pp. 377–384 (2008)

14. Fei, Y.: The Study of Multi-Layer Semantics of Chinese and the Design of Couplet System. Institution of Automation, CAS, Beijing (1999)

15. Yi, Y.: A Study on Style Identification and Chinese Couplet Responses Oriented Computer Aided Poetry Composing. Chongqing University, Chongqing (2005)

16. Bril, E.: Automatic grammar induction and parsing free text: a transformation-based approach. In: Proceedings of the ARPA Workshop on Human Language Technology, pp. 259–264 (1993)

17. Zhai, C.: Statistical language models for information retrieval a critical review. Found. Trends Inf. Retr. **2**(3), 137–213 (2008)

18. Zhang, K., Xia, Y., Yu, H.: The method of adding punctuation and analysis sentence based on conditional random fields. J. Tsinghua Univ. **49**(10), 163–166 (2009)

19. Yu, S.: Design and implementation of an automatic couplet answering system. J. Xiamen Technol. Univ. **19**(1) (2011)

20. Jiang, R.: Computer assisted Chinese poetry and couplet generation. Zhejiang University (2011)

21. Apple. IOS System (EB/OL), 30 October 2013. http://www.apple.com.cn/ios/what-is/

22. Chen, J., Huang, G.: Construction strategy and main technology of the mobile library APP-take iOS for instance. New Technol. Libr. Inf. Serv. **9**, 75–80 (2012)

Design and Implementation on Digital Display System of Tang Dynasty Women Costumes

Desheng Lyu$^{(\boxtimes)}$, Meng Guo, and Yuchao Sun

Key Laboratory of Interactive Media Design and Equipment Service Innovation in Ministry of Culture, Harbin Institute of Technology, Harbin 150001, China
{deshengl,mengguo,yuchsun}@hit.edu.cn

Abstract. As an excellent representation of Chinese traditional culture, the Tang Dynasty dress has unique artistic features, such as unique shape, rich colors and exquisite patterns. With the progress of the times and clothing innovation, Chinese traditional costume elements are less and less reflected in modern society, with the lack of public awareness of Chinese traditional costume culture. Chinese traditional dress is gradually fading away from our daily life. In view of this fact, this paper uses computer simulation technology to build a virtual exhibition system for traditional costumes. Based on interaction design principles, a digital simulation system for women costumes in Tang Dynasty has been designed and implemented, so as to modify the public learning approach to traditional culture, to express and spread the culture meanings of Tang Dynasty costumes through text, images and music, and to realize interaction with users by means of interactive effects.

Keywords: Digital cultural heritage · Traditional costumes in Tang Dynasty
Interaction experience

1 Introduction

Dominated by the Han culture and centering on the Chinese ceremonies, traditional costumes in Tang Dynasty present as good examples of "Splendid China" and "State of Ceremonies" [1]. Based on the traditional costume culture, in combination with costume elements of neighboring countries and other ethnic minorities, Tang Dynasty costume culture has its unique shapes, rich colors, distinct patterns and exquisite dress materials, illuminating the development process of Chinese costume culture. Tang Dynasty costumes embody the outstanding craftsmanship and timeless aesthetics of traditional Chinese costumes, reflecting the cultural connotations of the traditional Chinese costumes. However, as the elements of Chinese traditional costumes are less and less manifested in the modern society, while the general public lack critical awareness of their cultural connotations, traditional costumes are gradually fading out of our daily life. The tremendous advances in digital technology have provided more possibilities to disseminate culture and information, progressively affecting the habits and ways in which people acquire information. Since the monotonous way of literal

© Springer-Verlag GmbH Germany, part of Springer Nature 2018
Z. Pan et al. (Eds.): Transactions on Edutainment XIV, LNCS 10790, pp. 133–141, 2018.
https://doi.org/10.1007/978-3-662-56689-3_11

communication cannot meet their expectations, the general public are inclined to obtain information through images, animations and interactive media. Especially, the traditional media cannot meet their demands for knowledge [2] when the mass audience have gradually become accustomed to interaction and learning through multimedia. In order to help effectively carry forward the profound connotations of the traditional costume culture, this paper takes the traditional dresses of the Tang Dynasty as the research object and utilizes technologies of digital simulation system, with an aim to improve people's knowledge level of the traditional costume culture, to inherit and protect traditional costumes, and to explore effective ways to spread traditional culture. A combination of protecting traditional culture with the digital simulation system can not only spread the clothing culture but also enable the public to quickly grasp the traditional culture during entertainment activities. Apart from delicate visual effects that catch users' eyes, the developed simulation system also gives full consideration to the issues of feasibility and operation difficulty coefficient, in compliance with the principle of interaction design [3], both interesting and easy to operate [4, 5].

2 Positioning of Digital Simulation System of Women Costume in Tang Dynasty

The positioning should be properly identified before designing, as the digital simulation system is fundamentally targeted to meet the needs of users. In recent years, despite the fact that Chinese costume itself is supposed to carry forward our traditional clothing culture, only a few ethnic minorities have still insisted on their ethnic costumes [6] due to the deepened influence of Western-style apparel on Chinese clothing. In order to revive Chinese traditional costume culture and adapt it to the new times, it is appropriate to make corresponding adjustments to its transmission mode with the assistance of digital media technologies.

This study selects the traditional costumes in the Tang Dynasty as the object, as they are the most typical of traditional costumes of the Han nationality, representing the traditional aesthetic awareness, humanistic spirit and multi-cultures in costume and textile techniques of the Han people. At the same time, many clothing materials in Tang Dynasty have not been completely preserved, with a small number of cultural objects left over after Tang Dynasty that ended over 1,100 years ago. In order to ensure the authenticity and objectivity of costume appearance, this study centers on the *Court Ladies Adorning Their Hair with Flowers* that is attributed to Zhou Fang (active late 8th–early 9th century) in the Tang dynasty women clothing system, restoring the original picture and shape and physical forms and costume styles of the maids. The study involves different styles of clothing in early, mid and late Tang Dynasty, and also conducts vectorization of clothing design elements.

As to restoring costumes, first delineate the outside lines of the dress based on the body figure of maids, and then fill the dress patterns into the wire frame through processing the drawing software. This will naturally conform the two-dimensional clothing to physical forms of maids, providing a soft and flexible presentation of visual effect. In addition to the costume elements, the hairstyle and accessory elements of Tang Dynasty women in the system are in line with graphic illustrations in related books and pictures of cultural relics in museums, so that the displayed elements are authentic and verifiable. Besides, after properly processed, the displayed elements can provide a three-dimensional effect for users. The costume drawing is shown in Fig. 1.

Fig. 1. Costume drawing

While restoring the two-dimensional cultural elements, the interface design is also very critical. Different interfaces in the simulation system should be consistent with each other in terms of hue, composition, shape, etc., so that the target audience can learn about the Chinese traditional costume culture from various aspects such as scenes, colors, and elements.

The main page of the simulation system adopts the nude color, the same as that of the drawing paper. The figure is a maid dressed in a red garnet skirt and an outer orange-clad orange blouse. The color of the figure is consistent with that of the background. The display cabinet is an orange-red plank. For the gray mask layer, a combination of the main colors of red and gray reflects the restrained and implicit characteristics in Chinese traditional culture. The golden decorative pattern of display cabinet match well with the red color, which meets the aesthetic expectations of Chinese people in their pursuit of color. At the same time, a small amount of yellow color on the interface represents vitality and vigor. From the perspective of tone scale, featuring varied and vibrant colors, the design can enhance the degree of saturation and the sense of layers for costumes, so that users can focus attention into their experience. The costume experience interface is shown in Figs. 2 and 3.

Fig. 2. Costume experience interface (Color figure online)

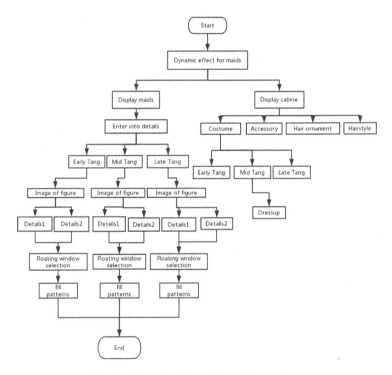

Fig. 3. Operation flow of simulation system

3   Realization of System Technology

The operation flow of the simulation system is shown in Fig. 3.

3.1   Development Environment

Operating system of Windows 8, editor of HBuilder 7.0.0. Install Ionic and AngularJS and create projects with Ionic. Once you've created the project, feel free to open the app's interface for real-time debugging in your browser, and display the Ionic project with the ionic serve-lab command. You can showcase different effects on both iOS and Android mobile devices by running both panels simultaneously.

3.2   Logical Framework of the Simulation System

As for the costume display, after opening the cabinet and clicking on the thumbnail of the costume elements, the selected dress pattern will replace the original dress on the maid. The dressup effect is thus completed.

```
$scope.changeCloth = function(type){

console.log(type);

if(type=="chutang"){

background.style.backgroundImage='url(./img/changecloth/1.png)';

    }

if(type=="shengtang"){

background.style.backgroundImage='url(./img/changecloth/2.png)';

       }

if(type=="wantang"){

background.style.backgroundImage='url(./img/changecloth/3.png)';

    }

}
```

The part of details on costumes and pattern fills is divided into three sections. Each section has character images of different periods. Slide around to switch to details on different costumes. The user can fill the blank costume patterns according to their own preferences.

4   System Functional Requirements

The digital simulation system is divided into four modules. First, the dynamic display of maids in *Court Ladies Adorning Their Hair with Flowers*. The display maintains the authenticity of original pictures, and injects dynamic features into the static figures, which stimulates curiosity and inspires users to further explore the product. The dynamic effect in the first module is shown in Fig. 4.

Fig. 4. Dynamic effect of static maids in the first module

The second module includes the restoration and introduction of costumes. The figure is the maid who puts fingers on her dress in *Court Ladies Adorning Their Hair with Flowers*. The wood cabinet slides onto the interface. It has different compartments that representing costumes, hairstyles, hair ornaments and accessories respectively. Click to open the cabinet drawers, and there will be three display cabinets with various design elements. This module aims to popularize and disseminate the unique costume culture in Tang Dynasty, as shown in Fig. 5.

The third module is dressup. The user can long press the dressing elements in the display cabinet, to put them onto the maid who puts fingers on her original dress. This module produces a stereoscopic effect on the two-dimensional and static vectorization elements, so that the user can observe the costume shapes and patterns in a clearer way, while gaining a vertical sense of costumes and a three-dimensional sense of hairstyles. This module enhances interaction with users, as shown in Fig. 6.

The fourth module comprises of the interface which introduces specific structures of the costumes, demonstrating cutting illustrations of five dress patterns of Served Ru,

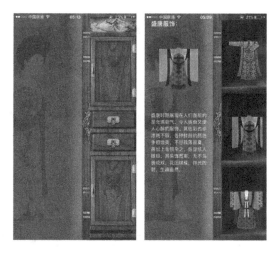

Fig. 5. Costume introduction interface

Fig. 6. Dressup for maids

dress, silk yarn, outer garment, half-arm shirt. Users can click on the lined and blank dress. And then the floating window will pop-up with three different patterns to choose from. Therefore, users can fill the blank dress according to their preferences, as shown in Fig. 7.

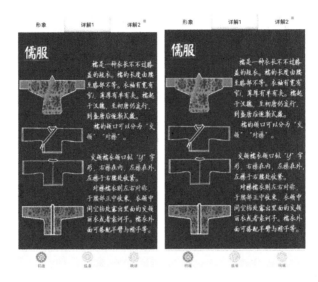

Fig. 7. Details on structures of costumes and pattern fills

5 Conclusion

Following the principle of interaction design, the digital display system of women costumes in Tang Dynasty meets the needs of the development of modern interactive new media devices. It used Hbuilder for encoding, while taking advantage of Ionic Framework and AngularJS, which can achieve aesthetic effects and interactive experience and ensure its integrity and operation. This design of digital products not only provides users with entertainment activities, but also subtly transmits the Chinese traditional clothing culture in daily life by integrating the cultural connotation of traditional costumes of the Han nationality in the Tang Dynasty with modern science and technology. Against the backdrop of the new media era, making full use of the positive and open potential of new media, this mode of design has demonstrated the infinite charm of Chinese traditional costume culture, and has to some degree made up for the shortcomings of traditional media in terms of time and space, while providing the possibilities for cultural sharing in a wide range of areas.

Acknowledgments. This research is funded by MOE (Ministry of Education in China) Project of Humanities and Social Sciences (Grant NO: 017YJAZH085).

References

1. Zhao, G.: A Study on Aesthetic Culture of Costumes in Tang Dynasty. Anhui University (2013)
2. Bo, Y.: A Digital Application Research on the National Costume Culture Based on Mobile Terminals. Beijing Institute of Fashion Technology (2016)

3. Zhou, P., Lv, Y.: Simulation analysis on co-site interference of vehicular digital communication system based on IM prediction method by BER. J. China Univ. Posts Telecommun. **1**, 31–41 (2016)
4. Jones, G.R., Lee, D., Holliman, N.S., et al.: Study and establishment of the digital-analog hybrid simulation system with FACTS devices. In: EEME, pp. 676–680 (2014)
5. Qin, J., Guan, Y., Lu, X.: Research on the interaction design methods of digital cultural heritage. In: IEEE International Conference on Computer-Aided Industrial Design & Conceptual Design, Caid & Cd., pp. 1452–1454. IEEE (2009)
6. Barwick, J., Dearnley, J., Muir, A., et al.: Playing games with cultural heritage: a comparative case study analysis of the current status of digital game preservation. Games Cult. J. Interact. Media **6**(4), 373–390 (2011)

Study of Animation Simulation Technology for Earthquake Escape Education

Weijian Hu[✉] and Yanyan Zheng

Institute of Engineering, Lishui University, Lishui, China
hwj@lsu.edu.cn

Abstract. China is an earthquake-prone countries, so it's important to carry out earthquake escape education which has practical significance. The traditional way of earthquake escaping education is not vivid enough, also lacking the sense of reality or interactivity, so to arouse the learner's interest proved to be very difficult. Based on the constructivism learning concept, a new educational method for assisting earthquake escaping was proposed based on animation simulation technology. Using virtual reality engine an animation game was developed, in which virtual scenes were created, animation character was modeled, the motion controlling method for virtual characters was constructed, and particle animation was used so as to achieve earthquake effects. The prototype of this demonstration system can run in a browser, which makes it easy to promote. Preliminary tests show that users prefer this new educational method for earthquake escaping to the old ones. Electronic document is a "live" template. The various components of your paper [title, text, heads, etc.] are already defined on the style sheet, as illustrated by the portions given in this document.

Keywords: Animation games · Simulation · Earthquake escaping
Virtual reality

1   Introduction

China is located in the junction of two major seismic zones, in which earthquake disasters are more frequent and severe. According to statistics, since 1900, the numbers of people died in the earthquake were up to as much as 550,000, accounting for 53% of global deaths.

In the last century, 20 million deaths were caused by two strong earthquakes in China. Survey showed that when earthquake occurring, it was most important to keep a clear mind and calm, and it was essential to take some necessary measures save themselves. A survey with Tangshan earthquake survivors shows that up to the rate of 73% had taken emergency measures for saving themselves, which means the promotion of public education for escaping the earthquake is very meaningful.

It is necessary to take some emergency measures to reduce losses in the earthquake escaping. In Chinese earthquake escaping education, written materials, escape drills were the popular ways for publicize and study, which couldn't make the participants experience the real environment during the earthquake. In contrast to these boring education forms, animation and game simulation technology can arouse more interests of the participants. There are not many studies on animation and game simulation

© Springer-Verlag GmbH Germany, part of Springer Nature 2018
Z. Pan et al. (Eds.): Transactions on Edutainment XIV, LNCS 10790, pp. 142–154, 2018.
https://doi.org/10.1007/978-3-662-56689-3_12

technology applied to earthquake escaping. In literature [1], J used virtual reality technology creating a seismic modeling virtual environment which can reduce children' panic in disaster environments through education. In literature [2], a virtual earthquake rescue simulation system was realized using ERT-VR, which can accelerate the efficiency and save the cost of the rescue by training. In literature [3], a virtual drilling rescue simulation system was developed by simulating earthquake scene. Study [5, 6] show that interactive virtual ways can improve the participants' interests and learning efficiency. In this paper, animation and game simulation technology was used to reproduce the earthquake scene, which allow participations can be drilled with an interactive way, increase their sense of immersion, and learn the correct way to escape more efficiently. In this paper, virtual scene and character models were built by 3dmax at first. Then, virtual characters interactive control was realized using Unity3d development tools. This system development process is showed in Fig. 1.

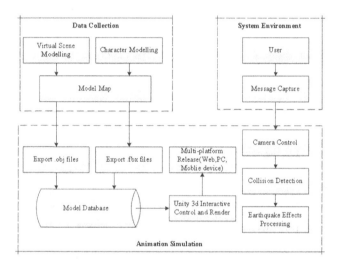

Fig. 1. System development process

In this paper, at first, the 3D scene models with textures maps were built in three-dimensional software, and exported to obj and .fbx format files. Then the resulting files were imported into unity3d to form model database. Users and the information capture device form the system environment. The above information was gathered into unity3d, interactive controlled, and collision detection, camera control and complete rendering of the scene, and finally the multi-platform release [7]. Using animation and game simulation technology can provide people with a feeling of having a real scene, and can enhance people to master more knowledge on rescue measure of earthquake escaping in entertaining study.

2 Components of the Simulation System

Since the complexity of earthquake escaping environment, and the variability of environment disasters [8]. We build a complex environment in the hospital where people escaping from earthquake following the story. First, the virtual characters in the hospital were waiting for medical treatment at waiting room, they felt hospital shaking, someone shouted earthquake, the hospital crowd stirred, with the earthquake shaking constantly increasing, and resulting in some buildings collapsed, and explosive objects burst into flames. Then the virtual protagonist begins to escape.

Through analyzing the real situation of the earthquake, we thought that six modules i.e. Virtual characters modules, virtual environment module, earthquake module, virtual doctor module, the virtual supporting part modules needed to be added to this earthquake evacuation simulation system. Each part of which contains its own unique way of movement and behavioral patterns, where the virtual actor is user-controlled module includes running, walking, crawling, standing, and maybe death action in the earthquake escape, virtual doctor module provides the earthquake escaping roles with some warnings and recommendations. Virtual disaster module includes some major earthquake disasters such as

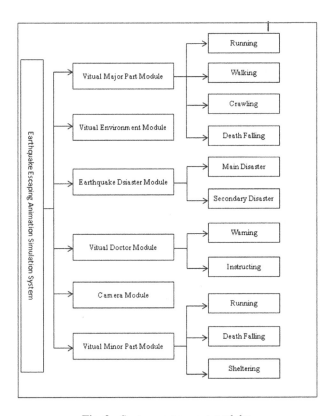

Fig. 2. System component modules

building collapses and secondary disasters such as fire, noxious gas leakage. System consists of modules are shown in Fig. 2.

3   Implementation of This Animation and Game Simulation System

3.1   Earthquake Scenario Building and Role Modeling

In order to achieve a realistic earthquake scenarios, enabling users a deep experience, according to content requirements of our system, in view of the complexity of the hospital scene, we use three-dimensional modeling software 3ds max to build a virtual scene (hospital), map and bake. Virtual hospital scene is a four-story building, including, departments, waiting room, reception, lifts connecting all floors, fire exits, and common hospital furniture. In order to achieve the authenticity of the hospital scenes, we use image processing software photoshop to process the captured photos from the actual scene, and adjust pixels and size of the images, so as to match them with the virtual scene of the furniture and architecture. In the complex environment of the hospital, which contains a very wide range of objects, in order to ensure the smooth operation of the system, we simplify the virtual scene [9]. Scene model output from 3ds max should be imported to unity3d, and then export formats supported by unity3d. In earthquake escaping education, varied action the role can increase the fun of the game animation and simulation; increase the user's sense of immersion, while making the scene more real and vivid. We design action and model of the virtual role by using 3ds max, adding bones to the virtual characters, also its skin, and bones moves by regulating key frames to achieve virtual characters motion libraries in earthquake escaping education. In animation game simulation, movements that user operate the actor include creeping, running, jumping and the virtual supporting part including head away, squatting down and other movements, as shown in Fig. 3.

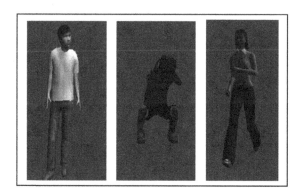

Fig. 3. Examples of virtual characters action

3.2   Creating Interactive Scene

Interaction is an important function in simulation system. It is also an important way to improve the effectiveness of education.

We used the Unity3d that is the popular game development engine to develop the interactive function. The earthquake escaping education system developed using unity3d can run not only on pc machine, but also smoothly on mobile devices. Interactive scenes were also created in unity3d, which supported not only static models, such as hospitals and a variety of furniture, but also dynamic models such as animated characters.

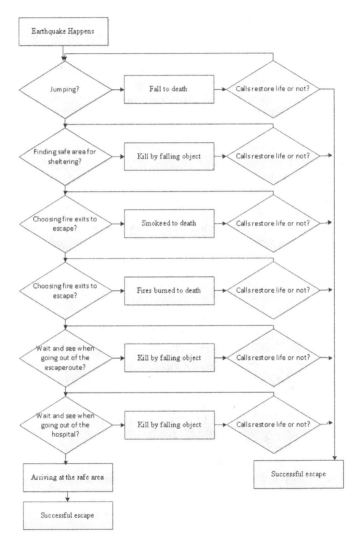

Fig. 4. System interactive processes

According to the system requirements, some objects in the scene need to add some properties when importing unity3d static scene. For example, the floor needs to add the properties of collision, so that the floor can support the virtual character motion when the virtual characters walking on the floor and the stairs, avoiding penetration. Directional light is added to improve the brightness of the environment, increase the realistic of the environment. The animation properties of virtual character need to be set when importing dynamic model. The character animation are adjusted through setting Animation attributes in the Inspector panel of the characters .rename different actions through setting the start and end of key frames. For example, the main action of the actor needed controlled by the user are divided into: Run, Walk, Die, Crew, Idle five states. At the same time, in order to processing interaction when virtual role interact with the virtual environment in the movement, virtual attribute is needed to add a character controllers for detecting collision of virtual characters with the floor and the building more easily.

3.3 Implementation of Interactive Features

According to the story, a virtual character interactive processes are designed based on the earthquake escaping knowledge, which includes whether to jump for escaping, or look for shelter, or through escaping route, fire put out or not when road closured by fire or detour, watch out when at the exit of the escaping route and other interactive dialogue. The interactive process is shown in Fig. 4, among which human machine interactive contains controlling virtual characters, collision of virtual character with the surrounding environment processing and human perspective processing.

Virtual character control section: Virtual character control
In this interactive system, the learner control virtual characters through keyboard, and then escape in the earthquake environment. Virtual characters' actions include Run, Walk, Die, Crew, Idle five states. Code control virtual characters to get ahead through keyboard are as follows:

```
If (Input.GetKey("w")||Input.GetKey("up"))
//keyboard event monitor
        {
            if(runState)
            {
            animation.Play("Run");//play animation
                if(!runSound.isPlaying)
                {
                runSound.Play();// play sound
                                            }
            }
CharacterController controller=GetComponent<CharacterController> ();
        //get character controller
    moveDirection=transform.TransformDirection (moveDirection);
        //local coordinate transform to global coordinate
        controller.Move(moveDirection * Time.deltaTime);//move
        }
```

First the system continuously monitor trigger events from the keyboard, once a run forward key triggered, it determine the operational status of the virtual character. If the state is Run, the system plays the animation of running of a virtual role, synchronized by sound effects. Then the running directions of the virtual characters are obtained. In order to making operation of the virtual character smooth and natural, Time.deltaTime method are used to gradually transit each frame of the virtual character movement.

Collisions with the surrounding environment processing

In order to simulate real virtual character movement, increasing the game's sense of immersion in the system, bounding box are added to detect the collision of virtual character with the surrounding objects. When virtual actor running on the floor, in order to make the virtual character run on the floor surface in time, increasing the avatar gravity properties and detect whether the avatar in contact with the ground in real-time. If virtual actors have no contact with the ground, "grounded" state is false; triggering gravitational properties of virtual characters, promoting the position of the virtual character down to contact with the floor, part of the code is as follows:

private bool grounded=false;// to determine whether contact with the ground

    moveDirection.y = jumpSpeed;// jump up

    If(!grounded)

    {

    moveDirection.y -= gravity * Time.deltaTime; // decline in direct contact with the ground

}

(1) *Virtual character perspective treatment:*

Virtual characters perspective in an interactive system is achieved through the camera, which contact user with virtual scene visually. The system ensures visual effects of virtual characters by setting the transition between the first angle and the third angle. At the same time, the visual angle of rotation direction is adjusted by mouse. In order to view more smoothly, the camera target always follows the virtual character and the virtual role rotation automatically rotates the camera, which makes the camera follows virtual characters motion.

3.4   Treatment of Seismic Effects

Seismic effect of simulation system mainly involves the building shaking, the building collapse, and secondary disasters triggered by the earthquake. Buildings shaking: In the past, earthquake shaking effect is usually achieved using the camera shaking, so effects of earthquake cannot be felt by the virtual character. These systems establish nodes to achieve the earthquake effects. Object with the same attributes being on the same node, the Script method are used to control the root node, and then the whole scene are brought to actual shaking. Therefore a realistic earthquake shaking effect is realized. The key codes are as follows:

```
Vector3 moveDirection=Vector3.zero;
//define the direction of building moving
    Bool earthquakeState;//
    Mark the earthquake
    if(earthquakeState==true)
    {//Randomly acquire moving distance of building in three directions
     moveDirection.x=Random.Range(-1f,1f);
     moveDirection.z=Random.Range(-1f,1f);
    moveDirection.y=Random.Range(-1f,1f);
    // building shaking
     transform.Translate(moveDirection*Time.deltaTime*3);}
```

Buildings collapse: the earthquake will inevitably lead to destruction; the collapse of the building can set off a complex environment for earthquakes escaping. In order to achieve realistic results, as well as collision effects of debris landing when buildings collapsed. On setting the collapse effect, the whole buildings are divided into irregular polyhedron using Ray Fire tool plug-in. To highlight the effect of the collapse of the collided building, box collider is added to increase the collision between different fragments. While the gravity attribute is added to reflect the gravity effect of the collapsed debris. Key codes are as follows:

```
GameObject[] stair=GameObject.FindGameObjectsWithTag("stair");
    //      Acquire the game object tagged stair
    for(int i=0;i<stair.Length;i++)
    {
    stair[i].AddComponent<Rigidbody>();//add component to object
stair[i].transform.rigidbody.useGravity=true;//activate attributes of gravity of object
```

Secondary disasters: In reality, the secondary disasters triggered by actual earthquake tend to bring some people obstacles and difficulties for escaping. We increase the difficulty of escape by adding secondary disasters triggered by earthquake and fire smoke. Unity3d provides a particle system which can adjust sophisticated effects [10]. We realize the dynamic flame and smoke effect using shade to render the particles and combining a particle system, which increase the realistic secondary disasters and an immersive simulation system. Smoking effects are shown in Fig. 5.

Fig. 5. Flame effects

3.5   AI of a NPC

In the hospital environment, the crowd unrest and panic could heighten the authenticity of the environment and increase participants' sense of tension. By increasing AI control method of the Non-Player Character to achieve the intelligence of the Non-Player Character. Non-Player Character could choose different behaviour according to the earthquake occurring time and different states. Non-Player Character's behaviour of finite state machine is shown in Fig. 6.

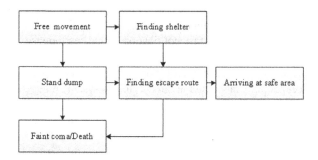

Fig. 6. Finite state machine of a NPC

In the animation simulation system, free movements of hospital's crowd before earthquake start randomly change the motion path. Motion status of the virtual man change when earthquake occur. According to the system requirements, when an earthquake occurs, some roles in an overwhelmed panic state, some find safe areas for shelter. When the earthquake slightly weakened, virtual characters find the escape paths in A * algorithm. Since the earthquake movement had a secondary disasters, AI role in the moving process may encounter road closures by obstacles, as well as fire barriers. AI characters need to judge and find a new safe escape route. If any role makes wrong judgment in finding path, this virtual role will be at risk of death. In the real disaster scenario, some roles will choose to follow the major part movement according to its judgment. In an inter active system, if the major part does correctly, AI characters can be led to normal escape, if the participant operate wrong, AI characters will calculate the nearest path point as the start point of escaping route, then the escaping route are calculated by a * algorithm, part of the codes are as follows:

```
for(int i=0;i<pd.Length;i++)
    {if(dis>Vector3.Distance(transform.position,pd[i].transform.position))
    {dis=Vector3.Distance(transform.position,pd[i].transform.position);
    //Record the nearest escape route point
    target=pd[i];//set escape target point
        }
    }
```

3.6   Audio and Other Effects Processing

Sound plays an important role in the simulation system. A good sound simulation system can increase the overall effect and enhance user's sense of immersion. Unity3d provides a powerful audio channel, which helps us to improve the effects of system's overall rendering. Adding Audio sound source to the system and connect our audio files can synchronize playback of sound and animation. In this system, we've added dozens of sound files, such as hospitals noise, broadcast notification sound, earthquake sound, running sound, cries, fires burning sound, etc.

Remain calm is an important condition for the success of disaster escape, but fear of disasters often affect people's mood and judgment. In this system, escape time constraints are added to increase the participants' sense of tension and to simulate the operation correctness of the participants under stressful conditions. At the same time, in order to increase participants' sense of crisis, bloodstains are added to the roles who are injured by falling objects to stimulate the participants vision and enhance their stress levels. These are shown in Fig. 8. Meanwhile, in order to give the participants a correct indication for escape, a virtual doctor will give participants correct instructions to help participant master correct escaping method.

3.7   Main Function of This Simulation System

The scene of earthquake disaster in the hospital were realized in this system, and a series of game rules were joined, therefore earthquake escaping knowledge could be learned and enhanced by participants in the entertainment. For example, jumping from building for escape when earthquake happens are forbidden, but one should look for the nearest triangle area for shelter as soon as possible. In complex Chinese hospital environments of this system, a large, panic crowd could cause character misjudge on escape, as shown in Fig. 7. There were also some roles following the character to escape in this system. Escape time was set to increase the participants' sense of tension in this system. Some sound effects were added to increase sense of immersion. Virtual doctor was added to guide participants to correctly choose for escape, or give tips of the danger, such as when fire approaching, virtual characters should be away from the fire source, or else he/she may be burned to death, which was shown in Fig. 7.

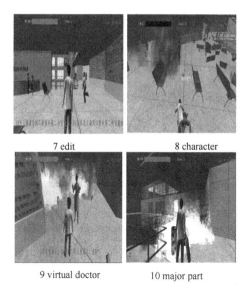

7 edit   8 character

9 virtual doctor   10 major part

Fig. 7. Main function of this simulation system

In order to make this simulation cartoon game system more interesting and interactive, participants are free to carry out some editing of the scene. Participants could add some objects in the environment, such as chairs, fire extinguishers, warning signs, flame, trash and other items, to increase the difficulty of escaping and to influence the judgment and choice of AI characters, while increasing judgment for choosing escaping route of substitute operated by participant, as shown in Fig. 7.

4 Conclusion

In real life, escaping the earthquake disaster cannot be reproduced, usual earthquake disaster evacuation drills cannot simulate the real disaster environment, participants cannot experience the real atmosphere of escape, and also with the issue of secondary disasters. Even the learned knowledge on escaping cannot turn into emergency measures in times of crisis.

Based on the analysis of the earthquake disaster, we used simulation techniques to reproduce animation game quake scene, as well as secondary disaster caused by the earthquake, in which participants can be drilled evacuation through virtual roles. Controlling the virtual character, participants can try out various escape plans. When it fails, the system will display a death screen of a virtual role in bloodbath, which gives participants a serious lesson, so as to let participant to be aware of the importance to master the correct escaping programs. The system uses a lot of sound effects, as well as smoke, fire and other particle effects to enhance realism of environmental disasters, while increasing function of regulating and interacting with the environment, enabling participants to adjust some objects in the environment, and participants' sense of immersion and fun.

Practice shows that the participants' earthquake escaping senses of reality are enhanced through animation and game simulation. Costs of previous escape training are reduced and training becomes safer, more interesting and more effective. The system can arouse users' enthusiasm of active learning and earthquake escape education through animation games simulation provides a new way of education.

References

1. Zhang, M., Bao, W., Xiong, Z., Xu, W.: ERT-VR: virtual simulation system for training earthquake rescuers. J. Syst. Simul. **16**, 3693–3696 (2007)
2. Jia, Q., Zhou, B.: Earthquake disaster scenario simulation technology. J. Comput. Res. Dev. **16**, 177–202 (2008)
3. Roussou, M., Oliver, M., Slater, M.: The virtual playground: an educational virtual reality environment for evaluating interactivity and conceptual learning. Virtual Real. **10**(3–4), 227–240 (2006). (S1359-4338)
4. Xuan, Y.: Unity 3d Game Development. People Posts and Telecom Press, Beijing (2012)
5. Sun, B.: The implementation of three-dimensional seismic damage simulation system. Earthq. Eng. Eng. Vibr. **5**, 1–8 (2010)
6. Liu, B., Wang, Z., Wang, L., Hua, W., Peng, Q.: Efficient modeling and real-time rendering of large-scale urban scenes. J. Comput. Aided Des. Comput. Graph. **9**, 1153–1162 (2008)

Online Game Bot Detection Based on Extreme Learning Machine

Xu Huang[1,2(✉)], Jing Fan[2], Shaowen Gao[2], and Wenjun Hu[1]

[1] School of Information Engineering, Huzhou University,
Huzhou 313000, Zhejiang Province, China
hx@zjhu.edu.cn
[2] College of Control Science and Engineering, Zhejiang University,
Hangzhou 310058, Zhejiang Province, China

Abstract. Some players of Massively Multiuser Online Role-Playing Games (MMORPG) manipulate game bots to accumulate property quickly in the game world, for getting a high-level experience quickly without spending too much time and energy. It has a great impact on the game experience of human players, and lead to an unfair phenomenon in games. We analyze and screen players in online games to quickly capture game bots, and let game operators do subsequent processing. First, we analyze game log data and arrange user behavior sequences to form a matrix with user information. Second, Extreme Learning Machine (ELM) is used for classification and screening. Some traditional classification methods, i.e. SVM and KNN, are used on the same data to verify the algorithm effect. Empirical study demonstrates that the proposed method is competitive with some traditional methods in terms of accuracy and efficiency.

Keywords: Extreme learning machine · Online game security
Game bot · MMORPG

1 Introduction

At present, the game industry has been unprecedented development. Single game, online games, mobile games, etc., continue to enrich people's lives and attract participants at all levels. Especially the Massively Multiuser Online Role-Playing Game (MMORPG) is a wide range of participation. In order to increase the interest and enhance the user's immersion, most of the Games simulate the real-life mode and set up a series of virtual production and virtual transaction links [1, 2]. Players can gain wealth and experience through various activities in the virtual game world. This series of virtual activities of the set, it is the charm of the game. As a result, game players usually invest a lot of time and effort in getting the money and equipment in the game, achieving levels of promotion, and gaining experience beyond real life. However, some game players often through the payment of real world money to buy virtual property, and even manipulate the game robot in the game world the rapid accumulation of property, in order to obtain high grade experience and avoid spending too much time and energy. Game robot is a computer program that represents human players to participate in the game. It has the ability to perform tasks without interruption, and also has a strong

Z. Pan et al. (Eds.): Transactions on Edutainment XIV, LNCS 10790, pp. 155–165, 2018.
https://doi.org/10.1007/978-3-662-56689-3_13

purpose and higher efficiency. Some players use game robots to accumulate wealth quickly in the game world and translate it into real world wealth, making the game less entertaining and degenerate into a means of making money. Obviously, this kind of behavior is unfair to the regular player, and it often hurts the enthusiasm of the human players to participate in the game, and affects the overall social effect of the game. So, most games do not allow game bots. Many game companies invest a lot of manpower in identifying and tagging game bots in order to get a clean human player group.

In order to quickly identify game robots from many players and terminate their operations, various methods for detecting game robots have been proposed [3, 4]. Game bot detection methods are divided into three categories in literature [3]. The game robot detection method is divided into three categories in this literature, client-side (Complete Automated Public Turing Test to Tell Computers and Humans Apart (CAPTCH) analysis), network-side (traffic analysis), and serve-side (user behavior analysis, moving path analysis, human observation proofs (HOP) analysis). The client-side bot detection method is similar to the Turing Test. It requests answers that can be easily provided by humans but not by game bots. This method is effective for detecting game bots, but it needs to interrupt the game to answer the question, so that the player's sense of immersion is greatly reduced [2]. Based on the difference of the network traffic generated by human players and by game bots, literature [5, 6] proposed a new method that distinguish between human players and robots by analysis the network traffic during the game. This approach has a low accuracy rate. In order to overcome the shortcomings of client-side and network-side detection methods, many studies analyze log data generated by players during the game process to distinguish between human players and game bots, known as server-side robot detection methods. In this approach, through the server-generated log generated by the player, can tap their important behavioral characteristics, used to distinguish between human players and game bots. Specific methods related to machine learning, user behavior analysis, task analysis and so on.

Thawonmas et al. [7] proposed a method of using the difference between action frequencies of game bot and human. Ahmad et al. [8] try to identify gold farmer using Bayesian Networks, Naive Bayes, KNN, etc. Yeung et al. [9] proposed a method of using the dynamic Bayesian Network (DBN) to model the detection accuracy in First Person Shooter (FPS). Lecture [10] showed that the idle time and active time is also a user feature. Varvello and Voelker [11] detected game bots by analysing the social connections of avatars in the social graph. At least, social network constructed by players in games was studied in some lectures. Kang et al. [3] studied the group action of players in a game, and tried to identify game bot based on the difference between other players and this group. Mitterhofer et al. [4] identified the game bots based on the repeat model of move sequences in games. Lecture [12] identified game bots by testing the frequency difference between movement angles of bots and human player. Thawonmas et al. [13, 14] proposed a method to test important states from general states. The actions of click, mouse moving, idle time, and mouse drag and release events are all collected. Lectures [15, 16] proposed that can test game bots using these events.

There are many factors such as high data dimension, complex structure, large amount of data, etc. in this process. The analysis and processing of a large number of log data [17] become the premise of solving this problem. Liu et al. proposed that the fast reduction algorithm with Rough Set [18] plays a good role in this kind of process. In addition, the performance evaluation of specific features is also an important process before data processing, and the methods proposed in document [19] can be used for reference.

However, when using machine learning tools to analyze log data, the differences are very small and difficult to implement by automatic mechanism. We proposed an efficient identification method for game bots with Extreme Learning Machine(ELM) [20] used to analyze game log data. This method was compared with traditional methods such as SVR and KNN in some experiments.

2   Basic ELM Method

Extreme Learning Machine is used to solve single hidden layer neural network. It is faster than traditional neural networks on the premise of ensuring the accuracy of learning [20, 21]. Unlike those traditional iterative implementation, ELM randomly selects input weights and implied preferences, and then analyzes the input weights of the SLFNs. The hidden layer nodes do not need to have the similar neurons. Unlike the traditional learning algorithm for a neural type, the ELM target not only achieves the minimum training error, but also achieves the minimum output weight norm. As a new fast learning algorithm for single hidden layer neural networks, ELM can initialize the input weights and offsets randomly and obtain the corresponding output weights. The ELM architecture is shown in Fig. 1.

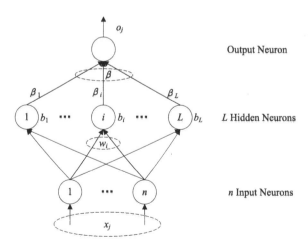

Fig. 1. ELM architecture

ELM's learning process consists of two steps, (1) random feature mapping: ELM randomly initializes the hidden layer and uses a nonlinear mapping function to map the input vector into the feature space; (2) linear parameter solving: ELM uses standard optimization methods to find solutions and minimize training errors.

It is assumed that there are N arbitrary samples (X_i, t_i) for a single hidden layer neural network. Where, $X_i = [x_{i1}, x_{i2}, \ldots, x_{in}]^T \in R^n$, $t_i = [t_{i1}, t_{i2}, \ldots, t_{im}]^T \in R^m$. Then a single hidden layer neural network with L hidden layer nodes can be represented as,

$$\sum_{i=1}^{L} \beta_i g(W_i \cdot X_j + b_i) = o_j, j = 1, \ldots N$$

Where, $g(x) = [g_1(x), g_2(x), \ldots, g_L(x)]$ is EML nonlinear feature mapping (activation function). It is an output vector in hidden layer about X, $g_i(x)$ is the output of hidden layer unit i. In real applications, you can choose,

$$g_i(x) = G(a_i, b_i, x), a_i \in R^d, b_i \in R$$

$G(a_i, b_i, x)$ is a nonlinear piecewise continuous function satisfying the theory of ELM universal approximation capability.

$W_i = [w_{i1}, w_{i2}, \ldots, w_{in}]^T$ is input weight, $\beta = [\beta_1, \beta_2, \ldots \beta_L]^T$ is the output weight vector between L hidden layer nodes and output nodes, $b = [b_1, b_2, \ldots, b_L]^T$ is the out bias of hidden layer, b_i is the bias of hidden layer unit i. $W_i \cdot X_j$ is the inner product of W_i and X_j.

The learning target of ELM is to minimize the output error,

$$\sum_{j=1}^{N} \|o_j - t_j\| = 0$$

That is to say, there are β_i, W_i, and b_i, it makes,

$$\sum_{i=1}^{L} \beta_i g(W_i \cdot X_j + b_i) = t_j, j = 1, \ldots, N$$

In matrix form, it can be represented as,

$$H\beta = T$$

Where, H is the output of hidden layer node, β is output weight, T is the expected output.

$$H(W_1,\ldots,W_L,b_1,\ldots,b_L,X_1,\ldots,X_L)$$

$$= \begin{bmatrix} g(W_1 \cdot X_1 + b_1) & \cdots & g(W_L \cdot X_1 + b_L) \\ \vdots & \ddots & \vdots \\ g(W_1 \cdot X_N + b_1) & \cdots & g(W_L \cdot X_N + b_L) \end{bmatrix}_{N \times L}$$

$$\beta = \begin{bmatrix} \beta_1^T \\ \vdots \\ \beta_L^T \end{bmatrix}_{L \times m}$$

$$T = \begin{bmatrix} T_1^T \\ \vdots \\ T_N^T \end{bmatrix}_{N \times m}$$

In order to train single hidden layer neural networks, we hope to get $\hat{W}_i$, $\hat{b}_i$ and $\hat{\beta}_i$,

$$\left\| H(\hat{W}_i,\hat{b}_i)\hat{\beta}_i - T \right\| = \min_{W,b,\beta} \| H(W_i,b_i)\beta_i - T \|$$

Where, $i = 1,\ldots,L$. It is equivalent to minimizing the loss function,

$$E = \sum_{j=1}^{N} \left(\sum_{i=1}^{L} \beta_i g(W_i \cdot X_j + b_i) - t_j \right)^2$$

In the ELM algorithm, once the input weight W_i and the offset b_i of the hidden layer are randomly determined, the output matrix H of the hidden layer is uniquely determined. The training single hidden layer neural network can be transformed into solving a linear system $H\beta = T$, and the output weight β can be determined,

$$\hat{\beta} = H^{\dagger}T$$

Where $H^{\dagger}$ is generalized inverse of matrix H. And it is proved that the norm of solution beta is the smallest and the only.

In addition, ELM has been widely used in clustering [22], feature selection [23] and other fields.

3   Game Bot Detection Method Based on ELM

We have collected more than 3 billion of the logs data from the hot game *New Qiannv Online* provided by NetEase. We expect to learn a model that correctly distinguishes robot players. In general, human players aim to achieve a good behavior experience by pursuing a sense of immersion in the game. Fighting monsters, making money, and upgrading are just the vehicles that build up this experience and witness this experience. The robot players use the high efficiency of the program, the virtual world of behavior gathered into the pursuit of wealth surge, and ultimately the virtual world of wealth into real life money. Therefore, a robot player is very different from what a normal gamer does. Based on this understanding, the game log data are analyzed. Logs record the behavior of game users. There is a huge difference in the density of the same behavior and the rate of increase and decrease of the wealth reflected by the two users. Switching of different behaviors of the same user also reflects the purpose of the user. Normal gamers have a variety of ways of combining behavior in pursuit of higher interest. However, robot players are heavily gathered in the fastest growing behavior of wealth.

In this paper, the user's daily logs are grouped according to the time period, and the frequency of each group is calculated. The user's feature description is constructed by using the time series of frequency. a temporal behavior matrix can be formed for each user. We believe that the matrix reflects the comprehensive features of the user and can reflect the difference between the robot player and the normal player. The structure of the user log information matrix is shown in Fig. 2.

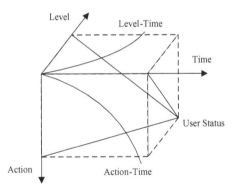

Fig. 2. The structure of the user log information matrix

The matrix has three dimensions, Time, Action, and Level. The Action-Time plane shows the changing law of user behavior over time. The Level-Time plane shows user updates. This paper focuses on the change of user's attributes on these two planes. In the Action-Time plane, for normal players, the frequency of user behavior is low, and the change curve is gentle. There are obvious peaks and valleys in a day. However, for the robot players, the behavior of money reproduction frequency is high, the peak valley phenomenon is not obvious. Therefore, in the Level-Time plane, the normal player's upgrade curve is smooth, while the robot player upgrade curve is steeper. In addition, the matrix can reflect the activities of users at different levels, and we will focus on these factors in the next experiment.

Based on the above considerations, this article divides game log information by hours. That is, a user's daily log information can be expressed as,

$$Log = \begin{bmatrix} (l_1, f(a_{11})) & \cdots & (l_N, f(a_{1N})) \\ \vdots & \ddots & \vdots \\ (l_1, f(a_{K1})) & \cdots & (l_N, f(a_{KN})) \end{bmatrix}$$

Where l_i is users' current level, $f(a_{ij})$ is the reproduction frequency of user behavior i at time j. $N = 24$. K is number of actions involved. The reproduction frequency is defined as the ratio of the total number of actions occurring in a period of time (1 h) to the total number of actions occurring in that time. Denoted by $f(\cdot) = \frac{t_a}{t_{all}}$.

There are two ways of reproducing frequency of user behavior.

(1) The maximum of elements of $f(a_{ij})$ in all row in matrix Log are selected and mapped to a N dimensional vector.

$$L^{LINE} = [(l_1, f(a_{x_1 1})), \ldots, (l_i, f(a_{x_i i})), \ldots, (l_N, f(a_{x_N N}))]$$

Where $f(a_{x_i i})$ marked with $x_i \in \{1, \ldots, K\}$ is the maximum in $\{f(a_{1i}), \ldots, f(a_{Ki})\}$. This method only examines the behavior with the highest reproduction frequency.

(2) Each row of the matrix A is sequentially connected to a $K \times N$ dimension vector.

$$L^{ALL} = [(l_1, f(a_{11})), \ldots, (l_N, f(a_{1N})), \ldots, (l_1, f(a_{K1})), \ldots, (l_N, f(a_{KN}))]$$

This approach will incorporate all actions into the scope of the investigation, and may be given more extensive information expression, but will pay more computing time.

In combination with the ELM architecture, the N dimension vector L^{LINE} or $K \times N$ dimension vector L^{ALL} are used as input vectors respectively. Represented as L. However, game robot recognition is a two kind of classification problem. That is, $m = 2$. Therefore, the ELM model for game robot identification can be represented as,

$$\sum_{i=1}^{L} \beta_i g(W_i \cdot L_j + b_i) = o_j, j = 1, \ldots N$$

Where, $g_i(x) = G(a_i, b_i, x), a_i \in R^d, b_i \in R, o_j = [o_{j1}, o_{j2}]^T$.

Besides ELM, SVM and KNN are also common classification methods. In this paper, SVM and KNN are used to compare experiments, Construction vectors set $\{(t_j, L_j)\}$ is used as training data. Where $t_j = [t_{j1}, t_{j2}]^T, t_{ji} \in \{0, 1\}$, represent normal players and game bots. $L_j = L_j^{LINE}$, or $L_j = L_j^{ALL}$.

In this paper, the general idea is to analyze the game log data first, sort out user behavior sequence, and then combined with the target type and user level, user log information matrix, followed by ELM and SVM, KNN method to classify, final classification effect analysis. The process is shown in Fig. 3.

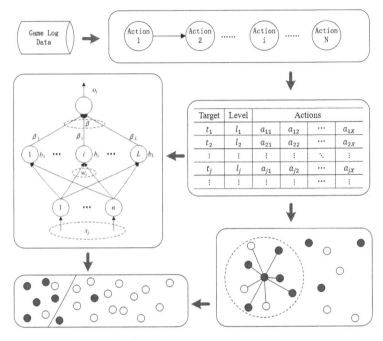

Fig. 3. Experimental process

Combined with the above experimental process, on the one hand, the ELM model parameters are solved and optimized, and the vertical promotion of classification effect is realized. On the other hand, it also compares with the traditional classification methods, and makes a horizontal comparison of the recognition effects in a timely manner.

4   Experiment and Result

We have collected some of the logs data from the hot game *New Qiannv Online* provided by NetEase. There are 468.5 G data, which contains 3,785,522,567 events and 38,793 effective players, distributed from level 1 to level 40. First, the log data is analyzed, the user behavior sequence is combed, and the user behavior matrix is constructed. Then ELM and KNN are used to cluster analysis. The algorithm is implemented on a machine configured as i5-2450 M 2.50 GHz CPU, and 16.0 GB memory, with the operating system is Ubuntu 14.04. These programs are developed with C language.

To deal with the reappearance of user behavior, two methods are used to test only the highest reproduction frequency and to examine all behaviors. In order to verify the effect of the algorithm, 1000, 10000 and 100000 log data were selected randomly for preliminary analysis. The experiment results of these two methods are shown in Table 1.

Table 1. Experiment Results

	Number of log data	Number of real bots	ELM		KNN		SVM	
			Actions	Users	Actions	Users	Actions	Users
For max value	1000	27	27	5	27	5	27	5
	10000	261	258	47	252	47	254	47
	100000	1255	1201	405	1196	401	1198	404
For all value	1000	32	32	5	32	5	32	5
	10000	314	311	50	303	51	308	48
	100000	1332	1296	443	1032	417	1276	426

The experimental results show that the three algorithms show good performance when the target is less. However, as the number of targets increases, the advantages of ELM are gradually highlighted. At the same time, under the condition of multiple targets, the experimental results using all the data are better than the maximum. This result shows that ELM has more advantages in terms of large amount of data and more parameters. However, in this experiment, KNN was not improved, probably due to the selection of similarity computation functions. Next, we will do further research on similarity function selection.

5   Conclusion

At present, the MMORPG is a wide range of participation. Some players of MMORPG manipulate game bots to accumulate property quickly in the game world, for getting a high-level experience quickly without spending too much time and energy. It has a bad effect on the normal users' experience. This is a problem to be solved urgently. ELM has some value in game robot detection. The recognition rate is higher than other methods such as KNN on the data set we selected. And it also shows some advantages in the recognition efficiency. Next, further research will be done on the promotion of recognition efficiency as well as ELM parallelization.

Acknowledgments. This work was partly supported by National Natural Science Foundation of China (61202290, 61370173, 61772198). We are grateful to the anonymous referees for their insightful comments and suggestions, which clarified the presentation.

References

1. Oh, J., Borbora, Z.H., Sharma, D., Srivastava, J.: Bot detection based on social interactions in MMORPGs. In: International Conference on Social Computing, vol. 10(1), pp. 536–543 (2013)
2. Novak, T., Hoffman, D., Duhachek, A.: The influence of global directed and experiential activities on online flow experiences. J. Consum. Psychol. 13(1-2), 3–16 (2003)
3. Kang, A.R., Woo, J., Park, J., Kim, H.K.: Online game bot detection based on party-play log analysis. Comput. Math Appl. 65, 1384–1395 (2013)
4. Mitterhofer, S., Krügel, C., Kirda, E., Platzer, C.: Server-side bot detection in massively multiplayer online games. IEEE Secur. Priv. 7(3), 29–36 (2009)
5. Chen, K.-T., Jiang, J.-W., Huang, P., Chu, H.-H., Lei, C.-L., Chen, W.-C.: Identifying mmorpg bots: a traffic analysis approach. EURASIP J. Adv. Signal Process. 2009, 22 (2009)
6. Hilaire, S., Chul Kim, H., Kim, C.-K.: How to deal with bot scum in mmorpgs? In: 2010 IEEE International Workshop Technical Committee on Communications Quality and Reliability (CQR), pp. 1–6 (2010)
7. Thawonmas, R., Kashifuji, Y., Chen, K.-T.: Detection of MMORPG bots based on behavior analysis. In: Advances in Computer Entertainment Technology, pp. 91–94 (2008)
8. Ahmad, M.A., Keegan, B., Srivastava, J., Williams, D., Contractor, N.S.: Mining for gold farmers: automatic detection of deviant players in MMOGS. In: CSE, vol. 4, pp. 340–345 (2009)
9. Yeung, S., Liu, J.-S., Lui, J., Yan, J.: Detecting cheaters for multiplayer games: theory, design and implementation. In: 3rd IEEE 2006 Consumer Communications and Networking Conference, CCNC 2006, vol. 2, pp. 1178–1182 (2006)
10. Chen, K.-T., Hong, L.-W.: User indentification based on game-play activity patterns. In: NETGAMES, pp. 7–12 (2007)
11. Varvello, M., Voelker., G.M.: Second life: a social network of humans and bots. In: Proceedings of the 20th International Workshop on Network and Operating Systems Support for Digital Audio and Video, NOSSDAV 2010, pp. 9–14. ACM (2010)
12. van Kesteren, M., Langevoort, J., Grootjen, F.: A step in the right direction: bot detection in MMORPGS using movement analysis. In: Proceedings of the 21st Belgian-Dutch Conference on Artificial Intelligence (BNAIC 2009) (2009)
13. Thawonmas, R., Kurashige, M., Iizuka, K., Kantardzic, M.: Clustering of online game users based on their trails using self-organizing map. In: Harper, R., Rauterberg, M., Combetto, M. (eds.) ICEC 2006. LNCS, vol. 4161, pp. 366–369. Springer, Heidelberg (2006). https://doi.org/10.1007/11872320_51
14. Thawonmas, R., Kurashige, M., Chen, K.-T.: Detection of landmarks for clustering of online-game players. IJVR 6(3), 11–16 (2007)
15. Kim, H., Hong, S., Kim, J.: Detection of auto programs for MMORPGs. In: Zhang, S., Jarvis, R. (eds.) AI 2005. LNCS (LNAI), vol. 3809, pp. 1281–1284. Springer, Heidelberg (2005). https://doi.org/10.1007/11589990_187
16. Gianvecchio, S., Wu, Z., Xie, M., Wang, H.: Battle of botcraft: fighting bots in online games with human observational proofs. In: Proceedings of the 16th ACM Conference on Computer and Communications Security, CCS 2009, NY, USA, pp. 256–268. ACM, New York (2009)
17. Choi, Y., Chang, S., Kim, Y., Lee, H., Son, W., Jin, S.: Detecting and monitoring game bots based on large-scale user-behavior log data analysis in multiplayer online games. J. Supercomput. 72, 3572–3587 (2016)

18. Yong, L., Wenliang, H., Yunliang, J., Zhiyong, Z.: Quick attribute reduct algorithm for neighborhood rough set model. Inf. Sci. **V271**, 65–81 (2014)
19. Jiang Yunliang, X., Yunxi, L.Y.: Performance evaluation of feature and matching in stereo visual odometry. Neurocomputing **120**, 380–390 (2013)
20. Huang, G., Huang, G.-B., Song, S., You, K.: Trends in extreme learning machines: a review. Neural Netw. **61**, 32–48 (2015)
21. Huang, G., Song, S., Gupta, J.N.D., Wu, C.: Semi-supervised and unsupervised extreme learning machines. IEEE Trans. Cybern. **44**(12), 2405–2417 (2014)
22. He, Q., Jin, X., Du, C., Zhuang, F., Shi, Z.: Clustering in extreme learning machine feature space. Neurocomputing **128**, 88–95 (2014)
23. Huang, G.-B.: An insight into extreme learning machines random Neurons, random features kernels. Cognit. Comput. **6**(3), 376–390 (2014)

Attention Decrease Detection Based on Video Analysis in E-Learning

Liying Wang$^{(\boxtimes)}$ (iD)

Department of Educational Technology, Nanjing Normal University,
Nanjing 210097, China
wangliying@njnu.edu.cn

Abstract. E-learning takes the advantages of lower cost and higher benefit. It becomes one of the educational research focus through learning behavior analysis to promote deep learning. In order to help learners overcome possible disadvantages in e-learning environment such as prone inattention and delayed response, one video analysis algorithm is designed to detect attention decrease situation, then feedback in time or warn early. The algorithm uses head posture, gaze, eye closure and mouth opening, facial expression features as attention observation attributes. Next machine learning classifiers are applied to code behavior features. Finally the time sequential statistics of behavior features evaluate the attention level and emotional pleasure degree. Experiments show that the algorithm is effective to find out the inattention cases to give desirable feedback. It may be applicable in adaptive learning and human computer interaction fields.

Keywords: E-learning · Video analysis · Attention observation model
Attention decrease

1 Introduction

Fast booming e-learning takes great educational advantages of openness, autonomy, equality, fun, promotion, lower cost and higher benefit compared to traditional learning. Engagement is closely related to cognition and behavior, and the high concentration on learning is the basic excellent quality for effective autonomous learning. Based on educational, cognitive and psychological theories, research on e-learning attention autonomous observation and decrease detection will promote the persistence of deep learning, meet the further demands of adaptive learning and human computer interaction.

1.1 E-Learning Interaction Demand

The current e-learning platform is facing the challenge of transformation from the "quantity" accumulation of teaching resources into the "quality" improvement of

---

L. Wang (1976-)—Female, Tongliao, Inner Mongolia, lecturer, doctor, research direction: virtual reality, network applications.

Z. Pan et al. (Eds.): Transactions on Edutainment XIV, LNCS 10790, pp. 166–179, 2018.
https://doi.org/10.1007/978-3-662-56689-3_14

teaching services. Based on the unified MOOCs resource system, multi-level, multi-mode, diversified learning ways can be realized, such as autonomous learning, interactive learning, blended learning, and flipped classroom [1]. Relevant research on learning resources, learning tools and learning effects are emerging greatly, but deep tracking and psychological analyzing learning activity are still in short. It is the spatial-time isolation between teachers and students causes many problems, such as motivation shortage, prone inattention interactive monotony, delayed response, weak monitoring and high dropout rate. All of these disadvantages restricts the long-term sustainable development of online education. The development of e-learning needs credit authentication policy design and teaching service quality assurance system, as well scientific requirements for student learning activities inspection, guidance and assistance [2].

Educational research in e-learning mainly bases on behaviorism and connectionism. Many factors affect e-learning effects, such as self-management, academic skills, social interaction, learning time, motivation, Internet accessibility and costs, learning organization types, learning efficiency and pleasure, self-evaluation, completed courses number [3]. Tracking the participation and completion in e-learning is the important aspect of evaluation to give certain pressure and maintain the learning motivation. In the early stage, the mouse click operation times and learning duration are simply accumulated. Presently it widely depends on the learning process data including courseware, homework, test, examination, question, discussion and mutual evaluation participation. Zheng et al. [4]. constructs learning comprehensive evaluation indicators which come from 5 dimensions including degrees of engagement, completion, initiative, control and connectivity. Learning results can be classified and predicted according to the teaching objectives taxonomic ranks, learning activities participation degree, interaction level, and knowledge mapping analysis [5]. On MOOCs platform, all information interaction, emotional support and reliability, cooperation and sharing cannot do without social common attributes, so enhancing social interactive strategy design is necessary to improve the course completion rate [2]. For example, emotional support by means of encouraging, praising, feedback and responding, technical support through providing resources to change the coordination among learners can be designed [2].

1.2 Affective Computing in E-Learning

Affective computing in e-learning promotes education research from behaviorism to constructivism. Affective computing [6] is an advanced goal of artificial intelligence. At present, the precise sensors, such as EEG, ECG, GSR and eye movement, are widely used in medical and psychological diagnosis. Emotional recognition applications have profound significance, such as understanding dyslexia [7, 8], monitoring epilepsy sudden death, preventing depression and so on. However, the negative impact of these sensors on the subject is unavoidable, large-scale normal application in education is nearly infeasible. To make up for emotional deficiency in e-learning, researchers have designed emotion sensors, such as facial expression recognition, fatigue detection, speech recognition and so on. Multi-channel interaction and control operation are applied by recognizing speech, eye movement, and hand gesture,

message event. For example, determine whether the mouse is located inside the course window to control whether the courseware is played or not. Asteriadis et al. [9]. proposed a behavior recognition system to find interest of attention based on gaze, head pose and hand tracking. Mixture reality and virtual reality technology is a future trend to create learning environment and conduct natural interaction. It is worth looking forward for intelligent tutoring system to have emotion recognition, understanding and cognitive response.

Learning analysis(LA) is sprouting since 2010. Siemens [10] defines LA is the technique which applies data mining and analysis model to discover the internal information and relationship, to predict and improve learning. The use of analytics in education has grown in recent years for four primary reasons: a substantial increase in data quantity, improved data formats, advances in computing, and increased sophistication of tools available for analytics. LA has several recent impacts on the learning sciences. One particularly useful area of that is in research on disengagement within educational software. Researchers used these detectors to study the relationship between these behaviors and learning. Detectors have also been embedded into intelligent tutors that adapt based on student disengagement.

Under quantitative study trend, the emotional state, learning behavior and psychological characteristics of the learner in the real situation has become the focus of study and analysis. The biological characterization data can present learner information more comprehensively and accurately. It is helpful to monitor human-computer interaction process to know individual emotional and cognitive states and has great potential value in the field of emotion modeling, learning activities tracking, behavior feature extraction and adaptive learning [11].

Personalized learning behavior analysis model in digital learning environment especially emphasizes learner's emotion states, expression analysis, attitude and content analysis, which considers the aspects of boredom, participation and attention; thus, individual differences and learning resources dynamic allocation will be fully considered, the traditional standard static learning path will be re-planning [4]. These works develops learning analysis and provides referable constructivism concept and design scheme.

1.3 Video-Based Emotion Recognition

Video-based sensing and recognizing method is the basic research of affective computing in e-learning. Using machine vision algorithm to understand the video captured by the camera has the advantages of low cost, comfort, efficiency, authenticity, and better result more than human judgment. Video analysis algorithm can easily determine whether users in front of the computer, but is still difficult to judge whether seriously study or wrongly understand. Currently facial expression recognition has made important progress, which relies on face detection, feature register, face tracking and relevant machine learning algorithms. Researchers from abroad CMU, MIT, UIUC, Microsoft, Google and domestic Sciences academy, Tsinghua University, Harbin industrial university have mastered advanced theories and technologies.

Large-scale real-time face recognition have been realized and can avoid too much psychological interference to the subjects. But it is also vulnerable to light, occlusion, rotation, glasses, background interference which increases the detection difficulties. Typical works from e-learning lab of Shanghai Jiao Tong University detected students drowsiness and attention detraction according to eye closure state [12, 13]. These works do not care for the relationship between attention and cognition. With the development of the computer deep learning technology, the accuracy of face detection and recognition reaches more than 90%. Meanwhile, many open source software and tools are easily adapted to develop own applications, such as Openface [14], Face++, Microsoft cognition service, faster-RCNN etc. Therefore, technological maturity provides opportunity for precise service of online education. The perception, recognition, understanding attention and emotion state would improve the intelligent interaction level so as to breakthrough monotonous text communication and inefficient control by self-consciousness in e-learning.

2   Learning Attention Observation Model

Learning attention evaluation complies with attention functional classification and psychological mechanism. Some evaluation methods include observation, investigation, questionnaire, pen and paper task test, computer software test and biological signal feedback. Related driving fatigue vigilance works could be referred, one detection method of which is based on the driver physiological reaction features. This paper uses the facial video of the learner in e-learning process to observe and measure his attention level.

Schloberg's emotional 3D pattern shown in Fig. 1 proposed learning mood has pleasure, attention and activation three dimensions including pleasant-unpleasant, attention-rejection and activation level. Based on this pattern, we observe attention activation level and pleasant degree. Furthermore, we use the basic hypothesis that the premise of attention is posture stability, and the appearance of irrelevant action represents distraction. The learning attention observation model is shown in Fig. 2. Therein, the physical characteristics are detected and extracted from the video captured by the camera, which mainly include head posture, gaze, eye closure, mouth opening and facial expression.

Fig. 1. Schloberg's emotion 3D pattern

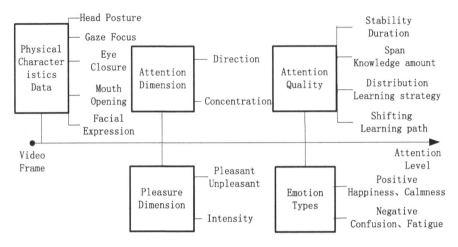

Fig. 2. Learning attention observation model

In the following paragraph, the correlation between observed characteristics and learning attention is described in detail. Attention dimension consists of direction and intensity. Directivity and concentration are the basic features of attention. Concentration represents attention intensity which is relevant to the activation level. Psychological research shows that arousal level is emotion activates the body's energy level, namely is the level difference between physical activity and mental alertness. Low arousal means sleep, tired, distraction, high arousal means awake, concentration and tension. The pleasure dimension consists of emotion type and intensity. Emotional types include happiness, confusion, and calmness expression.

Refer to the attention theory of cognitive psychology, attention level can be calculated from the learners' physical characteristics by observing the video. With the continuously tracking behavior changes in time can recognize the attention decrease cases, such as sleepiness, drowsiness, fatigue, distraction, shift and so on. The abnormal situations could be found out and given early warning.

2.1   Head Posture Estimation

In the learning process the mental activity of attention directs to a specific stimulus meeting the needs of current activities. Whether in the physical classroom or e-learning, regardless of which sensory input channel stimulation, the individual will pay attention to where the stimulation is taking place. Usually, attention direction and feelings change through tuning the head posture, maybe accompanied by eye movement. Head posture estimation has become one of the necessary approaches for attention decrease detection. Head posture consists of position and rotation in the camera 3D coordinate system. Head rotates around XYZ three axes to tune its posture. As shown in Fig. 3, rotation is represented by three Euler angles which namely are pitch, yaw, and roll angle. The positive angle of the rotation follows to the right-hand rule. In the head coordinate system, the positive angles are head up, turn left and tilt left.

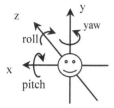

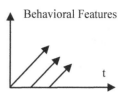

11	12	13	14	15
21	22	23	24	25
31	32	33	34	35
41	42	43	44	45
51	52	53	54	55

Fig. 3. Head posture   **Fig. 4.** Gaze focus encoding   **Fig. 5.** Attention level model

2.2   Gaze Focus Estimation

If the learner cannot follow the focuses in the learning situation, he is unable to achieve the best possible learning effect. In the camera coordinates, certain attention focuses in the context of learning is very necessary. The attention focuses can be simplified into space bounding boxes, such as computer screen displaying video, text for e-learning, traditional classroom multimedia screen, blackboard, and teachers so on. The attention focuses may also be dynamic. In learning process, the individual maintains following the attention focuses through adjusting the gaze direction with head posture and eyes movement. The gaze region is calculated according to the intersections of the attention focuses and the lines from the pupils' position along the gaze direction. If the eyes are closed, the sight line disappears. The gaze focuses are encoded as shown in Fig. 4 to describe whether the attention focus is.

2.3   Eye Movement Estimation: Closure and Blink

Eye movement delivers the most important information of the attention level. The cascade Adaboost classifier and Haar features were widely used to detect where faces and eyes located in the image. When the method is used to video, snapping images in a certain of interval is used to judge the sleepy states according to eye closure.

Blink is very important and straight forward feature in judging the attention level. When one blinks, the eyelid height is changing from large to small, then to large again. Normally people blink 15 times per minute, the interval of two blinks is about 4 s, the elapse time of each blink is between 0.1 and 0.3 s. When watching computer screen blink will be reduced to 10 times per minute because of the need for a long time staring at one place. In the fatigue, drowsy state, blink frequency will be higher. Previously the blink detection based on video analysis is still difficult due to landmark register difficulty. Now, video frame rate can be more than 15 fps so as to capture the blink to improve the diagnosis accuracy.

2.4   Mouth Opening and Yawn Estimation

Yawning is one distinct feature of fatigue and tired. Zhang [12] analyzed the learning state in terms of concentration, fatigue, safety and time aspect. Concentration was designed to judge the learner is inattention when detected face turning aside or recognizing mouth speaking. Fatigue state was estimated by detecting the yawning or closed eyes. In which, the mouth is positioned relative to the human eye position, and the mouth non-skin area is used to determine the mouth opening height and width. If the mouth is wide continuously more than 5 s in 6 s, it indicates that he yawned.

2.5   Facial Expression Recognition:Confusion and Happiness

In 1966, Paul Ekman, California University professor, summed up six basic expressions of human beings: anger, fear, happiness, sadness, disgust and surprise. Computer vision algorithms commonly used these 6 kinds of facial image samples for training facial expression recognition classifier. He also designed a facial action coding system (FACS) to identify emotions through the combination of action units (AU), such as frowning, smiling and so on.

Russell built a 2D ring learning emotion model including pleasure degree and intensity, which has 8 states: calm and cool, calm and satisfied, happy, excited and enthusiastic, nervous, sad, depression and fatigue. From 2004 to 2006, research on E-learning emotional measurement in Memphis University shows six kinds of emotional states that play important roles in the learning process are boredom, enthusiasm/attention, confusion, frustration, happiness and surprise. Two kinds of emotional states of low frequency are happiness and surprise. In 2010, Beck in CMU and Glazer in Memphis University compared these six kinds of emotion from three aspects of incidence, duration and effect. They found boredom, frustration are the 2 kinds of the longest duration states which are relevant with inefficient learning and problematic behavior, as well has negative influence on learning. Enthusiasm and confusion are the most ordinary states; happiness and surprise are the least states. They suggests frustration and boredom need be monitored and responded intensively. In 2012, they proposed a model of emotion transformation in e-learning based on above-mentioned Russell's model.

It can be seen that learning emotion is not equal to 6 basic expressions. It is enough to measure the pleasure degree by identifying the representative emotions such as calmness, confusion and happiness.

2.6   Attention Observation Model Summary

In brief, the attention observation features include head pose (position and rotation), gaze (viewpoint, gaze direction and gaze focus), eye movements (blink and closure), mouth opening (lip movement, yawning) and expression (confusion, happiness and calmness). Each video frame is quantitated by a vector to represent the values of the observed features, so as to identify the head, gaze, blink, eye closure, mouth movement, yawning, facial expressions and other behavioral characteristics. The vector changes in the time axis as shown in Fig. 5. The statistical features in the certain period evaluate the levels of attention and emotion. We consider 6 levels of attention: sleepiness, drowsiness, fatigue, shift, distraction, attention and concentration, as well 3 types of emotion: calmness, confusion and happiness. In the time axis, the attention level and emotional level will be quantified and evaluated to induce the attention quality in learning.

Below how to extract feature and classified for learning attention decrease detection by video analysis and machine learning algorithms are elaborated.

3   Attention Decrease Detection

Our attention decrease detection bases on Openface which provides video analysis results. The detection flowchart is shown in Fig. 6. Each of the steps is explained in detail as follows. The experimental video are recorded from subjects in e-learning process with upper body and facial behavior data. In addition, learning content and learning strategies data can be tracked in the captured computer screen video.

3.1   OpenFace Introduction

OpenFace [14–18] is the first open source tool capable of facial landmark detection, head pose estimation, facial action unit recognition, and eye-gaze estimation. The computer vision algorithms which represent the core of OpenFace demonstrate state-of-the-art results in all of the above mentioned tasks. Furthermore, the tool is capable of real-time performance and is able to run from a simple webcam without any specialist hardware. The tool can reach more than 15 fps, the accuracy rate reached 97%. The tracking results can be output as 431-dimension vector, which includes key data of each frame of video, such as head position and head euler angle, gaze vectors of both eyes, 68 facial landmarks (as shown in Fig. 7) indenfied by either pixel points in 2D image space or spatial position in 3D camera coordinates, 18 facial action units labeled by intensity and whether or not appear.

3.2   Observation Features Extraction

In order to detect attention level, a group of observation features are extracted from the initial features output by OpenFace. The observation features consist of head position, head posture, eyelid height, lip height, lip width, gaze direction, pupil position, the

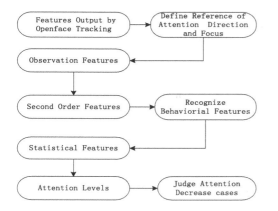

Fig. 6. Attention decrease detection flowchart

Fig. 7. OpenFace facial landmarks

facial action units of AU4, AU12 and AU17, which have 24 dimensions. For example, the height of eyelids is the mean distance between the upper and lower eyelids of the left and right eyes, the corresponding landmarks from No.37 to 48 among the 68 feature points are selected as the judgment points. The height of lips is the mean distance between the upper and lower lips these corresponding landmarks are from No. 50 to 60. No. 49 and 55 are used as the judgment points of lip width. The confusion is judged by AU4 and AU17, and the happiness is judged by AU12.

3.3   Behavioral Features Recognition

The observation features differences between the current frame and the reference frame and between two adjacent frames are calculated frame by frame, which is called the second order feature. Make use of the second order features and labels of the samples, the parameters of decision trees and SVM classifiers are trained to identify head position and head rotation, eye closure, mouth opening and facial expression characteristics. Each classifier recognizes a meaningful behavior, thus obtaining a 12 dimensional vector representing the identified behavioral features.

Taking head pose deviation in three axises as examples, including left and right, up and down, forward and afterward, pitch angle, yaw angle and tilt angle. After training, the frame with the left rotation angle greater than 30° is identified as 2, with head position afterwards displacement more than 10 cm is identified as 2, oppositely −2 means the head is forwards approaching the screen. Blink and yawn detection depend on the change of height, affected by the head posture and the tracking accuracy of openface. The gaze focus classifier is used to determine whether the gaze region is the attention focus.

According to PERCLOS eyelid distance, the curves of eye closure, blink and yawn are constructed as Fig. 8 shown.

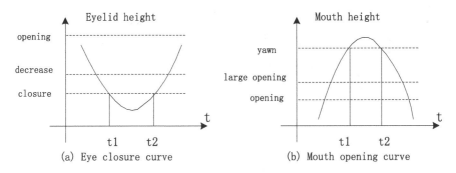

Fig. 8. Eyelid height and mouth height change in times

3.4   Classifier Samples Construction

The classifier parameters are trained from samples to obtain the criterion of classification, not by empirical threshold. Learning samples are constructed by manual annotation. After watching the video, the frame representing attention concentration is selected as the reference frame of the subsequent annotation from the beginning of the video. This means that the attention positive direction and focus region in camera coordinate system are defined. Normally, in e-learning, students stare at the screen in front of them, and the direction facing the screen is the attention positive direction, and the focus is the screen. If the head rotates, deviates greatly and the duration is longer than one threshold, it shows that the attention is distracted.

Table 1. Behavioral features encoding

Physiological reaction features	Quantity orders	Coding and meaning					
Head position and angle	5	0	−2	−1	1	2	
		Stable	Reversely large moving	Reversely small moving	Small moving	Large moving	
Eyelid height	3	0	1	2			
		Stable	Small decrease	Large decrease			
Mouth lips height and width	6	0	1	2	3	4	5
		Stable	Small opening	Large opening	Yawn	Pout	Clench
Gaze focus of left and right eyes	5	22 ∼ 44	1y	5y	x1	x5	
		Staring	Leftward deviation	Rightward deviation	Upward deviation	Downward deviation	
Emotion of confusion and happiness	2	0	1				
		Calm	Appearing				

Sample annotation includes video name, frame number, attention level and behavioral characteristics label which have 12 dimensions: including 3D head position, 3D head rotation, 1D eyelid movement, 1D mouth movement, 2D gaze points, 2D expression. The behavioral characteristics label encoding is shown in Table 1, with 9 indicating the uncertain situation, and two emotion types. The sample data come from all the above mentioned features.

3.5   Behavioral Features Statistics in Minutes

Behavioral features with 12 dimensions are taken in statistics in minutes to get the total number of frames and frequency times of the large deviation changes (or confusion and happiness appearance), stable states (or calmness). When eyelid height decreases largely, the blink case is detected if the duration is less than 0.7 s or the frame number is not more than 10 frames. Otherwise the case belongs to the eye closure.

3.6   Attention Level and Pleasure Degree Judgement

The attention level is divided into 6 levels: sleepiness, drowsiness, fatigue, distraction, shift, attention and concentration. Pleasure degree is divided into calmness, confusion and happiness.

When the frequency of eye closure is more than 6 times or eye closure duration is longer than 20% of a minute, the case is identified as sleepiness.

When the frequency of eye closure is more than 3 times or eye closure duration is longer than 10% of a minute, the case is identified as drowsiness.

When the frequency of blink is more than 15 times or yawn frequency is more than 2 times, the case is identified as fatigue.

When the total duration of head large rotation is more than 30% of a minute, the case is identified as shift.

When each of the total duration of head position is stable longer than 70%, and the total duration of head large rotation is less than 3%, and no gaze deviation, and no closed eyes and yawn, it is considered the case is identified as concentration.

When the total duration of head posture is stable longer than 70% no gaze deviation, and no closed eyes and yawn, the case is identified as attention.

Others are identified as distraction.

Through the video analysis these attention decrease cases can be detected, which include distraction, fatigue, drowsiness, sleepiness. Other abnormal situations of attention shift and emotional confusion can be also distinguished. Two situations should be warned early.

4   Experimental Results

One learner's facial behavior video is used to test our algorithm. The video lasts 48 min with 15 fps framerate and 1280*720 image resolution. For this video, 210 samples were manually annotated, which were used to train 12 classifiers including head, eyes, mouth, gaze and facial expression classifier. The classifier algorithm is realized in matlab. The prediction results can reach 92% accuracy.

The overall behavior of histogram features are shown in Fig. 9(a). The statistical features are shown in Fig. 9(b), (c) and (d) which respectively illustrate the large deviation of head and facial expression duration and frequency in minutes. The attention level and pleasure degree are shown in Fig. 9(e). It is found that the attention level of the experimental subject decreased continuously from 6 to 22 min, later it is still in the abnormal state of shift, distraction and sleepiness. Therefore, early warning should be declared in time.

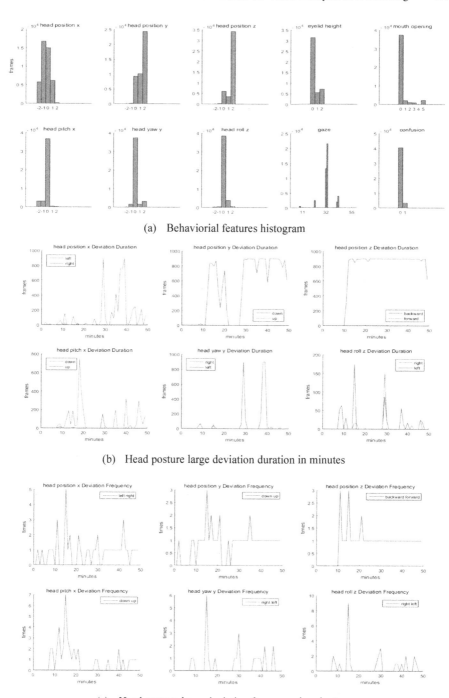

(a)   Behaviorial features histogram

(b)   Head posture large deviation duration in minutes

(c)   Head posture large deviation frequency in minutes

Fig. 9. Experimental results

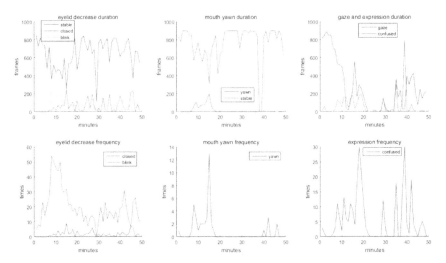

(d) Facial expression appearance duration and frequency in minutes

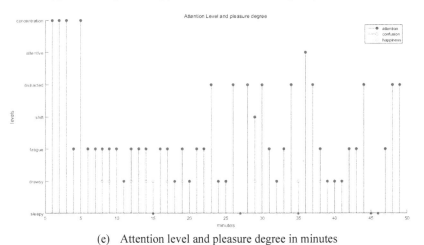

(e) Attention level and pleasure degree in minutes

Fig. 9. (*continued*)

5 Conclusions

Experimental results show that the proposed algorithm can effectively analyze individual learning attention level. In the experiment, samples were selected only from the video of a single experiment object, and the above threshold can be adjusted according to the actual situation.

The next step should consider the adaptability and robustness of the same learner under different cameras or the same learner under different cameras. Furthermore, the number and type of experimental objects and samples should be expanded to improve the generality of the algorithm.

Acknowledgments. The paper is supported by the educational science plan foundation "in 12th Five-Year" of Jiangsu province (B-a/2015/01/010).

References

1. Zheng, Q., Zhang, X., Chen, L.: Comments on the development of MOOCs and the design of core supporting policy in china. China Educ. Technol. **356**(9), 44–50 (2016). (in Chinese)
2. Zhang, X., Wang, M.: A study on the effecting factors and promotive strategies of social interaction among MOOC learners—the perspective of people's social attributes. China Educ. Technol. **354**(7), 63–68 (2016). (in Chinese)
3. Wei, S.: An analysis of online learning behaviors and its influencing factors: a case study of students learning process in online course "open education learning guide" in the Open University of China. Open Educ. Res. **8**, 81–90 (2012). (in Chinese)
4. Zheng, Q., Chen, Y., Sun, H., Chen, L.: Construction and application of the student-systematically evaluation reference indicator based on learning analytics technology. E-educ. Res. **356**(9), 33–40 (2016). (in Chinese)
5. Wu, F., Mou, Z.: The design research of learning outcomes prediction based on the model of personalized behavior analysis for learners. E-educ. Res. **348**(1), 41–48 (2016). (in Chinese)
6. Picard, R.W.: Affective Computing. MIT Media Laboratory Perceptual Computing Section Technical Report No. 321, pp. 1–16 (2000)
7. Yang, F.Y., Chang, C.Y., Chien, W.R.: Tracking learners' visual attention during a multimedia presentation in a real classroom. Comput. Educ. **62**(3), 208–220 (2013)
8. Bradski, G.R.: Computer Vision face tracking for use in a perceptual user interface. In: Proceedings of Fourth IEEE Workshop Applications of Computer Vision, pp. 214–219. IEEE, Berlin (1998)
9. Asteriadis, S., Tzouveli, P.: Estimation of behavioral user state based on eye gaze and head pose - application in an e-learning environment. Multimed. Tools Appl. **41**, 469–493 (2008)
10. Sawyer, K.: Cambridge Handbook of the Learning Sciences, 2nd edn, pp. 253–266. Cambridge University Press, Cambridge (2014)
11. Zhang, Q., Yang, L.: Learning measurement progress and trends in e-learning——based on eye movement application perspective. China Educ. Technol. **358**(11), 63–87 (2016). (in Chinese)
12. Xu, S.: The Detection of Students' Attention in a Real-time System, pp. 1–55. Shanghai Jiaotong University, Shanghai (2007). (in Chinese)
13. Zhang, J.: Research on learning states based on facial features, pp. 1–73. Taiyuan Science Technology University, Taiyuan (2013). (in Chinese)
14. Baltrušaitis, T., Robinson, P., Morency, L.-P.: OpenFace: an open source facial behavior analysis toolkit. In: IEEE Winter Conference on Applications of Computer Vision (2016)
15. Baltrušaitis, T., Robinson, P., Morency, L.-P.: Constrained local neural fiel. for robust facial landmark detection in the wild. In: IEEE International Conference on Computer Vision Workshops, 300 Faces in-the-Wild Challenge (2013)
16. Wood, E., Baltrušaitis, T., Zhang, X. et al.: Bulling rendering of eyes for eye-shape registration and gaze estimation. In: IEEE International Conference on Computer Vision (ICCV) (2015)
17. Baltrušaitis, T., Mahmoud, M., Robinson, P.: Cross-dataset learning and person-specific normalisation for automatic action unit detection. In: Facial Expression Recognition and Analysis Challenge, IEEE International Conference on Automatic Face and Gesture Recognition (2015)
18. https://github.com/TadasBaltrusaitis/OpenFace

Miscellaneous

Research on the Construction Mechanism of Collaborative Innovation Research Platform of Private Universities

Taking Jilin Animation Institute as an Example

Mingming Zhao[1(✉)] and Guangning Sui[2]

[1] Scientific Research Management, Jilin Animation Institute, Changchun, China
zhaomingming@jldh.com.cn
[2] Jilin Animation Institute, Changchun, China
17790085058@163.com

Abstract. The participation of private universities in collaborative innovation is of great significance to the academic development of scientific research work, the economic development of society and the implementation of the national collaborative innovation strategy. At first, this paper expounds on the connotation of the collaborative innovation research platform and its requested functions, and then illustrates the principles of building the collaborative innovation research platform. Also, it takes Jilin Animation Institute as an example to study the structure, safeguard mechanism and operation mode of its collaborative innovation research platform, providing effective basis for private universities to build the collaborative innovation research platform.

Keywords: Private universities · Collaborative innovation
Platform construction · Mechanism

In 2011, General Secretary Hu Jintao, on the centennial anniversary of Tsinghua University, delivered an important speech, pointing out the need for Chinese universities to carry out in-depth cooperation with research institutions and companies and to promote collaborative innovation enthusiastically. In the process of technological innovation, the private universities of our country are also endowed with important missions. In the early stage of the incorporation of private universities, the teachers' technological innovation consciousness is relatively weak due to that more attention is paid on teaching and less is paid on research. Therefore, the research bases of private universities have yet taken shape due to insufficient research funding, so the research work was limited and restricted, which further blocked the development of the universities. The collaborative innovation gives full play to the self advantages of private universities to build research platforms in order to promote the development of scientific research. So it is an effective way to address this problem.

Jilin Animation Institute, founded in the beginning of the 21st century, is the first private university focusing on cultivating application-oriented talents in cultural innovation fields such as animation games. Since its establishment, Jilin Animation

© Springer-Verlag GmbH Germany, part of Springer Nature 2018
Z. Pan et al. (Eds.): Transactions on Edutainment XIV, LNCS 10790, pp. 183–193, 2018.
https://doi.org/10.1007/978-3-662-56689-3_15

Institute has been attaching great attention to the innovation and development of science and technology while adhering to the integration path of academic research and development. This paper takes Jilin Animation Institute as an example to study how to construct collaborative innovation research platform for private universities.

1 Functions of Collaborative Innovation Research Platform

The research platform constitutes the mainstay for scientific and technological innovation, personnel training and social services, demonstrating the university level in teaching, research and talent cultivation. The collaborative innovation research platform has the following functions.

1.1 Resources Sharing

The institutions of higher learning can cooperate with other universities, research institutes and enterprises at home and abroad and realize the sharing of high-quality innovative resources among various organizations. All resources can be exchanged in members of the platform. All members can learn internally or mutually to complement each other's advantages in order to realize resources integration and optimization in the collaborative innovation research platform.

1.2 Talent Cultivation

Due to that the members are with different requirements for talents, the collaborative innovation research platform will undertake the integration and optimization of the teachers and teaching resources of universities to cultivate or train corresponding talents. At the same time, the technical personnel in the enterprise can collaborate with universities in carrying out technical training for students to improve students' practical ability; the teachers and students in universities can undertake internship or probation in the enterprise to combine the actual theory with the practical needs, cultivating high-quality talents in favor of the talent exchange among the platform members.

1.3 Achievement Transformation

By virtue of the collaborative innovation of scientific research platform, the institutions of higher learning, scientific research institutions and enterprises at home and abroad can share their work and conduct research and development for the key technology in research process. The members can work together to jointly create a diversified achievement transformation and radiation mode, thus promoting the development of the innovation industry and accelerating the adjustment of regional industrial structure.

1.4 Cultural Inheritance

Collaborative innovation research platform can realize the combination of universities discipline advantages with talent advantages. Academic exchanges can be made in all members of the platform, pushing the platform construction with multidisciplinary characteristics. In an innovative way of seeking cultural inheritance, it contributes to improving the national cultural strength.

2 Principles in the Construction of Collaborative Innovation Research Platform

Based on existing resources from institutions of higher learning, the collaborative innovation platform focuses on innovative studies on cutting-edge science and technology and other aspects required by our country in a collaborative way by collecting resources from other platform members. In the process of building collaborative innovation research platform, institutions of higher learning need to follow the following principles (Table 1).

Table 1. Construct the follow principle of collaborative innovation research platform

SN	Construction principles	Contents
1	Demand orientation	The contents of platform innovation research should be closely associated with the major needs of the country and the prospective field of science and technology development. Through collaborative innovation among the various members in the organization, the achievements are made in the frontier areas of science and technology, national and social development
2	Resources sharing	The members' high quality resources should be integrated and optimized, and the resources should be fully open and shared by all kinds of innovative powers in order to create a comprehensively open and diversified organization
3	Organic integration	The institutions of higher learning should deeply cooperate with all members in the organization, effectively utilizing the various resources in the platform to realize the deep integration of interdisciplinarity
4	Security mechanism	Effective management, communication, assessment and restraint mechanisms are the guarantee of the normal operation of the platform while reasonable benefit allocation and risk-sharing mechanisms are in benefit to the long-term development of the platform

3 Advantages of Private Universities to Build a Collaborative Innovation Research Platform

Owing to the separation of financial resources, manpower and material resources of private universities from government administration, the legal representatives of the private universities are granted to very large autonomy in university-running with its operation mechanism relatively flexible. This is a unique advantage in constructing collaborative innovation research platform. The following contents focus on Jilin Animation Institute to elaborate on the advantages of collaborative innovation research platform construction in private universities.

First, the talent introduction mechanism is flexible. Jilin Animation Institute places its double-teachers team in line with its strategic position of priority development. It employs more than 340 industrial or enterprise leaders with high professionalism and rich practical experience for its teaching and research work. Due to the relatively large amount of talent input and the reasonable flow of staff, the need of collaborative innovation research platform for talents is met.

Second, the target of personnel training meets the needs of the industry. In setting disciplines and majors, the demand for applied talents is given top priority. Through the integration of the talent cultivation mode, the innovative and applied professional talents with international vision are cultivated. The teaching work for freshmen and sophomores is on basic knowledge while juniors and seniors are trained to remove professional barriers. Following the individual interests, the students can freely choose the platform for practical lessons with an aim to improve the interdisciplinarity of culture, art, technology and market to realize seamless joint between talent training and market demand.

Third, the legal representatives have the right of autonomy and resource allocation. In order to promote the development of university's science and technology, the required software and hardware resources are reasonably utilized. During the operation of the platform, it behooves us to share the abundant resources of the universities with other collaborative members in promoting the innovation research work and the university development.

Finally, the international resource platform is effectively constructed. Jilin Animation Institute pays attention to international science and technology research and development, inviting famous scholars and experts from more than 20 countries such as China, the United States, Britain and France to participate in national and provincial scientific research and development project or the creation of animation film. The animated film Frog Kingdom, the animated cartoon Chicken Wants to Fly and other more than 100 works have won many domestic and foreign awards (Figs. 1 and 2).

Fig. 1. Film <*Frog Kingdom*>

Fig. 2. Cartoon <*Chicken Wants to Fly*>

4 Platform Structure of Collaborative Innovation Research System

As an innovation system for the research platform of private universities, the collaborative innovation research platform is to analyze the following contents by the introduction of Jilin Animation Institute.

4.1 To Construct Scientific Research Innovation Mode Highly Integrating Learning, Research and Production

Because of the relatively flexible operation mechanism of private universities, there are natural advantages in the research mode of construction, research and production integration. In 2011, Jilin Animation Institute and 24 universities, provincial scientific research institutions and enterprises jointly created "Jilin Provincial Animation Industry Technical Innovation Strategic Alliance"; in 2015, Jilin Animation Institute reached an agreement 'with 28 well-known universities and research institutions including Beijing Film Academy, Communication University of China, Automation of Chinese Academy of Science and Technology and built a major collaborative innovation center at the provincial level based on development need of cultural industry. By virtue of Jilin provincial animation cultural industry chain, the Alliance and the Center, by engaging in the new mechanism of cooperation on teaching, research and production, are committed to study the technology which blocks the development of animation and cultural industry to address talent bottleneck, boost the development of cultural industry and build Jilin provincial aircraft carrier in animation industry, thus achieving the win-win collaborative prosperity.

4.2 Building Academic Groups

As for the collaborative innovation research platform, the construction of the academic group is the intrinsic driving force to ensure its sustainable development. Jilin Animation Institute, based on the construction industry and the market demand, focuses on building the design discipline, drama and film discipline and interdisciplinary discipline of animation art and emerging technology so as to improve its academic quality, quantity and level, attributing to interdisciplinary complementary advantages, resources sharing, talents cultivation and technological innovation. It promotes the transfer of research results into production in the collaborative innovation research platform.

4.3 Building a R&D Center of High-End Technology

The university uses the R&D center as the platform and builds "Modern Animation Technology in Jilin Provincial Engineering Research Center of Institutions of Higher Learning", "Games and Interactive Media Technology in Jilin Provincial Engineering Research Center of Institutions of Higher Learning" and "Digital Animation Technology in Jilin Provincial Engineering Research Center". The research, backed by the advanced science and technology, through the application of engineering and industrialization, focuses on promoting the upgrading of university technology in favor of the further in-depth development of collaborative innovation mode.

4.4   Building an Internationally Shared Resource Base

Jilin Animation Institute, for the sake of building an internationally shared resource base, by virtue of its own advantages, strengthens its ties with overseas universities, research institutions and international companies from the United States, France, Britain, Germany, Russia, Canada, South Korea, New Zealand, Australia and Singapore. Through the establishment of the international joint laboratory, participation in international projects, inter-university exchanges, organization of international exhibitions and attending international forums, Jilin Animation Institute successfully built an international resource base including information, talents and equipments (Fig. 3).

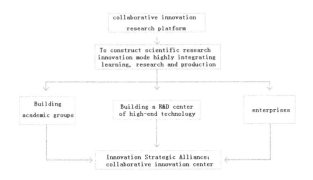

Fig. 3.   Platform structure of collaborative innovation research system

5   Security Mechanism of Collaborative Innovation Research Platform

The sustainable development of any platform should be closely associated with the effective security mechanism. In order to enable the collaborative innovation research platform of private universities to function properly, the security mechanism is summarized as follows.

5.1   Seeking Diversified Collaborative Innovation Modes

In order to promote collaborative innovation among its members, private universities should resort to collaborative innovation research platform in finding the right collaborative innovation mode. Here are a few different collaborative innovation modes for reference.

Mode one: talents and resources shared by various universities. In the principle of fairness and mutual benefit, the innovation resources and talent reserve of various universities will be shared in the collaborative innovation research platform.

Mode two: cooperation between private universities and enterprises. According to various market demand and innovation purpose, corresponding cooperation should be done between private universities and enterprises. For example, private universities and enterprises conduct joint research, private universities sponsor the research enterprises, private universities attends the enterprises' research, etc.

Mode three: the enterprises will be responsible for the transformation of the research and innovation achievements for private universities. Private universities and enterprises will realize resources & risks sharing by combining research innovation achievements with funds to accelerate the process of innovation research.

Mode four: cooperation between private universities and the government. Within the scope of this mode, the research binding upon private universities should tally with the national demand, backed by active participation in the innovation activities advocated by the government (Fig. 4).

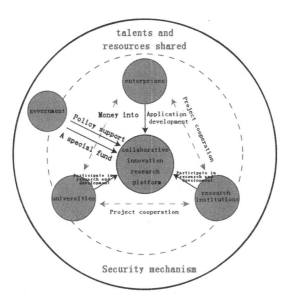

Fig. 4. Diversified collaborative innovation modes

5.2 Establishing of Management and Communication Mechanism

First, the private universities should be responsible for optimization of the talent management mechanism. A sound talent management mechanism should be built and the assessment method should be modified in order to give full play of the inner potential of innovation personnel and make the talents in private universities or research institutions to better work for the collaborative innovation research platform.

Second, the innovation members of the collaborative innovation research platform should jointly establish a management organization to ensure the normal operation of the platform.

Third, a perfect communication mechanism should be established among the innovation members of the collaborative innovation research platform. The collaborative innovation research platform, based on the purpose of mutual benefit and win-win results, should be granted a right approach to build a complete communication network in order to realize the sound communication on research tasks and interpersonal relationship.

At last, we should strengthen cultural exchanges within the platform and promote the convergence of values among its members. In the process of platform operation, we should eliminate the habitual defense psychology of researchers, strengthen mutual trust and promote the sustainable development of the platform.

5.3   Establishing Assessment and Restraint Mechanisms

When the collaborative innovation research platform is built, the assessment mechanism should also be established to restrain the behaviors of innovation members. The assessment mechanism should involve the third parties to ensure the fairness and justice of the mechanism. The assessment of each member should be evaluated in various task stage according to the task allocation and the final benefit should be allocated according to the result. The assessment system should be made in a fair and reasonable manner to promote the capability of collaborative innovation as the target, while promoting the healthy competition of innovation and setting up a good working atmosphere.

At the same time, it is imperative to establish the corresponding restraint mechanism for the innovation members to restrain behaviors such as default and dishonesty. And punishment will be made through asking for compensation and ordering to dismiss in order to promote the development of platform.

5.4   Establishment of a Reasonable Risk-Sharing Mechanism and Profit Distribution Mechanism

Because the collaborative innovation research platform involves multiple innovation members with specific pursuit of interests. Therefore, the appropriate mechanism should be established so that the interests and risks of each member can be shared.

First, establishment of the risk-sharing mechanism of the platform requires defining the respective responsibilities, obligations and innovation tasks. In the principle of risk-sharing and in accordance with relevant policies, the input of each member should be taken into consideration with corresponding indicators being formulated to clarify the risks shared by each member through amicable negotiation, thus a risk-sharing mechanism is established.

Second, setting up the interest distribution system of the platform should start from the promotion of the cooperation and innovation. According to the relevant policies, The total input and actual contribution of each member should be considered to confirm the basis of benefit sharing. Then a benefit sharing system should be formulated with clarified distribution ratio. And this system should be continuously adjusted negotiated in the research so as to ensure reasonable allocation of interests.

The huge risks borne by the enterprises in the process of research results transformation should be comprehensively considered and the value of innovation results should be calculated objectively and fairly, enabling each member in the platform to get satisfied benefit in the process of collaborative innovation, thus promoting the healthy development of collaborative innovation research platform.

5.5   In Pursuit of a Long-Term Collaborative Innovation Mechanism

In order to ensure the sustainable development of the collaborative innovation research platform, it is necessary to construct a long-term mechanism suitable for platform development. Through establishing the management and communication mechanism, assessment and restraint mechanism of the platform, the collaborative innovation research platform can be operated normally. Establishing a learning organization and fostering an innovative culture are the guarantee of the long-term operation of the platform, providing the driving force for improving the performance and core competitiveness of the platform.

First, the management personnel of each member in the platform should build an environment suitable for learning, where each innovative member can improve his own ability through continuous learning and practice. At the same time, members should learn from each other by keeping a frequent touch and eventually form a learning organization. The establishment of learning organization is to improve the innovation capability of the platform and enhance the competitiveness of the team.

Second, the management personnel of each member in the platform should start from the perspective of fostering the innovative culture, create a democratic, harmonious, fair and free learning atmosphere in the learning organization, promote the convergence of values of the members, improve teamwork awareness, strengthen the members' mutual trust, hence strengthening their coagulative power. The construction of innovative culture serves as a stimulant to the innovation capability of the platform, increasing the core competitiveness of the platform and promoting its long-term development.

6   Operation Mode of the Collaborative Innovation Research Platform

The essence of the collaborative innovation research platform of private universities is to improve the innovation capability of subjects, scientific research and high-quality talents. The operation mode of collaborative innovation of scientific research platform serves as a stimulant to the integration of private universities, scientific research institutions at home and abroad, the government and related enterprises. Based on private universities discipline advantages and talent reserves, the platform integrates resources and seeks a variety of collaborative innovation modes. The platform should be operated in the following ways.

6.1   Knowledge Innovation Mode

The platform operation focuses on the cutting-edge science and technology and social development of major issues. Private universities, on the basis of their special advantage disciplines, closely cooperates with the domestic and foreign high-ranking universities, research institutes and related industrial enterprises and integrate the absorbed excellent innovation resources to build a good learning atmosphere and cultivate innovative talents for the purpose of a better implementation of research and development innovation, thus improving the quality of innovation talents and consolidating the position of collaborative innovation research platform.

6.2   Technology Transfer Mode

Through in-depth cooperation between private universities and domestic and overseas research institutions and relevant enterprises, a research platform, in which its innovation members cooperate, various techniques are integrated and all kinds of resources are shared, can be built. Thus, a technology transfer mode which integrates discipline, research and production can be established. This operation mode not only leads to improvement of the industrial production technology but also promotes the collaborative innovation research platform to become the mainstay platform of scientific and technological innovation.

6.3   Achievement Transformation Mode

We should give our support and assistance to institutions of higher learning with the various approaches to render unremitting services for social and regional economic development, and encourage local government to lead private universities to seek friendly ties with other members for joint innovation cooperation based on local economic development. This operation mode can form a transformation mode and radiation mode for the diversified innovation achievements. It can promote the transfer of the service type of private universities, promote the development of the industrial structure and push the integration of the industrial structure. At the same time, the operation mode can also serve the decision-making process of local governments, making the collaborative innovation research platform play an important role in regional innovation.

6.4   Culture Inheritance Mode

We should take the philosophy and social science as the main body and integrate the unique talent reserves and discipline advantages of private universities through the strong cooperation between private universities and other industrial organizations such as research institutions, local government and relevant industries, institutions of higher learning, international academic institutions, etc. This operation mode can not only foster Chinese culture but increase the soft power of Chinese culture.

7 Conclusion

The participation of private universities in collaborative innovation is of great significance to the development of scientific research, the economic development of society and the implementation of the national collaborative innovation strategy. Through collaborative innovation, we give full play to the unique advantages of private universities and establish dedicated research platforms, thus promoting the development of scientific research as an effective way to address problems concerned. This paper firstly elaborates on the connotation of the collaborative innovation research platform and its practicality. Then it illustrates the principle of constructing the collaborative innovation research platform. Focusing on Jilin Animation Institute, it summarizes the advantages of the private universities on building the collaborative innovation research platform. And based on this research, it studies the platform structure and presents the security mechanism and its operation mode, providing an effective basis for private universities to build the collaborative innovation research platform.

Acknowledgements. This paper is one of the staged achievement attributed to "Thirteenth Five-year" Plan of Jilin Province Ministry of Education in social science research project which is titled "Research on the Construction of Collaborative Innovation Research Platform of Private Universities" with its project number: JJKWHZ [2016] 523).

References

1. Hu, J.: Speeches in Centennial Anniversary of Tsinghua University. People's Daily, 25 April 2011
2. Tang, Z., Wang, J., Wang, H.: A case study on the operation mechanism of Industry-university-research cooperation. Sci. Stud. (1), 154–160 (2015)
3. You, S., Hui, Y., Cui, Y.: A study on the cross-disciplinary development path in collaborative innovation of universities. Educ. Res. (4), 94–99 (2014)
4. Xue, D.: Analysis on the policy of collaborative innovation and innovative talent cultivation in universities. China High Educ. Res. (12), 26–31 (2012)
5. Zhang, L.: Strategic significance and policy direction of collaborative innovation of Industry-university-research cooperation. Educ. Res. (7), 18–21 (2011)
6. Ning, B.: The Status and Role of Universities in Collaborative Innovation. People's Daily, 19 April 2012
7. Wang, Y.: Building Collaborative Innovation Mechanism to Cultivate Innovative Talents. China Education Daily, 23 April 2012
8. Zeng, P., Li, X.: Overview of Industry-university-research cooperation: theoretical perspective, cooperative mode and cooperation mechanism. Sci. Manag. Res. (22), 28–32 (2014)

A Bibliometric Analysis on the Published Papers in Journal of Technology Enhanced Foreign Language Education (TEFLE) from Year 2006 to 2015

Xiu-Yan Zhong[(⊠)]

School of Foreign Languages, Huizhou University, Huizhou 516007, China
zhongbetty@126.com

Abstract. This Paper presents a bibliometric analysis of the papers published in the journal of Technology Enhanced Foreign Language Education (TEFLE), a core professional academic journal in China, during the years from 2006 to 2015. Our result aims to provide a clear view of the evolution of literature in the research field of technology enhanced foreign language learning over the past decade, intending to put forward a preliminary framework for TEFLE to improve its publication quality and at the same time foster better technology enhanced foreign language education in China. Bibliometric indicators of paper amount, author information, total citations, and frequency of keywords have been analyzed with the use of tools of BICOMB and SPSS and methods of co-word and cluster analysis, which indicates that, over the past decade, both of the quality of the published papers and the paper evaluation system has been improved. The statistics also reveal that the authors in TEFLE are mainly from eastern China, a research group that has been formed with more researchers constantly joining in, and a number of papers have been highly cited, bringing further interest in the related disciplines. Currently, the reform of foreign language classroom teaching with technological aids appears the hotspot topic in the related applied field. An effort is made to demonstrate that the research method has shifted to a new way that places equal emphasis on both quantitative and qualitative study in technology enhanced learning (TEL) and technologies have a bigger influence on foreign language learning in China, but in the meantime, there is an imbalance in the distribution of authors from different national geographic areas in TEL research.

Keywords: Technology Enhanced Foreign Language Education (TEFLE)
Bibliometric analysis · Co-word analysis · Cluster analysis
Technology enhanced learning (TEL)

1 Introduction

The academic journal of *Technology Enhanced Foreign Language Education (TEFLE)*, directed by the education department and sponsored by Shanghai International Studies University [1], has been, so far, the only academic journal for the scholarly researches on both foreign language education technologies and foreign language teaching ontology.

© Springer-Verlag GmbH Germany, part of Springer Nature 2018
Z. Pan et al. (Eds.): Transactions on Edutainment XIV, LNCS 10790, pp. 194–206, 2018.
https://doi.org/10.1007/978-3-662-56689-3_16

Founded in 1979, it is mainly designed for foreign language teaching researchers in universities and colleges, aiming to probe into foreign language teaching and foreign language research in the context of modern information technology. This journal especially explores foreign language teaching ontology, teaching process and teaching content based on the background of foreign language instructional technologies, focusing on foreign language teaching theory and the related principles, covering every language-skill instructions: listening, speaking, reading and writing from university, middle school to primary school, and all the courses from listening (audio-visual), oral English, reading, writing, vocabulary acquisition, pronunciation, translation, research on literature to linguistics, so as to guide the trend of domestic foreign language teaching research and keep the staff in grasp with the latest development in their fields. It has set up lots of columns consisting of volumes on foreign language audio visual teaching, network and foreign language teaching, researches on foreign language teaching, corpus-based teaching and English testing, network classroom teaching case selection, college English teaching, specialized English teaching, new horizons in language research, new genres of foreign language teaching methodology, trends in foreign technology aided teaching and introductions to the new theory in foreign language educational technology development. TEFLE has been continuously selected for Chinese Social Science Citation Index (CSSCI) source journal directory and the Chinese Core Journals Directory of Peking University, becoming the leading academic exchange front of research on TEL and the important channel for tracing the development and evolution of technology enhanced foreign language education in China.

This Paper links bibliometric measures to the study of this journal, providing the visualizations of the specific features in the portfolio of papers published over time and an quantitative evaluation to its academic quality in order to influence decision-making or policy formulation through the provision of empirically-driven feedback, and therefore, point a right way for further academic research [2]. This Paper presents the measured statistics from a bibliometric analysis of the papers published in TEFLE during the years from 2006 to 2015, intending to put forward a preliminary framework for TEFLE to improve its publication quality and at the same time foster better technology enhanced foreign language education in China [3, 4].

2   Data Resources and Research Tools

2.1   Data Resources

TEFLE is a bimonthly journal containing 80 pages with nearly 19 to 15 papers in every issue from 2004 and it has published 60 issues in total during the ten-year period from 2006 to 2015. Our data were selected from Chinese Academic Journals Database (CNKI), by using the method of standard retrieval and taking TEFLE as the source journal. We retrieved 986 relative papers under time span from 2006 to 2015. To ensure the validity of the research objects, we have taken up manual screening to delete 136 papers that do not meet the standards including the annual general directory, contribution notice, letters for contributors, meeting notice, training notice and book information, and chose 850 papers as data samples.

2.2 Research Tools and Procedures

The main research tools used in this topic is the BICOMB co-word analysis software [5, 6] developed by China Medical University and SPSS statistical software [7]. The research conforms to the following procedure: importing 850 research papers into BICOMB co-word analysis software; extracting and counting the authors, companies, journals, particular years and keywords of papers; extracting and selecting high-frequency keywords in the papers and setting up co-occurrence matrix and the similarity matrix of the high-frequency keywords; importing high-frequency keywords' co-occurrence matrix and the similarity matrix into SPSS statistical software, then selecting the applicable system clustering method and conducting clustering analysis on high-frequency keywords.

3   Research Results and Analysis

3.1 Statistics of Published Papers and Result Files

The published volume of academic journal reflect the information content, information transfer capability of the journal directly, and on the other hand, indirectly reflect the academic quality of the published papers. The key specifications in evaluating the published volume of academic journal are the total papers, the average number of pages and the density of papers in each issue. Table 1 is the report of the published papers in TEFLE.

As we can see from Table 1, the biggest number of the total annual published papers in TEFLE is 92 and the smallest one is 76 in the past ten years, and the statistics show a downward trend year by year, especially from 2013 to 2015 showing a dramatic decrease in annual published papers. The average number of pages of published journal papers is 5.67, showing an upward trend, and also a rapid increase from 2013 to 2015. The data above indicates that the journal TEFLE has developed steadily, and under the situation of keeping page number of each issue unchanged, the annual published papers of the journal have decreased in recent years coupling with page number increase of each article which means that the published papers are becoming longer, reflecting that the journal is making gradual improvement in these aspects, such as article resources, article quality and review quality.

3.2 Analysis of Author

850 papers published on TEFLE are written by 946 authors from 2006 to 2015 (for details see Table 2). It shows that 736 authors publishing a single article on the journal, accounting for 77.8%; 132 authors participating in writing 2 papers account for 13.95%; 45 authors have 3 published papers, accounting for 4.75%; 10 authors have 4 papers, accounting for 1.06%; 23 authors have over 5 (including 5) papers, accounting for 2.43%. It can be seen that the number of experts, scholars or organizational personnel who concern about the research on TEL is large in China, and the source basis of researcher is wide. Judging from these author output active period and duration, we can find that core authors of the research on TEFLE have formed well organized

Table 1. List of published papers in TEFLE during 2006–2015

Year	Number of papers each year	Number of papers each issue	Average pages of the papers	Density	Rate (%)
2015	76	12.67	6.32	0.16	8.94%
2014	77	12.83	6.23	0.16	9.06%
2013	80	13.33	6.00	0.17	9.41%
2012	88	14.67	5.45	0.18	10.35%
2011	86	14.33	5.58	0.18	10.12%
2010	88	14.67	5.45	0.18	10.35%
2009	90	15.00	5.33	0.19	10.59%
2008	84	14.00	5.71	0.18	9.88%
2007	89	14.83	5.39	0.19	10.47%
2006	92	15.33	5.22	0.19	10.82%
小计	850	14.17	5.67	0.18	

Table 2. Numbers of the papers published and authors in TEFLE during 2006–2015

No. of the papers published	No. of the authors	Percent	Accumulated percent
5 (or above)	23	2.43	2.43
4	10	1.06	3.49
3	45	4.76	8.25
2	132	13.95	22.20
1	736	77.80	100.00
Total	946		

academic echelon, if we see those authors who have taken part in writing over 5 papers as core authors. What' s more, the high activity and the long duration of core authors indicate that the research in TEFLE from China has developed a core group of researcher. For example, Chen Jianlin from China Foreign Language Strategic Research Center in Shanghai International Studies University has produced 16 papers, Zheng Xinming from Institute of International Education in Shanghai International Studies University has produced 13 papers and Hu Jiasheng from Shanghai Foreign Language Audiovisual Publishing House has produced 12 papers. In addition, the statistics also indicate that there is a group of authors who have published fair number of papers but are late in active period in TEFLE, such as Cai Jigang from Foreign Language Institute in Fudan University producing 10 papers and both Ma Wulin from Foreign Language Teaching Department in Sichuan International Studies University and Yang Yonglin from foreign language department in Tsinghua University being listed into the group of active authors with 7 published papers. This kind of author can be judged as the new emerging group of the research on TEL, illustrating that research on TEL is showing the situation of continuous inheritance and development (Table 3).

Table 3. List of authors publishing over 5 papers as core author in TEFLE during 2006–2015

Name	Total papers	Active years	Adherence period
Chen Jinlin	16	2006–2015	Whole period
Zheng Xinmin	13	2006–2015	Whole period
Hu Jiasheng	12	2006–2015	Whole period
Cai Jigang	11	2009–2015	Middle and late period
He Gaoda	11	2006–2015	Whole period
Wang Linhai	10	2006–2015	Whole period
Liang Maocheng	9	2006–2015	Whole period
Wang Lifei	9	2006–2015	Whole period
Yang Yue	8	2006–2015	Whole period
Wen Qiufang	8	2006–2014	Whole period
Wang Kefei	7	2006–2014	Whole period
Dong Hongxue	7	2007–2015	Whole period
Ma Wulin	7	2008–2014	Middle and late period
Yang Yonglin	7	2006–2013	Earlier and middle period
Zou Shen	7	2006–2014	Whole period
Chen Bingbing	6	2007–2014	Whole period
Mao Wenwei	6	2007–2013	Whole period
Xiong Wenxin	6	2007–2013	Whole period
Cheng Dongyuan	5	2007–2011	Whole period
Wang Na	5	2008–2013	Middle and late period
Shi Guangxiao	5	2009–2013	Middle and late period
Huang Fang	5	2007–2013	Middle period
Wang Xuemei	5	2006–2014	Whole period

3.3   Analysis of Author Source Organization

Conducting statistical analysis on author source organization help us learn about geographic spatial distribution attributes of the authors in TEFLE. In the statistics, second class units from the same first class unit are merged into same institution, for example, Graduate Division in Shanghai International Studies University and English Institution in Shanghai International Studies University are seen as the same unit which is Shanghai International Studies University. Literature survey study has found that author source organization of TEFLE has shown two main features from 2006 to 2015. One is that the author source organization has wide coverage. Researchers mostly come from domestic key language schools, such as Shanghai International Studies University, Beijing Foreign Studies University and Guangdong University of Foreign Studies, and other key universities that have developed well in foreign language education, like Yan Shan University, Shanghai Jiaotong University and Fudan University. The other is that the proportion of contributions from universities in Shanghai is large. In the ranking of author source organization, Shanghai International Studies University is listed in the first place with 142 papers, accounting for 16.71%, while Shanghai Jiaotong University listed in forth with 20 papers, Fudan University listed in fifth with 16 papers and

Shanghai Polytechnics listed in tenth with 13 papers respectively, which indicates that authors from universities in Shanghai account for great proportion in the statistics of author source organization in TEFLE. The main reason of it is that Jiangsu region represented by Shanghai is the forefront of reforming and opening in China and its frequent foreign trade and exchange, becoming one of the most important region of developing foreign language talents and foreign language education research. Furthermore, many teachers and students have conducted further research into TEL, achieving great success, hence the output of academic research results is large which results in ranking in the front. On the other hand, the host of TEFLE is exactly Shanghai International Studies University, resulting in more contributions coming within university and from universities in Jiangsu. However, too many contributions coming within Shanghai International Studies University itself will do harm to academic exchange and have the effect on the quality of the journal. Hence, we should make more efforts to expand the source of great contributions outside the university, forming the situation of the radiation across the country and enhancing the influences of the journal.

Table 4. Author source organization distribution in TEFLE during 2006–2015

No.	Author source organization	Total papers	Percentage %
1	Shanghai International Studies University	142	16.71%
2	Beijing Foreign Studies University	39	4.59%
3	Yan Shan University	24	2.82%
4	Shanghai Jiaotong University	20	2.35%
5	Fudan University	16	1.88%
6	Guangdong University of Foreign Studies	15	1.76%
7	University of International Business and Economics	14	1.65%
8	Shandong University	14	1.65%
9	South China Agricultural University	13	1.53%
10	University of Shanghai for Science and Technology	13	1.53%
11	Xidian University	13	1.53%
12	Tsinghua University	11	1.29%

3.4   Analysis on the Attention Degree of the Published Papers

Until November 18th, 2016, the journal of TEFLE during 2006–2015, cited the highest frequency. There are twelve papers in Table 4 above, which were cited for more than 150 times. From the publishing time of the 12 papers above, we know that most of the high-rate citations are in prior period during 2006–2015, which is mainly focused in 2006 (which has 4 papers, account for 33%), in 2007 (which has 3 papers, account for 25%). Many of the high frequency citation are influential papers. The paper *The analysis of multimedia and multimodal learning* [8] ranked first, which was written by Gu Yueguo, the professor of China Foreign Language Education Research Center, while *Multimodal Construction of Meaning - A Discourse Analysis of a PPT Demonstration Contest* [9] ranked second, whose first author Hu Zhuanglin is the professor of Peking University English Department. It should be noted that *"Micro-class-based"* *Flip classroom "Model of College English Teaching in the Application of the Feasibility Analysis"* [10] published in 2014, but in reference frequency ranked No. 3, which reflects the micro-class, flip classroom theme has become a hot topic in today's research. Analysis on the attention degree of the theses indicates that there exists hysteresis nature and Matthew effect in TEFLE. At the same time, the higher cited frequency papers also reflect the high quality of the journal in this period (Table 5).

Table 5. List of higher cited frequency papers in TEFLE during 2006–2015

No.	Title	Author	Year	Total citations	Total downloads
1	*The analysis of multimedia and multimodal learning*	Gu Yueguo	2007	983	6068
2	*Multimodal Construction of Meaning - A Discourse Analysis of a PPT Demonstration Contest*	Hu Zhuanglin; Dong Jia	2006	383	3676
3	*"Micro-class-based" Flip classroom "Model of College English Teaching in the Application of the Feasibility Analysis"*	Lu Haiyan	2014	299	18386
4	*Organic Integration of Computer Networks and Foreign Language Courses in the New College English Teaching Model - An Ecological Study on Computer Assisted Foreign Language Teaching*	Chen Jianlin	2006	289	3328
5	*A Corpus - based Study of Chunk Use Patterns in English Argumentative Writing by College Students*	Wang Lifei; Zhang Yan	2006	276	2979
6	*ELE or ESP, Further Discussion on the Development of College English in China*	Cai Jigang; Liao Chunzhao	2010	214	4396
7	*Present Situation and Prospect of Multimedia Foreign Language Teaching in China*	Zhuang Zhixiang; Huang Wei; Wang Le	2007	204	2467
8	*On the Basis and Countermeasures of College English Teaching Reform*	Cai Jigang	2010	184	3089

(continued)

Table 5. (*continued*)

No.	Title	Author	Year	Total citations	Total downloads
9	*Multimodalization and College Students' Multi-reading Ability*	Wei Qinhong	2009	174	2237
10	*A New Interpretation of the Requirements of College English Teaching in the 07th Edition*	Chen Jianlin; Gu Zhizhong	2008	154	1518
11	*Content-based Approach (CBI) and Compound Foreign Language Teaching - A Case Study of Business English Teaching*	Lei Chunlin	2006	154	2867
12	*The Comprehensive Application of Autonomous Learning Mode and Classroom Teaching Mode in Computer Network Environment*	Gu Shimin	2007	151	2587

3.5 Extraction and Analysis of High Frequency Keywords

For convenience of searching and using the content of the literature, we selected 3–8 words as keywords in each article of the TEFLE journal. A total of 2239 valid keywords were extracted from the 850 literatures by using the BICOMB tool. The total frequency of keywords is 3257 times, and the average is 3.83. With reference to the usual practice of domestic high frequency word division and considering the representativeness of keyword extraction results, we extracted the frequency of occurrence of greater than or equal to 5 as candidates for high frequency keywords. Meanwhile, to ensure the validity of the study's results, we extracted the candidate high-frequency keywords for the second screening, and deleted the generalization of the meaning of keywords. Besides, we also merge the synonyms so as to obtain a total of 26 effective high frequency keywords. See Table 6 for details. These 26 keywords reflect the trends of our foreign language teaching and development, which to a large extent represent the foreign language teaching research hot spots for the past 10 years.

3.6 Cluster Analysis of High-Frequency Keywords

In order to further study the structural relationships between high frequency keywords and research hotspots, In this article, the co-word visualization analysis method [11] was used to cluster analysis, and the clustering results were presented intuitively in the form of cluster tree. Keywords clustering is the process of classifying keywords into different classes or clusters, so key words in the same cluster have great homogeneity, and vise-versa, keywords in different clusters have great heterogeneity. By means of the analysis of high frequency keyword clustering, the closely related high frequency

Table 6. Statistics of High Frequency Keyword in TEFLE during 2006–2015

No.	Keywords	Frequency	No.	Keywords	Frequency
1	College English	53	14	Foreign language teaching	11
2	Corpus	51	15	The Internet	11
3	Foreign language teaching	48	16	Translation	10
4	Teaching mode	28	17	Curriculum integration	9
5	Information technology	24	18	Language teaching	8
6	Self-learning	23	19	Curriculum	8
7	College English teaching	20	20	Teaching reform	8
8	Constructivism	19	21	Technology enhanced education	8
9	Web environment	17	22	English-teaching	8
10	English writing	16	23	Validity	8
11	Multimedia	14	24	Teachers' role	8
12	Multi-modal	12	25	Network teaching	8
13	College English teaching reform	11	26	Language learning	8

keywords are clustered together to form different classes, and then to express the foreign language teaching and research of the various branches.

The methods of clustering analysis are as follows: first of all, the BICOMB software is used to select co-occurrence matrixes whose frequency is greater than 5. Then the matrix is exported to text file, so as to import the text file into the SPSS software, which at the same time, the keywords are deleted and the synonyms are merged to finalize the key points. Finally, the 26 high-frequency keywords that highly related to the research connotation of computer-assisted foreign language teaching are ascertained. We use the software SPSS to systematically cluster the matrix. The cluster method selects "Ward method", while the metrics use "interval: square Euclidean distance", to transform the value according to variable Z and obtain the cluster analysis tree diagram which could be checked as Diagram 1. In the cluster analysis tree diagram, the far left maker marks 26 high-frequency keywords, and the scale with a digital (0 to 25) shows the distance between the keywords clustering objects. According to the structure of the cluster analysis tree diagram, all the high-frequency keywords could be divided into three parts: no. 18, 26, 21, 14, 20, 3 high-frequency keywords could be combined into a same category, named Category A; no. 22, 24, 5, 6, 9, 16, 23, 2 high-frequency keywords could be combined into another category, named category B; and the third category is the Category C with a maximum quantity no., including no. 7, 12, 11, 15, 10, 4, 17, 13, 8, 25, 1, 19 high-frequency keywords. In Category A, the aggregation of the high-frequency keywords such as 'Language Learning', 'Language Teaching', and 'Language Reform' demonstrates that this category mainly gathers together the research object of technology in foreign language education; in Category B, the aggregation of the high-frequency keywords such as "Validity", "Text Corpus" shows that this category mainly involves the research methods of technology in foreign language education; in Category C, the aggregation of the high-frequency keywords such as "Multimedia", "Network" and "Multi-modal" shows that this category mainly involves the main technological means of technology in foreign language education. Based on the high-frequency keywords cluster tree diagram in the years 2006–2015 in TEFLE and taking into account the correlations degree of the high-frequency keywords, this article summarizes the current research on technology in foreign language education, providing academic reference for scholars to conduct further in-depth study and improve the quality of foreign language education.

(1) **The research objects in TEL.** In recent ten years, technology in foreign language education focuses more on taking the computer and other technology as an auxiliary teaching means, giving full play of the computer's role as information retrieval tool, communication tool, information storing tools and others roles in foreign language education. It also focuses on applying this technology means to the classroom teaching and mode reform of technology in foreign language education, including applying this means in various scenarios such as classroom teaching, autonomous learning, and language learning.

(2) **Research methodology in TEL.** Pedagogy research methods can usually be divided into two categories, qualitative research and quantitative research. The early study of TEFLE focused on qualitative methods, which was to describe, to generalize and to summarize the problems. However, in middle-late stages, it pays more attention to quantitative method studying the subject. And this stage, TEFLE publishes a large number of experimental studies on teaching reform, which aims at the solution of the domain problem, by carrying out the teaching experiment and analyzing empirical data to arrive at a conclusion. Therefore, the key terms involved in data analysis, such as "corpus", "validity" and other keywords in the published papers appear in high frequency, which shows that the domestic foreign language teaching research is from qualitative to speculative-based research, and gradually transformed into qualitative, quantitative and research model.

(3) **Technical means in TEL.** Technology enhanced learning must be carried out by means of specific educational technical means, which includes traditional audio and video, radio and television, multimedia, in addition to network, artificial intelligence, virtual reality technology. In the recent years, with the popularization and application of the campus network in China papers in TEFLE has emerged a large number of keywords directly or indirectly related to the computer network [12], which shows that domestic scholars have gradually migrated to the study of the network environment, with the help of the Internet and other technical means of special attention to the impact of research networks on foreign language learning.

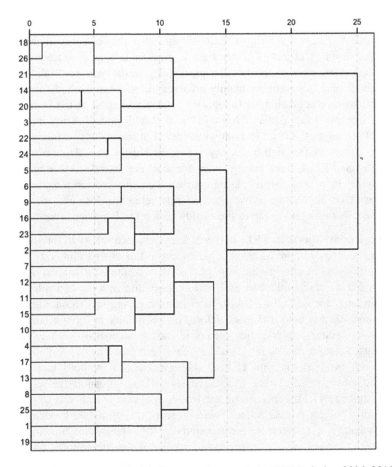

Diagram 1. Cluster-tree of high-frequency keywords in TEFLE during 2006–2015

4   Conclusion

An bibliometric analysis of papers in TEFLE (2006–2015) shows that the journal have been improved year by year over the past decade in the resources of manuscripts, the quality of papers and the reviewing quality. The authors of this journal come mainly from Eastern China based on Shanghai. By now, they have formed a core research group and more and more researchers join the camp constantly. The papers published are all of higher academic level, some of which are even frequently cited and have a great effect on the academic circles with their high quality. The papers published reflect the researching hotspot and frontier in each field, laying particular emphasis on classroom teaching mode of technology enhanced foreign language education. They also reflect that the research of TEL gradually turns to a kind of qualitative and quantitative researching mode. What's more, they also show that Internet plays a more and more important role in language learning. But at the same time, the econometric analysis also shows the distribution imbalance of the research areas in TEL. Therefore, the journal still need to publish good papers and improve its quality.

In this paper, a bibliometric analysis of Technology Enhanced Foreign Language Education is made with the method of literature metrology. The methods used include word frequency analysis, clustering analysis and so on. It describes the academic development in this field in the recent ten years. The results of the research have some certain reference value for domestic scholars to catch up with the latest development trend of domestic foreign language audio-visual teaching and for the journal of TEFLE to improve its quality. To more deeply and comprehensively describe this journal, which is considered the only journal to integrate modern educational technology and foreign language teaching, we can also further introduce more advanced analysis methods and tools in the field of information science, such as Co-citation Analysis, Network Analysis and Mapping Knowledge Domain, in order to get richer information.

Acknowledgments. This paper is funded by the 2016 Guangdong Provincial Research Project of Teaching Reform "Reform and Practice of English Reading Teaching based on PBL" (No.【2016】236).

References

1. Yu, F.: Strengthening the characteristics of running a publication and promoting the scientific development of foreign language teaching research - celebrating the 30th anniversary of technology enhanced foreign language education. Technol. Enhanced Foreign Lang. Educ. **1**, 3–5 (2012)
2. Junping, Q.: Bibliometrics. Scientific and Technical Documents Publishing House, Beijing (1988)
3. Yang, C., Li, X., Zhang, Y.: Analysis of computer-assisted foreign language teaching research in China - taking the papers published in foreign language teaching (2009–2013) as an example. Examination and Evaluation, College English Teaching and Research **4**, 82–88 (2014)
4. Dong, J., Yan, Z., Zhang, L., et al.: Hot trends and trends in the teaching of foreign languages in the past fifteen years - based on the analysis of the subject headings of two authoritative journals. Mod. Educ. Technol. **8**, 67–73 (2015)
5. Department of Medical Informatics in China Medical University: Brief Introduction to the BICOMB Bibliographic Co-occurrence Analysis System [EB/OL] (2016-11-01), 20 November 2016. http://www.cmu.edu.cn/bc/
6. Wang, C.: Research on the measurement analysis of international educational management based on BICOMB. J. Yunnan Agric. Univ. (Soc. Sci. Edn.) **6**, 40–45, 60 (2012)
7. Sun, Y.: SPSS software was used to analyze the correlation between variables. J. Xinjiang Educ. Inst. **2**, 120–123 (2007)
8. Yueguo, G.: The analysis of multimedia and multimodal learning. Technol. Enhanced Foreign Lang. Educ. **2**, 3–12 (2007)
9. Zhuanglin, H., Jia, D.: Multimodal construction of meaning - a discourse analysis of a ppt demonstration contest. Technol, Enhanced Foreign Lang. Educ. **3**, 3–12 (2006)
10. Lu, H.: "Micro-class-based" Flip classroom "Model of college english teaching in the application of the feasibility analysis". Technol. Enhanced Foreign Lang. Educ. **4**, 33–36 (2014)

11. Qin, Z., Feicheng, M.: Research on the structure of knowledge management in China - based on co-word analysis. J. China Soc. Sci. Tech. Inf. **27**(1), 93–101 (2008)
12. Lei, W., Dianlong, W.: New exploration of foreign language electrification teaching mode in network. J. Changchun Normal Univ. **12**, 128–130 (2007)

Fuzzy Comprehensive Evaluation for Rural Public Sports Services

Qiuhong Han[1(✉)] and Shen Qing[2]

[1] School of Physical Education, Huzhou University, Huzhou 313000, China
hqh@zjhu.edu.cn
[2] School of Information Engineering,
Huzhou University, Huzhou 313000, China

Abstract. Establishing a performance evaluation system for rural public sports services is the basis for setting up a scientific administrative control system for public sports services. Questionnaire survey, Delphi method and mathematical statistics technique were conducted. Based on relevant theories and principles, exploratory factor analysis was adopted, and the performance evaluation system for rural public sports services along with the weights of indicators was determined. This evaluation system consisted of three primary indicators, eight secondary indicators and thirty tertiary indicators. Rural areas of five prefecture-level cities in Zhejiang Province were taken as the research objects. An empirical study was conducted regarding the performance evaluation system for public sports services in rural areas using the fuzzy comprehensive evaluation method. The results showed that the comprehensive score for the performance of public sports services in rural areas of Zhejiang was 70.087, indicating a moderate level, which was intermediate between "satisfactory" and "neutral". The respondents were satisfied or above with three indicators, namely, public sports organization and administration services provided by the local public sports sector, current number of public sports facilities, and usage of public sports facilities. However, the respondents were most unsatisfied with two indicators, namely, service attitude of rural public sports administrators and development and exploitation and utilization of rural public sports resources.

Keywords: Rural public sports services · Performance evaluation system
Fuzzy comprehensive evaluation

1 Introduction

Performance evaluation is an effective administrative tool [1]. Wei and Wang conducted a comprehensive performance evaluation of China's public sports services from three dimensions, namely, evaluation subjects, contents and perspectives [2]. Later, Wei and Wang constructed a performance evaluation system for China's public sports services using the "resources utilization-benefit" model. This evaluation system consisted of two primary indicators, six secondary indicators and eleven tertiary indicators [3]. Wang et al. carried out literature research method, survey, entropy weight method and built a binary logistic regression model. Based on an analysis of the meaning of performance evaluation of public sports services and value orientation, the performance

© Springer-Verlag GmbH Germany, part of Springer Nature 2018
Z. Pan et al. (Eds.): Transactions on Edutainment XIV, LNCS 10790, pp. 207–224, 2018.
https://doi.org/10.1007/978-3-662-56689-3_17

evaluation system for public sports services was established [4]. Zhao applied factor analysis and DEA model to the construction of a performance evaluation system for public sports services. This evaluation system was used for the empirical analysis of the performance of public sports services in ten cities in southwest China [5]. However, most of the above-mentioned studies only make a theoretical exploration in the field of evaluation system and performance evaluation of China's public sports services. However, few researches are devoted to performance evaluation of rural public sports services, not to mention the construction of a performance evaluation system or empirical studies in this aspect. Along with the maturity of China's socialist market economy and the reform of grassroots social structure, public sports services in rural areas now play an increasingly important role. It is a widespread hope that a rural public sports administrative system that adapts to the economic system reform and provides improved services can be built up soon.

2   Objects and Methods of Research

2.1   Research Objects

China has a vast territory and a large rural population. China's rural public infrastructures are weak and the level of rural economic development varies greatly from one region to another. Therefore, it is not reasonable to use a uniform set of indicators for the performance evaluation of rural public sports services. Under the flexibility principle, rural areas in Zhejiang Province where the economy is generally developed were chosen as the research objects. Five prefecture-level cities (Huzhou, Jinhua, Quzhou, Jiaxing and Wenzhou) were randomly selected by stratified sampling from a total of eleven prefecture-level cities in Zhejiang Province. Three to five villages under the administration of one county under each of the five prefecture-level cities were selected randomly. Questionnaire survey was conducted among 500 rural residents aged above 18 years old. The survey data were used to verify the established evaluation system.

2.2   Methodology

First, literature research method was used to collect and sort the documents, policies, laws and regulations concerning rural public sports services from 2000 to 2016. Twelve books on performance evaluation of public sports services were also reviewed to preliminarily establish the performance evaluation system for rural public sports services.

Second, Delphi method [6] was employed to collect opinions from a panel of experts. The results were used to check and give weights to the performance evaluation indicators for rural public sports service established above. Forecasts were obtained.

A questionnaire survey was conducted among 500 rural residents in Zhejiang Province. The feasibility of the established performance evaluation system was verified. Considering the differences in educational background among the rural residents, members of the research group were first trained before going to the rural villages for the survey and guidance. In 500 copies of questionnaire distributed, 486 copies were retrieved. Excluding the unfinished ones and those with several answers given to one question, there were 479 valid copies, and the valid rate was 95.8%, which conformed to the requirement.

Data collected by questionnaire survey were analyzed statistically using SPSS 20.0 software. The performance evaluation system for rural public sports services was built using fuzzy comprehensive evaluation method.

3 Construction of Performance Evaluation System for Rural Public Sports Services

3.1 Theoretical Basis

3.1.1 Based on Actual Demands in Developing Rural Public Sports Services

Firstly, establishing the performance evaluation system for rural public sports services should be based on national conditions and the demands of local economic development. Any administration and services should be oriented towards the demands of local residents, specifically, the daily life and entertainment demands of the rural residents. And establishing the performance evaluation system for rural public sports services is no exception. This evaluation system should contribute to the development and improvement of comprehensive quality of rural public sports services, and also to the increase of local residents' satisfaction with public sports services. Therefore, the performance evaluation system for rural public sports services should be fully based on the demands of rural residents for public sports services while conforming to the national conditions.

Secondly, the rural residents' demand for public sports services should be satisfied. Along with the implementation of national fitness strategy, rural sports fitness project and the snow-charcoal project, the grassroots rural public sports infrastructure has been greatly improved. In spite of these efforts, the true sports demands of rural residents are not fully satisfied. Much more should be done to promote the forming of a sustainable sports life-style as well as the prosperity of rural public sports. As the progress of new urbanization has been accelerating, the conventional farming lifestyle no longer exists in many rural districts. Farmers have more leisure time, which can be spent on sports activities. This brings about changes in rural residents' sports demand. In addition to public sports facilities, rural residents are also in need of services in fitness instruction, sports events organization, physical fitness monitoring and sports information. Rural residents' sports demand is the driving force for rural public sports services. The performance evaluation system for rural public sports services should consider all aspects of rural residents' sports demands. This is the precondition for promoting the continuous development of rural public sports services.

3.1.2 Based on the New Public Management Theory

New public administration theory upholds the principles of customers first and public-oriented. In other words, public sectors should provide services and constantly improve service quality base on these two principles, so as to increase customer satisfaction [7]. The behaviors and values of public sectors should be fully oriented towards provide all-around services for the public. The performance evaluation of public sports services is in itself an administrative mechanism oriented towards services and public. It can promote public's trust in government and administrative departments for public sports by embodying the principle of public-oriented.

Public satisfaction is the core dimension of government performance evaluation, as reiterated by many experts. Performance evaluation system for rural public sports services is also part of the public sector performance evaluation. Therefore, public-oriented principle should be fully embodied in the performance evaluation of rural public sports services by placing rural residents as the subjects and the administrative departments of sports and rural sports organizations as the objects. Rural residents' satisfaction should be the standard of evaluation, and the products of rural public sports services the contents of evaluation.

3.2   Principles for Constructing the Performance Evaluation System

3.2.1   Target-Oriented Principle

Target-oriented principle consists of using the black box method to assess the actual achievements in a certain field while controlling and guiding the behaviors of the objects of evaluation so that the target can be met [8]. The target of establishing a performance evaluation system for rural public sports services is to arouse the attention of rural public sports administrators towards public opinions. This evaluation system can remind the public sports administrators of every link and every influence factor of rural public sports services. The public sports administrators will be urged to do more to encourage the participation of rural public in sports activities and to increase the quality of rural public sports services. The ultimate goal is to promote the healthy development of rural public sports services.

3.2.2   Comprehensiveness Principle

Comprehensiveness principle refers to the adaptability and flexibility of the performance evaluation system for rural public sports services in the purpose of realistically reflecting rural residents' satisfaction towards rural public sports services. The evaluation indicator system should be comprehensive while highlighting the key points of performance [9]. This principle is crucial for improving the performance of rural public sports services.

3.2.3   Operability Principle

The performance evaluation system for rural public sports services should have a high discrimination ability, thereby facilitating the questionnaire survey and the acquisition of reliable data. The indicator system must not be cumbersome, which will otherwise impede data collection and assessment.

3.2.4   Public Service-Oriented Principle

The vitality of public sports services lies in meeting the sports demand of rural residents. The fundamental goal of a performance evaluation system for rural public sports services is to promote the quality of rural public sports services, which is in turn the key measure of the performance. The performance evaluation system for rural public services should be oriented towards rural residents' sports demand and public services. This evaluation system should be built by centering around rural residents' satisfaction.

3.2.5 Flexibility and Contingency Principle

Flexibility and contingency principle is an important part of the administration science. It refers to the necessity of adjusting to the changing internal and external circumstances for an organization in administration practice. There is nothing that is fixed or universally good, but only something that is suitable based on specific conditions [10]. China has a vast territory and a large population. There is a high level of variability across the regions in natural conditions, economic development, social structure and people's living standard. Therefore, the performance evaluation system for rural public sports services should be established based on flexibility and contingency principle and a comprehensive consideration of local economic development level, natural resources and sports demand.

3.3 Building an Evaluation Indicator System

To estimate the structure validity of the evaluation system, the evaluation indicators were analyzed first and those that did not reach a significance level were deleted. Then KMO test and Bartlett's sphericity test were performed based on the selected samples. The KMO value was 0.930, and the factory analysis was conducted [11]. The result of Bartlett's sphericity test was $x_2 = 2867.286$, $P = 0.000$ ($P < 0.05$), and the null hypothesis was rejected. This means the tested variables were not mutually independent and suitable for factor analysis. After that, the evaluation indicator system for rural public sports services (represented by A) was built based on the above-mentioned principles, administration theories and exploratory factor analysis. This evaluation system consisted of three primary indicators (A_1, A_2, A_3), eight secondary indicators (B_{ij}) and thirty tertiary indicators (C_{ijk}), as shown in Table 1.

Table 1. Evaluation indicator system for rural public sports services

Primary indicator	Secondary indicator	Tertiary indicator
A_1: Cost of rural public sports services	B_{11}: Input cost	C_{111}: Input in rural public sports infrastructure
		C_{112}: Cost of rural public sports organization and administration
		C_{113}: Cost of rural public sports technology services
		C_{114}: Cost of legal maintenance for rural public sports
		C_{115}: Annual gross salary of working staff
		C_{116}: Investment in specific rural sports service projects

(continued)

Table 1. (*continued*)

Primary indicator	Secondary indicator	Tertiary indicator
A_2: Rural sports services performance	B_{21}: Sports organization service	C_{211}: Density of public body-building sites
		C_{212}: Service attitude of working staff of rural public sports sector
		C_{213}: Service efficiency of working staff of rural public sports sector
		C_{214}: Organization and administration services provided by rural public sports sector
	B_{22}: Public sports site and facility services	C_{221}: Current number of public sports sites and facilities
		C_{222}: Usage of public sports facilities
		C_{223}: Maintenance of public sports sites and facilities
		C_{224}: Safety of public sports sites and facilities
		C_{225}: Update cycle of public sports sites and facilities
	B_{23}: Public sports instruction services	C_{231}: Instruction services provided by public sports instructor
		C_{232}: Consulting services provided by public sports instructor
		C_{233}: Number of public sports instructors
	B_{24}: Sports fitness knowledge service	C_{241}: Physical training safety knowledge
		C_{242}: Health-enhancing knowledge dissemination
	B_{25}: Sports activity organization and promotion	C_{251}: Sports events promotion
		C_{252}: Dissemination speed of sports events news
		C_{253}: Number of sports events
		C_{254}: Degree of standardization of sports events
		C_{255}: Implementation Number of sports events
	B_{26}: Physical fitness monitoring services	C_{261}: Indicators of physical fitness monitoring
		C_{262}: Number of physical fitness monitoring
		C_{263}: Feedback of results of physical fitness monitoring
A_3: Rural sports organization and administration	B_{31}: Rural sports administration services	C_{311}: Exploitation and utilization of rural sports resources
		C_{312}: Mode of funding for rural sports services

Depending on the degree of contribution and importance of each indicator with respect to the target layer, different weights are given to different indicators. Analytic hierarchy process (AHP) is the most commonly used method for weight determination. The form of expert questionnaire survey was compiled based on the evaluation indicators. Expert opinions were pooled and the mean values of expert scores were taken [12, 13]. The judgment matrix for each layer was constructed, and the weights of each indicator were calculated. The weights for the indicator layer are shown in Tables 2 and 3.

Table 2. Weights of indicator layer with respect to the criterion layer

Criterion layer		A_1	A_2	A_3	Weights of indicators with respect to the criterion layer
		0.1866	0.7134	0.1000	
Indicator layer	B_{11}	1			0.1866
	B_{21}		0.1306		0.0932
	B_{22}		0.2799		0.1997
	B_{23}		0.1339		0.0954
	B_{24}		0.1571		0.1121
	B_{25}		0.1758		0.1254
	B_{26}		0.1227		0.0876
	B_{31}			1	0.1

Table 3. Weights of program layer with respect to the target layer

Indicator layer		B_{11} 0.1211	B_{21} 0.0988	B_{22} 0.2467	B_{23} 0.0919	B_{24} 0.1234	B_{25} 0.1186	B_{26} 0.0757	B_{31} 0.1237	Weights of indicators with respect to the criterion layer
Indicator layer	C_{111}	0.3268								0.0396
	C_{112}	0.2642								0.0320
	C_{113}	0.1158								0.0140
	C_{114}	0.0790								0.0096
	C_{115}	0.1502								0.0182
	C_{116}	0.0640								0.0078
	C_{211}		0.2516							0.0249
	C_{212}		0.0967							0.0096
	C_{213}		0.0967							0.0096
	C_{214}		0.5550							0.0548
	C_{221}			0.2603						0.0642
	C_{222}			0.1696						0.0418
	C_{223}			0.1166						0.0288
	C_{224}			0.3976						0.0981
	C_{225}			0.0559						0.0138
	C_{231}				0.3694					0.0338
	C_{232}				0.2241					0.0206
	C_{233}				0.4065					0.0374
	C_{241}					0.5000				0.0617
	C_{242}					0.5000				0.0616
	C_{251}						0.3657			0.0434
	C_{252}						0.1634			0.0194
	C_{253}						0.2365			0.0280
	C_{254}						0.0746			0.0088
	C_{255}						0.1598			0.0189
	C_{261}							0.4021		0.0304
	C_{262}							0.3294		0.0249
	C_{263}							0.2685		0.0203
	C_{311}								0.6000	0.0742
	C_{312}								0.4000	0.0495

Reliability is a measure of the consistency and stability of an evaluation system. Besides validity, reliability was also tested for the established evaluation system. Reliability is divided into premeasurement, replacement form and internal consistency reliability. Internal consistency reliability is the most commonly used measure and was adopted in this study. Cronbach's alpha was estimated as the measure of internal consistency reliability in the present paper, and the test results of internal consistency for the common factors is shown in Table 4.

Table 4. Internal consistency test of the evaluation indicator system for rural public sports services

Common factor	Cronbach's Alpha
Input cost	0.8375
Sports organization	0.8632
Public sports sites and facilities	0.8368
Public sports instruction	0.7722
Sports fitness knowledge	0.8325
Sports event organization and promotion	0.8787
Physical fitness monitoring	0.8615
Rural public sports administration	0.8451

It can be seen from Table 4 that the values of Cronbach's alpha for all eight common factors are above 0.8, which is much than the acceptable level of 0.70. This suggested the feasibility of the performance evaluation system for rural public sports services.

4   An Empirical Study on the Performance Evaluation System for Rural Public Sports Services

Based on the evaluation system and weight determination, rural villages in five prefecture-level cities of Zhejiang Province were taken as the research objects. The model for fuzzy comprehensive evaluation of rural public sports services was established, and an empirical study was conducted using this model.

4.1   Results of Questionnaire Survey on Performance Evaluation of Rural Public Sports Services

The fuzzy comprehensive evaluation matrix used for the evaluation was based on the comment set obtained through the questionnaire survey, which was conducted among some local residents in Zhejiang Province. The comments on the performance of rural public sports services are shown in Table 5.

Table 5. Comment set of performance evaluation of rural public sports services (%)

Primary indicator	Secondary indicator	Tertiary indicator	Very satisfied	Satisfied	Neutral	Unsatisfied	Very unsatisfied
A_1: Cost of rural public sports services	B_{11}: Input cost	C_{111}: Input in rural public sports infrastructure	20.3	23.2	26.5	10.3	19.7
		C_{112}: Cost of rural public sports organization and administration	11.5	13.4	29.4	33.2	12.5
		C_{113}: Cost of rural public sports technology services	14.3	4.2	28.6	25.5	27.4
		C_{114}: Cost of legal maintenance for rural public sports	19.1	5.5	31.9	19.7	23.8
		C_{115}: Annual gross salary of working staff	22.2	11.5	25.9	18.8	21.6
		C_{116}: Investment in specific rural public sports programs	19.7	23.8	31.9	19.5	5.1
A_2: Rural sports services performance	B_{21}: Sports organization service	C_{211}: Density of public body-building sites	3.1	13.4	36.1	33.2	14.2
		C_{212}: Service attitude of working staff of rural public sports sector	2.5	7.3	35.1	38	17.1
		C_{213}:Service efficiency of working staff of rural public sports sector	2.1	8.1	35.5	37	17.3
		C_{214}: Organization and administration services provided by rural public sports sector	16.7	37.8	30.7	12.1	2.7
	B_{22}: Public sports site and facility services	C_{221}: Current number of public sports sites and facilities	14.8	36.1	32.2	14	2.9
		C_{222}: Usage of public sports facilities	13.6	36.7	34.4	12.7	2.6
		C_{223}: Maintenance of public sports sites and facilities	15.7	33.2	39.7	9.6	1.9
		C_{224}: Safety of public sports sites and facilities	13.2	35.1	34.0	14.8	2.9
		C_{225}: Update cycle of public sports sites and facilities	16.9	33.4	37.2	10.2	2.3
	B_{23}: Public sports instruction services	C_{231}: Instruction services provided by public sports instructor	17.1	29.4	37.4	13.8	2.3
			11.7	33	38.4	14.6	2.3

(*continued*)

Table 5. (*continued*)

Primary indicator	Secondary indicator	Tertiary indicator	Very satisfied	Satisfied	Neutral	Unsatisfied	Very unsatisfied
		C_{232}: Consulting services provided by public sports instructor					
		C_{233}: Number of public sports instructors	12.3	11.1	35.1	38.6	2.9
	B_{24}: Sports fitness knowledge service	C_{241}: Physical training safety knowledge	13.4	11.7	36.5	35.7	2.7
		C_{242}: Health-enhancing knowledge dissemination	15.0	9.4	38.6	33.8	3.2
	B_{25}: Sports activity organization and promotion services	C_{251}: Sports events promotion	16.7	7.7	39.7	32.8	3.1
		C_{252}: Dissemination speed of sports events news	14.8	32.8	41.5	7.7	3.2
		C_{253}: Number of sports events	13.6	9.8	39.9	33.8	2.9
		C_{254}: Degree of standardization of sports events	2.4	8.1	42.2	32.4	14.9
		C_{255}: Implementation Number of sports events	2.9	8.1	40.3	37	11.7
	B_{26}: Physical fitness monitoring services	C_{261}: Indicators of physical fitness monitoring	3.3	9.2	42.0	33	12.5
		C_{262}: Number of physical fitness monitoring	3.8	7.9	43.4	32.4	12.5
		C_{263}: Feedback of results of physical fitness monitoring	3.8	7.5	43.6	32.6	12.5
A_3: Rural sports organization and administration	B_{31}: Rural sports administration services	C_{311}: Exploitation and utilization of rural sports resources	2.5	7.3	35.1	38	17.1
		C_{312}: Mode of funding for rural sports services	3.4	10.1	39.8	35	11.7

4.2   Determining the Number of Grades of Evaluation

Grade of evaluation is a fuzzy concept for the evaluation of each indicator. Either too many or too few grades should be avoided. Generally the number of grades is above 4 and below 9.

Let the comment set be V, and the grades of evaluation are

$V = \{\mu_1, \mu_2, \mu_3, \mu_4, \mu_5\} = \{$very satisfied, satisfied, neutral, unsatisfied, very unsatisfied$\}$

To provide a more intuitive picture of the performance of rural public sports services, the grades of evaluation were quantified by giving different scores to each grade. That is, the scores of 90, 80, 70, 60 and 60 were given to different grades, respectively, thus forming the quantitative comment set:

$$V = \{90, 80, 70, 60, 50\}$$

4.3   Single-Factor Fuzzy Evaluation

Through evaluation on a single factor μ_i ($i = 1, 2, \ldots, n$), the fuzzy subset (R_{i1}, R_{i2}, $\ldots$, R_{im}) is obtained on V and $\sum_{j=1}^{m} R_{ij} = 1$, where R_{ij} is the degree of membership of factor μ_i to grade μ_j. Thus the fuzzy evaluation matrix $R = (r_{ij})_{n \times m}$ is obtained from U to V [14].

4.3.1   Tertiary Indicator Evaluation Matrices

Based on questionnaire survey, the fuzzy evaluation matrix R_{ij} for each secondary indicator B_{ij} (including input cost and sports organization services) is constructed:

$$R_{11} = \begin{bmatrix} 0.203 & 0.232 & 0.265 & 0.103 & 0.197 \\ 0.115 & 0.134 & 0.294 & 0.332 & 0.125 \\ 0.143 & 0.042 & 0.286 & 0.255 & 0.274 \\ 0.191 & 0.055 & 0.319 & 0.197 & 0.238 \\ 0.222 & 0.115 & 0.259 & 0.188 & 0.216 \\ 0.197 & 0.238 & 0.319 & 0.195 & 0.051 \end{bmatrix}$$

$$R_{21} = \begin{bmatrix} 0.031 & 0.134 & 0.361 & 0.332 & 0.142 \\ 0.025 & 0.073 & 0.351 & 0.380 & 0.171 \\ 0.021 & 0.081 & 0.355 & 0.370 & 0.173 \\ 0.167 & 0.378 & 0.307 & 0.121 & 0.027 \end{bmatrix}$$

$$R_{22} = \begin{bmatrix} 0.148 & 0.361 & 0.322 & 0.140 & 0.029 \\ 0.136 & 0.367 & 0.344 & 0.127 & 0.025 \\ 0.157 & 0.332 & 0.397 & 0.096 & 0.019 \\ 0.132 & 0.351 & 0.340 & 0.148 & 0.029 \\ 0.169 & 0.334 & 0.372 & 0.102 & 0.023 \end{bmatrix}$$

$$R_{23} = \begin{bmatrix} 0.171 & 0.294 & 0.374 & 0.138 & 0.023 \\ 0.117 & 0.330 & 0.384 & 0.146 & 0.023 \\ 0.123 & 0.111 & 0.351 & 0.386 & 0.029 \end{bmatrix}$$

$$R_{24} = \begin{bmatrix} 0.134 & 0.117 & 0.365 & 0.357 & 0.027 \\ 0.150 & 0.094 & 0.386 & 0.338 & 0.032 \end{bmatrix}$$

$$R_{25} = \begin{bmatrix} 0.167 & 0.077 & 0.397 & 0.328 & 0.031 \\ 0.148 & 0.328 & 0.415 & 0.077 & 0.032 \\ 0.136 & 0.098 & 0.399 & 0.338 & 0.029 \\ 0.024 & 0.081 & 0.422 & 0.324 & 0.149 \\ 0.029 & 0.081 & 0.403 & 0.370 & 0.117 \end{bmatrix}$$

$$R_{26} = \begin{bmatrix} 0.033 & 0.092 & 0.420 & 0.330 & 0.125 \\ 0.038 & 0.079 & 0.434 & 0.324 & 0.125 \\ 0.038 & 0.075 & 0.436 & 0.326 & 0.125 \end{bmatrix}$$

$$R_{31} = \begin{bmatrix} 0.025 & 0.073 & 0.351 & 0.380 & 0.171 \\ 0.034 & 0.101 & 0.398 & 0.350 & 0.117 \end{bmatrix}$$

4.3.2 Secondary Indicator Evaluation Matrices

Secondary indicator evaluation matrix is $B_i = (B_{ij})^{\mathrm{T}}$, where B_i is the secondary indicator and B_{ij} is the result of tertiary indicator evaluation with weights. Compositional operation is conducted for the tertiary indicator evaluation results through the following form of fuzzy transformation:

$$B_{ij} = W_{ij} \cdot R_{ij} = (b_{i1}, b_{i2}, \ldots, b_{i5})$$

The calculation of B_{11} is taken as an example:

$$B_{11} = W_{11} \cdot R_{11} = (0.3268 \quad 0.2642 \quad 0.1158 \quad 0.0790 \quad 0.1502 \quad 0.0640)$$

$$\begin{bmatrix} 0.203 & 0.232 & 0.265 & 0.103 & 0.197 \\ 0.115 & 0.134 & 0.294 & 0.332 & 0.125 \\ 0.143 & 0.042 & 0.286 & 0.255 & 0.274 \\ 0.191 & 0.055 & 0.319 & 0.197 & 0.238 \\ 0.222 & 0.115 & 0.259 & 0.188 & 0.216 \\ 0.197 & 0.238 & 0.319 & 0.195 & 0.051 \end{bmatrix}$$
$$= (0.1743 \quad 0.1529 \quad 0.2819 \quad 0.2072 \quad 0.1837)$$

Similarly, we obtain B_{21}, B_{22}, ..., B_{31}. Thus the secondary indicator evaluation matrices are obtained:

$$B_1 = [0.1743 \quad 0.1529 \quad 0.2819 \quad 0.2072 \quad 0.1837]$$

$$B_2 = \begin{bmatrix} 0.1049 & 0.2584 & 0.3295 & 0.2232 & 0.0840 \\ 0.1418 & 0.3532 & 0.3444 & 0.1337 & 0.0269 \\ 0.1394 & 0.2279 & 0.3671 & 0.2406 & 0.0250 \\ 0.1420 & 0.1055 & 0.3755 & 0.3475 & 0.0295 \\ 0.1238 & 0.1239 & 0.4032 & 0.2959 & 0.0532 \\ 0.0360 & 0.0832 & 0.4289 & 0.3269 & 0.1250 \end{bmatrix}$$

$$B_3 = [0.0286 \quad 0.0842 \quad 0.3698 \quad 0.3680 \quad 0.1494]$$

4.3.3 Primary Indicator Evaluation Matrices

Using the above principles, the weights of primary indicators are multiplied by the secondary indicator evaluation matrices, respectively, to obtain the primary indicator evaluation matrix: $A_i = W_i \cdot B_i = (a_{ij})^T$, where Ai is the primary indicator.

$$A_1 = W_1 \cdot B_1 = 1 \cdot [0.1743\ 0.1529\ 0.2819\ 0.2072\ 0.1837]$$
$$= (0.1743\ 0.1529\ 0.2819\ 0.2072\ 0.1837)$$
$$A_2 = W_2 \cdot B_2 = (0.1306\ 0.2799\ 0.1339\ 0.1571\ 0.1758\ 0.1227)$$

$$\begin{bmatrix} 0.1049 & 0.2584 & 0.3295 & 0.2232 & 0.0840 \\ 0.1418 & 0.3532 & 0.3444 & 0.1337 & 0.0269 \\ 0.1394 & 0.2279 & 0.3671 & 0.2406 & 0.0250 \\ 0.1420 & 0.1055 & 0.3755 & 0.3475 & 0.0295 \\ 0.1238 & 0.1239 & 0.4032 & 0.2959 & 0.0532 \\ 0.0360 & 0.0832 & 0.4289 & 0.3269 & 0.1250 \end{bmatrix}$$

$$= (0.1205\ 0.2117\ 0.3711\ 0.2455\ 0.0512)$$
$$A_3 = W_3 \cdot B_3 = 1 \cdot [0.0286\ 0.0842\ 0.3698\ 0.3680\ 0.1494]$$
$$= (0.0286\ 0.0842\ 0.3698\ 0.3680\ 0.1494)$$

Thus, the primary indicator evaluation matrix is written as

$$A = (A_I)^T = \begin{bmatrix} 0.1743 & 0.1529 & 0.2819 & 0.2072 & 0.1837 \\ 0.1205 & 0.2117 & 0.3711 & 0.2455 & 0.0512 \\ 0.0286 & 0.0842 & 0.3698 & 0.3680 & 0.1494 \end{bmatrix}$$

4.3.4 Comprehensive Evaluation Matrix

The comprehensive evaluation matrix is $C = W \cdot A = (C_1, C_2, C_3, C_4, C_5)$, where C_1, C_2, C_3, C_4, C_5 are the degrees of membership of performance to each of the five grades, respectively.

$$C = W \cdot A = (0.1866\ 0.7134\ 0.1000)$$
$$\begin{bmatrix} 0.1743 & 0.1529 & 0.2819 & 0.2072 & 0.1837 \\ 0.1205 & 0.2117 & 0.3711 & 0.2455 & 0.0512 \\ 0.0286 & 0.0842 & 0.3698 & 0.3680 & 0.1494 \end{bmatrix}$$
$$= (0.1213\ 0.1881\ 0.3543\ 0.2506\ 0.0857)$$

4.3.5   Results of Fuzzy Comprehensive Evaluation

The fuzzy comment set only qualitatively reflects the degrees of membership to each grade. This set is then quantified to obtain the quantitative comment set $V = \{90, 80, 70, 60, 50\}$. The final score of comprehensive evaluation is calculated:

$$D = C \cdot V^T = (0.1213 \quad 0.1881 \quad 0.3543 \quad 0.2506 \quad 0.0857) \begin{bmatrix} 90 \\ 80 \\ 70 \\ 60 \\ 50 \end{bmatrix}$$

$$= 70.087$$

As seen from above, the overall performance of rural public sports services belonged to a moderate level, which was intermediate between "satisfied" and "neutral".

4.3.6   Analysis of the Fuzzy Comprehensive Evaluation Results

Statistical treatment was performed to the performance evaluation system using fuzzy comprehensive evaluation method and the overall score was 70.087, which was intermediate between "satisfied" and "neutral". To facilitate the analysis, the comment sets for "very satisfied" and "satisfied" were combined together to become "above the neutral category"; those for "unsatisfied" and "very unsatisfied" were combined together to become "below the neutral category". Local residents thought that the performance of rural public sports services was moderately good. For the three indicators, namely, organization and administration services provided by the rural public sports sector, current number of public sports sites and facilities and usage of public sports sites and facilities, over 50% of the respondents thought the performance was moderately good. However, the proportions for all other indicators were below 50%. Local residents were most unsatisfied with the service attitudes of public sports administrator and exploitation and utilization of rural sports resources. More details are provided below.

(1) Cost of rural public sports services

Cost of rural public sports services as the primary indicator consisted of one secondary indicator and six tertiary indicators. An analysis on comment sets indicated that the respondents were most satisfied with "input in rural public sports infrastructure" and "investment in specific rural public sports programs". As to the performance of the primary indicator, 43.5% of the respondents were satisfied or above; 24.9% of the respondents were satisfied with the cost of rural public sports organization and administration; as to the cost of legal maintenance for rural public sports, 24.6% of the respondents were satisfied or above; as to the annual gross salary of the working staff, 33.7% of the respondents were satisfied or above; as to the cost of rural public sports technology services, only 18.5% of the respondents were satisfied or above. In some rural areas of Zhejiang Province, there were no special sports activity sites ten years ago. With the implementation of new rural construction, rural sports fitness project and snow-charcoal project, many villages now have fitness paths, tables for table tennis, and basketball fields. Some sports fields of primary and middle schools are open to the public on holidays. A growing investment in rural public sports infrastructure has boosted satisfaction among local residents. The investment in specific rural public sports programs has been expanding as well. For example, Dadou Village of Changxin County attaches great importance to "blind dragon", a Chinese sports specialty. A certain amount of money is invested in the development of "blind dragon" every year, and the village committee organizes the rural residents to practice "blind dragon" on holidays. That is why the local residents are most satisfied with the input in rural public sports infrastructure and specific rural public sports programs.

(2) Performance of rural public sports services

Performance of rural public sports services as a primary indicator consisted of six secondary indicators and twenty-two tertiary indicators.

Among indicators of public sports organization services, the respondents were most satisfied with the organization and administration services provided by the rural public sports sector, accounting for 54.5%; 16.5% were satisfied with the density of public body-building sites; 10.2% were satisfied with the service efficiency of the working staff in the rural public sports sector. The lowest number of respondents was satisfied with the service attitude of the working staff, accounting for only 9.8% and below 10%. Although the rural public sports sector will organize and supervise some sports activities, the service attitude of the working staff is not pleasant. It is urgent to increase the service awareness of the working staff, so as to improve the overall service quality.

Respondents were generally satisfied with indicators related to public sports site and facility services. As to the current number of public sports sites and facilities, 50.9% were satisfied or above; as to the usage of public sports sites and facilities, 50.3% were satisfied or above; as to the maintenance of public sports sites and facilities, 48.9% were satisfied or above; as to the safety of public sports sites and facilities, 48.3% were satisfied or above; as to the update cycle of public sports sites and facilities, 50.3% were satisfied or above. The above figures indicate that a sufficient amount of high-quality rural sports sites and facilities have been built up in China and they can basically satisfy the sports demand of rural residents.

Among the indicators of services provided by public sports instructors, 46.5% were satisfied or above with the performance of the instruction services provided by public sports instructors; as to the performance of counseling services provided by public sports instructors, 44.7% were satisfied or above; as to the number of public sports instructors, 23.4% were satisfied or above.

Among the indicators of sports fitness knowledge services, 25.1% were satisfied or above with the physical training safety knowledge services; 24.4% were satisfied or above with the performance of health-enhancing knowledge dissemination. The satisfaction was generally low with sports fitness knowledge services, and more should be done to promote the dissemination of knowledge on sports and fitness.

Among the indicators of sports events organization and promotion services, the respondents were most satisfied with the dissemination speed of sports event news;

47.6% were satisfied or above with the dissemination speed of sports event news. This is because every rural household has a TV set, and most have PC and smart phones. Rural residents can know about sports event news via the Internet and TV. As to the sports activity promotion, 24.4% were satisfied or above; as to the number of sports events organized by the local public sports sector, 23.4% were satisfied or above; as to the degree of standardization of sports events, 10.5% were satisfied or above; as to the number of public sports programs, 11% were satisfied or above.

Respondents were not very satisfied with physical fitness monitoring services. As to the performance of physical fitness monitoring indicators, 12.5% were satisfied or above; as to the number of physical fitness monitoring, 11.7% were satisfied or above; as to the feedback of physical fitness monitoring result, 11.3% were satisfied or above. Our research team conducted interviews with some of the public sports administrators, who admitted that the physical fitness monitoring services need to be improved. Some rural areas organize free physical fitness monitoring for local residents every year from October to November. However, not many people receive physical fitness monitoring, not to mention the rural residents. The reasons are two-fold. On the one hand, not enough promotion programs have been conducted concerning physical fitness monitoring; on the other hand, awareness about physical fitness monitoring is low among rural residents.

(3) Rural public sports organization and administration

Rural public sports organization and administration as a primary indicator consisted of one secondary indicator and two tertiary indicators. An analysis of the comment sets indicated that the respondents were usually unsatisfied with rural public sports organization and administration. As to the exploitation and utilization of rural public sports resources, 9.8% were satisfied or above; as to the mode of funding for rural public sports services, 13.5% were satisfied or above. Much needs to be done to improve the exploitation and utilization of rural public sports resources and the mode of funding for rural public sports services.

5 Conclusions

The methods used in this study included questionnaire survey, Delphi method, and mathematical statistics method. The actual demands in developing rural public sports services and new public administration theory are the bases for the construction of the performance evaluation system for rural public sports services. Moreover, the principles involved in the construction were target-oriented, comprehensiveness, operability, and public-oriented principles. Based on exploratory factor analysis, the performance evaluation system for rural public sports services was established. This evaluation system consisted of three primary indicators: cost of rural public sports services, performance of rural public sports services, and rural public sports organization and administration. The eight secondary indicators were input cost, public sports organization, public sports site and facility services, services provided by public sports instructors, sports fitness knowledge services, sports event organization and promotion services, physical fitness monitoring services, and performance of rural public sports services. There were thirty tertiary indicators. Weights of the indicators were determined using AHP.

Based on the performance evaluation system and weight determination, rural villages under the administration of five prefecture-level cities in Zhejiang Province were taken as the research objects. The performance evaluation model was established using fuzzy comprehensive evaluation method. Statistical treatment of this model indicated that the overall score was 70.087, which belonged to a moderate level intermediate between "satisfied" and "neutral". The respondents were satisfied or above with three indicators, namely, public sports organization and administration services provided by the local public sports sector, current number of public sports facilities, and usage of public sports facilities. However, the respondents were most unsatisfied with two indicators, namely, service attitude of rural public sports administrators and development and exploitation and utilization of rural public sports resources.

Acknowledgment. This work was partly supported by 2016 Planned research topics in philosophy and social science of Huzhou City, Zhejiang Province (Grant number: 2016XJXM44); special research topics of rural development of Huzhou University (Grant number: 2016XJXM44).

References

1. Medori, S.D.: A framework for auditing and enhancing performance measurement systems. Int. J. Oper. Prod. Manag. **20**(5), 520–523 (2000)
2. Wei, W., Wang, J.: Construction of a theoretical framework for performance evaluation system for China's public sports services. Sports Culture Guide **9**(9), 19–24 (2015)
3. Wei, W., Wang, J.: Performance evaluation system construction of Chinese public sports service and empirical research. China Sport Sci. **35**(7), 35–47 (2015)
4. Wang, X., Li, X., Lu, Y., et al.: Construction of performance evaluation system for public sports services based on citizen satisfaction. J. Nanjing Sport Inst. **28**(4), 41–46 (2014)
5. Zhao, N.: A research on performance evaluation of public sports services based on DEA model. J. Chengdu Sport Univ. **34**(6), 8–14 (2008)
6. Zhang, X.: Performance Evaluation of Public Sectors, vol. 8, pp. 147–149. China Commerce and Trade Press, Beijing (2006)
7. Chen, Z.: Public Administration: A Research Approach Different from the Conventional Administration Science, vol. 3, pp. 47–49. China Renmin University Press, Beijing (2003)
8. Ma, G.: Government Performance Management, vol. 6, pp. 78–102. Fudan University Press, Shanghai (2005)
9. Hu, X., Pedrycz, W., Wang, X.: Granular fuzzy rule-based models: a study in a comprehensive evaluation and construction of fuzzy models. IEEE Trans. Fuzzy Syst. **25**(5), 1342–1355 (2017)
10. Williams, R.: Organizational Performance Management, vol. 5, pp. 79–93. Tsinghua University Press, Beijing (2002)
11. Lei, F., Quan, D.: A Course on Sports Statistics, p. 1. Science Press, Beijing (2012)
12. Acharyya, M., De, R.K., Kundu, M.K.: Extraction of features using M-band wavelet packet frame and their neuro-fuzzy evaluation foe multitexture segmentation. IEEE Trans. Pattern Anal. Mach. Intell. **25**(12), 1639–1644 (2003)

13. Wei, X., Luo, X., Li, Q., Zhang, J., Xu, Z.: Online comment-based hotel quality automatic assessment using improved fuzzy comprehensive evaluation and fuzzy cognitive map. IEEE Trans. Fuzzy Syst. **23**(1), 72–84 (2015)
14. Xie, J., Liu, C.: Fuzzy Mathematics Method and Its Application, p. 10. Huazhong University of Science and Technology Press, Wuhan (2005)

Studies on Artistic Style of Chinese Ink Deckle-Edged Paper-Cutting Animation

Xiaoli Dong$^{(\boxtimes)}$

Jilin Animation Institute, No. 168 BoShi Road, Advanced Technology District,
Changchun, Jilin, People's Republic of China
417463493@qq.com

Abstract. This article elaborates processes of the production and development of ink deckle-edged paper-cutting animation and summarizes its artistic style. The overall style of ink deckle-edged paper-cutting animation has the unique beauty of artistic conception of Chinese traditional arts, modeling of character is featured on fine and delicate, and has characteristic of shading in Chinese ink painting. Its theme is refined and rich in philosophy. At the same time, this article also explores problems existed and future development of ink deckle-edged paper-cutting animation.

Keyword: Artistic style of ink deckle-edged paper-cutting animation

1 Introduction

Chinese ink deckle-edged paper-cutting animation is a unique form of paper-cutting animation in China, it creatively uses hand-tearing to form deckle edge and ink dot-dyeing process to make paper-cutting animated characters, making its characters natural, delicate, plush and cute. Its rich national characteristics and unique artistic style are favored by the majority of the audience, and won several international awards, making a glorious chapter in the history of Chinese animation.

However, with the passage of time, animation technology is changing with each passing day, and ink deckle-edged paper-cutting animation technology is not advancing with the times, coupled with the death of ink deckle-edged paper-cutting animation master, the techniques of ink deckle-edged paper-cutting animation are lack of heritage and successor, and is at risk of losing. This article tries to sort out and summarize the artistic style of Chinese ink deckle-edged paper-cutting animation, hoping to promote the inheritance and development of this precious national animation.

Xiaoli Dong (1983-), female, Huanren, Liaoning province, lecturer of Jilin Animation Institute, major research direction is ink deckle-edged paper-cutting animation.

© Springer-Verlag GmbH Germany, part of Springer Nature 2018
Z. Pan et al. (Eds.): Transactions on Edutainment XIV, LNCS 10790, pp. 225–231, 2018.
https://doi.org/10.1007/978-3-662-56689-3_18

2 Production and Development of Ink Deckle-Edged Paper-Cutting Animation

2.1 Paper-Cutting Animation

Paper-cutting animation comes from the Chinese folk shadow play, and shadow play as far as written records, has more than 2,000 years of history. China's truly paper-cutting animation appeared in the late 50s of last century, in 1957, Shanghai Animation Film Studio was set up, Wan Guchan formed a paper-cut film testing group, collaborating with Hu Jinqing, Zhan Tong, etc., they divided the role into head, body, limbs and combined them, making it moving by manually adjusting the location of the various parts of the role. After more than a year of effort, Wan Guchan et al. successful shot China's first paper-cutting animation "Zhu Bajie eats watermelon", for the first time taking paper-cut and shadow art in the design and production of animation, refreshing the audience and created China's first paper-cutting animation in the history. Since then, technology of paper-cutting animation has become more and more mature, Animation Film Studio successively shot "Ginseng Doll", "The Fishing Child", "Golden Conch", "Lift The Donkey" and a series of excellent paper-cutting animation [1] (Figs. 1 and 2).

Fig. 1. Zhu Bajie eats watermelon

Fig. 2. The Fishing Child

2.2 Ink Deckle-Edged Paper-Cutting Animation

During the Cultural Revolution, China's animation industry was basically in a state of stagnation. In 1976, the Cultural Revolution ended, Chinese animation art breathed new life, animated masters burst into a huge creative enthusiasm, and the ink deckle-edged paper-cutting animation was born in this period. Hu Jinqing and other animation masters applied the new ink deckle-edged technology to the creation of paper-cutting animation characters, thus created this unique form of paper-cutting animation, the ink deckle-edged paper-cutting animation, which gained unanimous praise both at home and abroad. From 1976 to the beginning of 1980s, it was the development period of ink deckle-edged paper-cutting animation, China's first ink deckle-edged paper-cutting animation was "Bamboo Shoots in the House", taken in 1976; in the 80's, the flourishing period of ink deckle-edged paper-cutting animation, many good animations such as "Scarecrow", "Struggle Between Snipe and Clam", "Monkeys Grasp for the Moon" were created during this period, and won a number of domestic and foreign awards; in the 90's, due to the great changes in social economy, Chinese animation wholly trended to decline, ink deckle-edged paper-cutting animation works were basically gone, "Snow Fox", whose content was miserable, was the last work of paper deckle-edged paper-cutting animation [2] (Figs. 3, 4, 5 and 6).

Fig. 3. Struggle Between Snipe and Clam

Fig. 4. Monkeys Grasp for the Moon

Fig. 5. Scarecrow

Fig. 6. Scarecrow

3   Artistic Style of Ink Deckle-Edged Paper-Cutting Animation

3.1   The Overall Style Has the Unique Beauty of Artistic Conception of Chinese Traditional Arts

The ink deckle-edged paper-cutting animation looks fresh, natural, elegant and has a naive and simple ink taste, which exudes a rich traditional Chinese culture charm. When audiences enjoy the animated film, it looks like reading an ancient text, concise speech, lively spirit and charm, make sense reasonable and meaningful. For example, in the film of "Struggle Between Snipe and Clam", mountains seem like smoke, reeds are green, all of the things are misted, a fisherman alone fishing in the river quietly with a Chinese ancient raincoat and hat, happy and contented, fishes lively and vivid. The picture is simple and natural, ethereal and elegance, the man is in harmony with nature, full of poetic. Although the whole film does not have a line, people cannot help but think of Zhang Zhihe's "Fishing Boat" (a Chinese Song Poetry), which describes vividly the fisherman's quiet and comfortable, interest of fishing and nature.

3.2   Modeling of Character Is Featured on Fine and Delicate

Hu Jinqing, the founder of ink deckle-edged paper-cutting animation, believes that "fine and delicate" is the most important artistic characteristics of ink deckle-edged paper-cutting animated characters [3]. Modeling of paper-cutting animated character is angular, lines are too simple, having apparent cutting traces, and color on the edge is blunt. Hu Jinqing and other older animation artists give full play to creativity, they uses Chinese mulberry paper as the main material, firstly paints the outline of characters on the page, and then tear the characters down along the outline, which cleverly let the long fibers in the paper scattered on the edge of the characters, so that ink colors can shading naturally along the fibers, thus making the lines of characters soft and full, colors on the edge shading naturally and transmitting harmoniously, especially when depicting animal images, it making small animals seem plush, cute and lifelike.

For example, the image of golden monkey in the film of "The Naughty", with the application of ink deckle-edged paper-cutting technology, making the golden monkey's fur appears supple naturally and vivid. In the ink deckle-edged paper-cutting animation "Scarecrow", the animated masters make full use of this style, in order to make the water bird's long neck rotating flexibly, after several experiments, the water bird's neck is divided into more than a hundred joints, and then linked together with hair, so that the water bird's neck can move smoothly.

3.3   It Has Characteristic of Shading in Chinese Ink Painting

Chinese ink painting is a painting artistic form that expresses Chinese people's cultural feelings, and has unique aesthetic spirit and aesthetic taste of Chinese people. Chinese scholar-bureaucrats are the main body in creation of Chinese ink painting, having profound traditional culture background, they emphases on transmitting feelings by paintings, painting follow their hearts, getting back to nature, totally natural, so that they often do not pay attention to be similar in appearance and ask for similarity in spirit, they put their own ambitions and feelings into the ink painting and focus on the overall artistic conception and charm.

Ink deckle-edged paper-cutting animation makes a good use of drawing methods of Chinese ink painting, it uses ink painting techniques to express their feelings with poetic style. The overall style of ink deckle-edged paper-cutting animation is fresh and natural, for example, in the film of "Struggle Between Snipe and Clam", the ink deckle-edged style is further improved, the snipe has a feeling of fluffy, with the use of ink painting techniques, style of the whole film is fresh and beautiful, filled with poetic, as well as rich in philosophy [4].

3.4   Its Theme Is Refined and Rich in Philosophy

Although process of making deckle-edged paper-cutting animation is more simple than ink animation, the process is still cumbersome, its production cost is still high, and its cycle is relatively long. Therefore, the ink deckle-edged paper-cutting animation is not suitable for stories whose plot is too complex, so that characters cannot be too much, and its subject matter is relatively short, small and refined. However, Chinese classical literature and folk tales are just good at narrating a philosophical story by means of a short and condensed script. For example, the ink deckle-edged paper-cutting animation of "Struggle Between Snipe and Clam" is derived from the "Strategies of the Warring States", the whole story has only 65 words. At that time, Su Dai just persuades the king of Zhao state not to invade Yan state by means of this short story; Meanwhile, the film of "Monkeys Grasp for the Moon" comes out of Chinese folk tales. Other works like "Scarecrow" and "The Naughty" are also similar to Chinese classical literature and folk tales, though they are originally created by screenwriters. They all have short story, uncomplicated content, vivid plot and enrich in philosophy, which make audience impressed and memorable [5].

4 Problems Existed and Future Development

Chinese traditional ink deckle-edged paper-cutting animation is a highlight of Chinese national animation, ink animated character created by use of deckle-edged paper-cutting technique, not only maintains feelings and charm of ink animation, but also makes modeling of animated character natural, delicate, plush and cute, it has distinctive national features and unique artistic style. However, the traditional ink deckle-edged paper-cutting animation has complex production process, great technical difficulties, long production cycle, low efficiency and high cost, it can only produce a small amount of works, which can not meet the requirements of modern animation industry, which greatly limits the development of ink deckle-edged paper-cutting animation. After the 90's, ink deckle-edged paper-cutting animation gradually disappeared [6].

We must protect, inherit and develop the traditional ink deckle-edged paper-cutting animation, otherwise, the precious national animation art is at risk of dying. On one hand, we should collect, organize and summarize materials of ink deckle-edged paper-cutting animation, research and inherit its production techniques, and cultivate special talents. On the other hand, we should explore ways to combine modern computer animation production technologies and tradition ink deckle-edged paper-cutting animation technology, on the basis of ensuring its art style and quality, to simplify process, improve efficiency and reduce cost, so that to meet needs of modern animation industry and promote the development of ink deckle-edged paper-cutting animation.

Acknowledgments. One of the results of "Applied Research of Combination Between Traditional Ink Deckle-Edged Paper-Cutting Animation Art and Modern Digital Technology", key project of social science research of Jilin Department of Education "13th Five Year Plan", project number: Jilin ESC [2016], No. 525.

References

1. Xia, X.: On the development of paper-cutting animation. Art Sci. Technol. **6**, 80 (2010)
2. Li, B.: Recalling the wonderful work of Chinese art film: paper-cutting film. J. Fine Arts **12** (2), 72–74 (2012)
3. Jin, B.: Record of My mind track - interview with Hu Jinqing. Film Art **3**, 50–54 (1993)

4. Cao, G., Sui, C.: On the development of Chinese paper-cutting animation and artistic characteristics of each period. Movie Rev. **41**(10), 27–34 (2009)
5. Yang, Y.: Paper-cutting animation and cultural inheritance in the new media. Cult. Commun. Educ. **2**, 151–152 (2017)
6. Liu, H.: Research on paper-cutting animation under the new media. Art Sci. Technol. **9**, 46 (2016)

Usability Study of CAD for Clothing Thermal Computational Design Education

Mingliang Cao[1(✉)], Yi Li[2], Josephine Csete[3], and Zhigeng Pan[4]

[1] Guangdong Academy of Research on VR Industry,
Foshan University, Foshan 528000, China
merlin.cao@connect.polyu.hk
[2] School of Materials, The University of Manchester, Manchester M13 9PL, UK
henry.yili@manchester.ac.uk
[3] Educational Development Center,
The Hong Kong Polytechnic University, Hong Kong, China
josephine.csete@polyu.edu.hk
[4] Digital Media and Interaction (DMI) Research Center,
Hangzhou Normal University, Hangzhou 310012, China
zgpan@cad.zju.edu.cn

Abstract. This paper describes a usability study of CAD for teaching and learning clothing thermal computational design (CTCD) for university students of fashion and textiles. The CAD helps students to learn the clothing thermal computational design through computational design simulations (CD-Sims). The pedagogical strategies of employing CAD, and learning process and pedagogical implementation of CD-Sims are discussed. In addition, a user study employing the CD-Sims with CAD indicated that they enhanced students' learning outcomes on pre-test and post-test clothing thermal computational design scores.

Keywords: CAD · Clothing Thermal Computational Design · Education
Computer-assisted instruction

1 Introduction

Consumers are increasingly concerned about the thermal functions and performance of clothing, which in turn encourage universities and companies to conduct research in this area. It becomes necessary to teach design for clothing thermal functions and performance to university students of fashion and textiles before they go into the industry. An insufficiency of traditional methods of teaching and learning is drawing more and more attentions from university educators and researchers. With the development of mathematical modeling and computational technology, Computer Aided Design (CAD) technology provides a potential way for fashion and textiles educators to teach design for clothing thermal functions and performance.

Design for clothing thermal functions and performance is a functional design process for creating conceptual (paper-based) or prototype (model) apparel that achieves desirable thermal functions and performance for people living in a range of

© Springer-Verlag GmbH Germany, part of Springer Nature 2018
Z. Pan et al. (Eds.): Transactions on Edutainment XIV, LNCS 10790, pp. 232–243, 2018.
https://doi.org/10.1007/978-3-662-56689-3_19

climates and weather conditions. Traditional educational practices of this functional design process include user surveys, user requirements, garment design, garment assembly, testing & analysis (bench scale testing or field trials) and production [1]. The conventional procedure for the functional design process without CAD technology is based largely on the designers' experience and intuition, which have the following disadvantages [2]: experience-based design; long-term process of making interactive decisions; and incapability in predicting parametric design before real product.

In consideration of the above-mentioned problems, the computational design CAD software [3], based on mathematical models, was developed as an engineering design tool for technicians and designers as well as educators to conduct clothing thermal computational design (CTCD) in a scientific and quantitative way. The advantages of applying this CAD software over traditional design methods have been discussed [2]: (a) it is a model-based method; (b) it is an efficient decision-making method; and (c) it is a scientific quantitative method. In order to take advantage of this CAD technology in higher education in fashion and textiles, the learning approaches had to be initiated. For instance, Cao et al. [4] conducted a pilot study employing the CAD software to help students to analyze the apparel market potential with quantitative simulation data in a subject titled 'Fashion Product Development'. In a further study, Cao et al. [5] investigated the pedagogical effects and students' feedback about learning with the CAD software. It was found there were positive effects for the students to achieve the key learning objective. At the same time, it was also found there were some difficulties in students' learning, such as a lack of back-ground knowledge, learning materials and activities.

Different from the traditional CAD software in fashion and textiles which aims at pattern design, garment construction, fashion design, and physical fitting simulation, the CAD software employed in this study focuses on 'design' in terms of the thermal functions and performance of clothing than on fashion. In this paper, the CAD software is employed for university students of fashion and textiles to learn clothing thermal computational design (CTCD) through computational design simulations (CD-Sims) learning. The key objectives of the study include: (a) pedagogical strategies of employing the CAD software; (b) pedagogical implementation and learning process of the CD-Sims with CAD; and (c) pedagogical effects of the CD-Sims with CAD for students' outcomes in CTCD.

2   Related Work

In this section, the work that is related to CAD employed in this study is reviewed. First, CAD in apparel design education is reviewed. Second, pedagogical approaches in teaching CAD in fashion and textiles are reviewed. Third, learning with computer simulations is reviewed since, in this study, the CD-Sims with CAD is employed for university students of fashion and textiles to learn CTCD.

2.1 CAD in Apparel Design

Computer Aided Design (CAD) technology is becoming increasingly apparent in textiles and apparel industries due to the competitive nature of businesses in the sector [6, 7], with the aim of saving on production time and improving quality [8]. Apparel products require speedy development which can be achieved through effective and efficient operations [7]. Apparel CAD technology in designing started to receive a lot of attention as a creative design tool and by the end of 1980s, researchers were actively looking at ways to integrate this tool more effectively. Although CAD programs have been developed specifically for apparel industry and apparel CAD training, fashion design students mostly used basic CAD design programs. These basic CAD programs were also available to students of fashion and textiles and included Adobe Illustrator, CorelDraw and Adobe Photoshop which allow students to communicate their designs professionally [9]. Technically, an apparel product life cycle with computers can be divided into the following main sections: conceptual design, CAD, CAM, and selling and follow-up. CAD involves all the processes of conceptualizing, designing, analyzing, prototyping and actual manufacturing in a project assisted by a computer. It can unleash the designers' creativity with many powerful functions and software capabilities. In the apparel industry, with its growing development and creation of new fibers, new machines and new processing, and the increasing demand for new designs, there are bigger challenges in apparel design than ever before. The adoption of CAD technology makes it possible to meet new consumer requirements.

2.2 Pedagogical Approaches for Teaching CAD in Fashion and Textiles

There are several pedagogical approaches used in teaching CAD to students of fashion and textiles [10]: constructivism, problem-based learning, experiential learning, and global-scope learning. The application of constructivism includes self-regulation and instructional scaffolding [11]. Self-regulation refers to planning, checking, and evaluating. Instructional scaffolding refers to the sufficient support to help learners to focus on and master the key features of the task quickly. By employing constructivism to teach CAD to fashion and textiles students, it is hoped that the students can construct their own questions and seek possible answers by themselves rather get direct instruction from their teachers. Through problem-based learning, students learn the necessary skills to deal with real-life problems that they have to face in the real world [12]. Problem-based learning can be useful to teach CAD to fashion and textiles students because this subject undergoes rapid changes every day. There is a large amount of material to be learned and it is conceptually complex. In teaching CAD to fashion and textiles students using experiential learning, students must take responsibility to investigate the nature of the design problem. Global-scope learning has involved into formal exchange programs, virtual universities, and double degrees between global institutions [13]. According to Hui [10], there are three main challenges of teaching CAD to fashion and textile students: changes of industry needs, changes of computer technology, changes of global working environment for fashion and textiles, and absence of standardized jargon in fashion and textiles.

2.3   Learning with Computer Simulations

de Jong and van Joolingen [14] described a computer simulation as 'a program that contains a model of a system (natural or artificial) or a process'. Computer simulations offer the opportunity to learn within a professional context [15], to refine the existing knowledge into functional schemata [16], and to provide background knowledge [17]. By using computer simulations, the learner gradually infers the features of the concept model whilst he/she proceeds through the simulation, which may lead to changes in his/her original concept [14]. By exploring and discovering during learning with computer simulations, learners can be retained longer in learning-by-doing than in learning-via-listening, reading, or seeing [18]. On one hand, previous research has demonstrated the effectiveness of computer simulations in facilitating student learning [19, 20]. On the other hand, some researchers have found problems with teaching and learning using computer simulations [21, 22].

3   Clothing Thermal Computational Design CAD

The CAD software (Fig. 1) was employed to teach CTCD. With the CAD software, users can perform multi-layer CTCD to simulate and preview the thermal performance of the clothing wearing system at the whole level, and to identify and improve their designs before making any real garments. Through the software, the user can consider fundamental physical/chemical properties and structured features of fibers, yarns, and fabrics in the computational design simulation to generate solutions that are very close to practical situations. As a virtual tool for the users to conduct CTCD, the software has several advantages compared to the traditional trial-and-error design method, such as speeding up the design process, saving time and money, and in-creasing productivity. A typical computational design simulation case includes three modules: pre-processing, computation, and post-processing. Several steps need to be followed to get a pre-processing case file: (1) 'What to do' to select the activity and the duration time of the activity (Fig. 1b); (2) 'Environment' to specify the environment for the activity (Fig. 1c); (3) 'Human body' to set up basic information about the human body (Fig. 1d); and, (4) 'Garment' to design the style, fitness, fiber and fabric properties of the garment (Fig. 1e). The key idea of employing the software is to help students to conduct CTCD with the first-hand experience of collecting, inputting and analyzing with quantitative data.

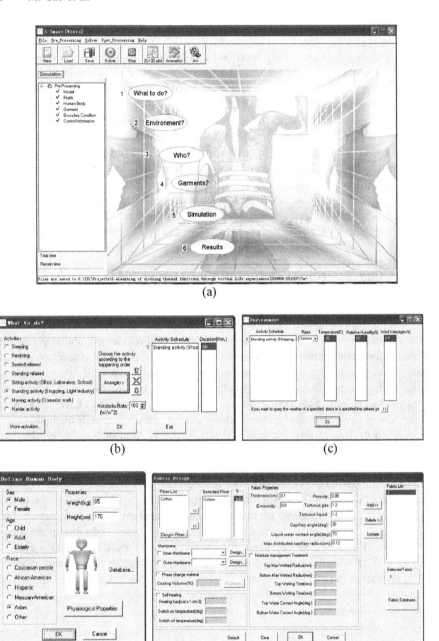

Fig. 1. The clothing thermal computational design CAD software, a: main interface; b: interface of 'What to do'; c: interface of 'Environment'; d: interface of 'Human body'; e: interface of 'Garment'

4 Pedagogical Strategies of Employing CAD

In this study, three pedagogical strategies were used to employ the computational design CAD software for students' learning. They are described in the following section.

4.1 As a Tool of Transmission for Knowledge

The CAD software can be employed as a tool for the transmission of knowledge. Through the CAD software, the following can be introduced or explored.

(1) The framework for CTCD can be introduced with procedural steps (e.g. what to do, environment, human body, and garment design).
(2) The parameters, key concepts and background science, and knowledge of CTCD can be explored by students through self-reflection or discussion with teachers. An example is the 'moisture management treatment', built in the 'garment design' step, which is a very important part of the CTCD.
(3) The knowledge is built constitutively and all parameters can be explored with logical identification. Similarly, in previous research, it has been suggested that computer simulations provide a professional context [15] or background knowledge [17] for learning, and refine the existing knowledge into functional schemata [16].

4.2 As an Experiential Learning Tool for Skills Development

The CAD software can be employed as an experiential learning tool for students to practice skills. According to Akpan [18], computer simulations retain learners longer in learning-by-doing than learning-via-listening, reading, or seeing. In the study, by using a group of computational design simulation cases, the students were able to practice how to conduct the CTCD. In addition, after each practice, the teacher organized a debriefing session for the students to discuss their learning experiences. They had an opportunity to share their feelings and experiences with each other.

4.3 As a Computational Design Tool for Application

The CAD software can be employed as a computational design tool for the design of new apparel products. Through the software, students learn to design new apparel products using a computational design approach. After learning the key knowledge and skills of CTCD, students are requested to design new products with the CAD software. By using the software, students prepare information and data for the target product, evaluate the pilot design, compare different conceptual designs, analyze with quantitative computational design simulation data, and select and finalize the best design for a prototype. According to de Jong and Van Joolingen [14], computer simulations lead to changes in learners' original concepts. In this study, the key difference between traditional design processes and the computational design method is the type of evaluation method. The computational design method can provide scientific quantitative data to evaluate the clothing functions and performances rather than the traditional qualitative method with (field-based) wear trials. The new method will lead to changes in the students' original concepts in designing new apparel products.

5   Learning Process of CD-Sims

The learning process of CD-Sims (Fig. 2) for university students of fashion and textiles consists of five steps: (1) an introduction to the background knowledge about the target topic; (2) the CD-Sims instruction for the target topic; (3) experimentation with the target topic; (4) reflection on the imitation of the CD-Sims for the target topic; and (5) the interpretation of the results of the CD-Sims for the target topic. In this study, learning process of CD-Sims with CAD is a repeated process for each study topic. The basic idea of applying the learning process is 'factor-control' case study. For each topic, through the learning process, the students are expected to learn the specific knowledge and influence of target factor for the final clothing thermal functions and performance. The learning process is explained further in the following:

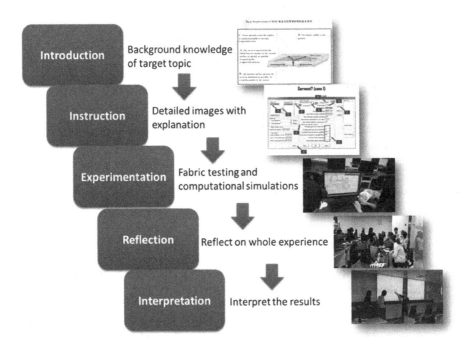

Fig. 2. Leaning process of CD-sims

(1) *Introduction* - The students are given a brief introduction to the background knowledge about the target topic. The aim of this introduction step is to prepare the students before their further study of the target topic. The key contents include the definition, the role, and the potential influence of the target topic.

(2) *Instruction* - The CD-Sims instruction gives very detailed images and explana-
tions. The aim of the instruction step is to provide specific learning instruction.
The key contents include the design of the CD-Sims cases, the operational steps of
each case, and the collection of key results.

(3) *Experimentation* - The students are asked to do fabric testing and CD-Sims by
themselves according to the instructions. The key contents include fabric testing
for CD-Sims, input and output CD-Sims data and collection of the key results.

(4) *Reflection* - Students are asked to reflect on the whole experience of doing
CD-Sims. The aim of the reflection step is to help students to reflect on what they
have experienced and connect what they have learned and what they have
experienced. The key contents include reflection on the process of the CD-Sims,
reflection on the data of the CD-Sims and reflection on the relationship between
theoretical knowledge and quantitative CD-Sims.

(5) *Interpretation* - An interpretation of the results of the CD-Sims is given. The aim
of the interpretation step is to help students to learn quantitative analysis of the
CD-Sims. The key contents include interpretation of case design, protocol of the
CD-Sims, and interpretation of the results.

6 Pedagogical Implementation of CD-Sims

The key pedagogical implementation of the CD-Sims was designed according to
multi-level skills for CTCD. These multi-level skills are organized from low to high
levels: operational, analytical and experimental (Fig. 3):

Learning with CD-Sims	Topic	Objective	Content
Operational level	Physical activity; Environment; Human body	To help students to learn the basic operational skills of designing CD-Sims	Introduction; **Instruction**[*]; Experimentation; Reflection; Interpretation
Analytical level	Clothing style; Clothing fit; Clothing layer; Fabric thickness; Fabric breathability; Fabric thermal conductivity; Fiber type	To help students to learn the analytical skills of analyzing CD-Sims results	Introduction; Instruction; Experimentation; Reflection; **Interpretation**[*]
Experimental level	Fabric moisture management	To help students to learn the experimental skills of testing fabric data for CD-Sims	Introduction; Instruction; **Experimentation**[*]; Reflection; Interpretation

Fig. 3. Multi-level educational use of the CD-Sims with CAD. *: the key content in each level.

(1) *Operational level* – to help students to learn the basic operational skills of designing CD-Sims.
(2) *Analytical level* – to help students to learn the skills of analyzing CD-Sims results.
(3) *Experimental level* – to help students to learn the experimental skills for testing fabric data for CD-Sims.

7   User Studies

To assess students' learning outcomes in CTFD by using the CAD software, the subject 'Design for Functions and Performance', with a total of 48 undergraduates from the Institute of Fashion and textiles in The Hong Kong Polytechnic University, was taught twice for two terms. There were 28 students in Class 1 in Term 1, and 20 in Class 2 in Term 2. The same pre- and post-test questions about CTCD were used for both classes. First, in Class 1 of Term 1, the students demonstrated a significant improvement from the pre- to post-test (mean scores: 56 ± 12 vs 83 ± 8, p < .001). Second, in Class 2 of Term 2, the students demonstrated a significant improvement from the pre- to post-test (mean scores: 48 ± 10 vs 72 ± 10, p < .001). Although these pre- to post-test gains indicate significant improvements in the students' understanding of CTCD, the study design did not allow us to claim that this CAD method is better than traditional approaches in design for clothing functions and performance. A controlled experiment in which some students would not be allowed to use CAD was considered unethical and the author did not collect pre- and post-test data on students in the same subjects from previous cohorts; ongoing research has literally opened up new areas of content that must be taught to students, and CTCD is an example of this. The CAD software was developed to help students learn CTCD that had never been taught before, so there was no prior student group against which to compare. However, what the author can claim from these results is that the students demonstrated a high level of retention of key CTCD skills soon after having received the instruction. Furthermore, as the main method used to help the students acquire the new skills was hands-on experiential learning using the CAD software (approximately 60% of class time with access available outside of class time), the author is comfortable in claiming that the CAD software was the main way for the students to acquire the skills of CTCD.

8   Discussion

In this section, the design, application and debriefing of learning tasks in CAD study are discussed. The Experiential Learning Theory is the foundation of this learning approach. The learning task is the main way to facilitate students' learning by using the CAD software. There are several considerations to be taken into account in designing the learning tasks: exploration, reflection and communication.

(1) *Exploration* - The learning tasks are expected to provide the chance for students' self-exploration with a guided instruction.
(2) *Reflection* - The learning tasks are expected to provide the chance for students' self-reflection on the target task, based on what they have learned in the class.

(3) *Communication* - The learning tasks are expected to provide the chance for students to communicate with each other or with the teacher.

The key feature of the application of the learning tasks in the CAD study is flexibility. The learning tasks can be applied flexibly according to the following factors.

(1) *Topic of subject* - The learning tasks can be applied for different topics (i.e. 'Design for Functions and Performance', 'Fashion Product Development', 'Apparel Product Development', 'Equipment (s) in Infection Control';
(2) *Duration of class* - The learning tasks can be applied as a learning module according to the duration of the class (i.e. 4 weeks, 7 weeks, 14 weeks);
(3) *Level of study* - The learning tasks can be applied according to different levels (i.e. operational, analytical, experimental).

Debriefing about the learning tasks is very important. The teacher organized a debriefing session after each learning task and posed a series of progressive questions for the students to reflect on what they had experienced. The teacher provided important insights, linked to the key objectives of the learning tasks, about the potential future use. These debriefing sections were a very important part of the learning tasks in learning by using the CAD software.

The CD-Sims with CAD proposed in this study does have some technical and educational limitations. First, its quality is limited by the mathematical models and engineering design of the CAD software. Second, the CD-Sims with CAD only employs limited typical 'case' studies to demonstrate specific domain knowledge and skills in CTCD. Third, the CD-Sims with CAD seems to require too much 'doing' work for the students.

9 Conclusion

This paper has described the CAD software for university students of fashion and textiles to learn the clothing thermal computational design (CTCD). The computational design simulations (CD-Sims) with CAD can provide three levels (operational, analytical and experimental) of skills by using three groups of topic-oriented case studies. A study of students using the CD-Sims with CAD indicated that it significantly enhanced their CTCD learning outcomes. Future work on the CD-Sims with CAD for CTCD education will focus on improving and extending more topic-oriented cases, and evaluating its educational implementation to support university students of fashion and textiles via additional user studies.

Acknowledgments. We would like to thank the Hong Kong Innovation and Technology Commission and the Hong Kong Research Institute of Textiles and Apparel for providing funding support to this research through projects ITP/002/07TP, ITP/030/08TP and ITP/015/11TP, as well as The Hong Kong Polytechnic University through project 8CGT. Also, we would like to thank the support of the EU Horizon 2020, University of Manchester and national NSFC through projects with project codes 644268-ETEXWELD-H2020-MSCA-RISE-2014, AA14512 and 61332017.

References

1. Gupta, D.: Design and engineering of functional clothing. Indian J. Fibre Text **36**(4), 327–335 (2011)
2. Li, Y., Dai, X.Q.: Biomechanical Engineering of Fashion and Textiles. Woodhead Publishing Limited, Abington Hall, Abington (2006)
3. Li, Y., et al.: P-smart - a virtual system for clothing thermal functional design. Comput. Aided Des. **38**(7), 726–739 (2006)
4. Cao, M.L., Li, Y., Csete, J.: Computer thermal functional simulation to enhance students' learning on fashion product development. In: Proceedings of the 2nd Textile Bioengineering and Informatics Symposium, Hong Kong, pp. 663–671 (2009)
5. Cao, M.L., Li, Y., Csete, J.: Effects of an E-learning case computer simulation on student's learning of clothing functional design and students feedback. In: Proceedings of 3rd Textile Bioengineering and Informatics Symposium, Shanghai, pp. 1284–1294 (2010)
6. Hardaker, C.H., Fozzard, G.J.: Toward virtual garment: three dimensional computer environment for garment design. Int. J. Cloth. Sci. Tech. **10**(2), 114–127 (1998)
7. Glock, R.E., Kunz, G.I.: Apparel manufacturing: sewn product analysis, 4th edn. Prentice Hall, Upper Saddle River (2005)
8. Hunter, A., King, R., Lowson, R.H.: The Textile/Clothing Pipeline and Quick Response Management. The Textile Institute International, Manchester (2002)
9. Ryder, C.: Visual communication in fashion and textile design. John Moore's University, Liverpool (2005)
10. Hui, P.C.L.: Approaches to teaching computer-aided design (CAD) to fashion and textiles students. In: Computer Technology for Textiles and Apparel. Woodhead Publishing Limited (2011)
11. Bruning, R.H., Schraw, G.J., Ronning, R.R.: Cognitive Psychology and Instruction, 3rd edn. Merrill/Prentice Hall, Upper Saddle River (1999)
12. Uden, L., Beaumont, C.: Technology and Problem-Based Learning. Information Science Publishing, Hershey and London (2006)
13. Ankerson, K.S., Pable, J.: Interior Design: Practical Strategies for Teaching and Learning. Fairchild Books, New York (2008)
14. de Jong, T., Van Joolingen, W.R.: Scientific discovery learning with computer simulations of conceptual domains. Rev. Educ. Res. **68**(2), 179–201 (1998)
15. Kneebone, R.: Evaluating clinical simulations for learning procedural skills: a theory-based approach. Acad. Med. **80**(6), 549–553 (2005)
16. Winberg, T.M., Berg, C.A.R.: Students' cognitive focus during a chemistry laboratory exercise: effects of a computer-simulated prelaboratory. J. Res. Sci. Teach. **44**(8), 1108–1133 (2007)
17. Chang, K.E., Chen, Y.L., Lin, H.Y., Sung, Y.T.: Effects of instructional support in simulation-based physics learning. Comput. Educ. **51**(4), 1486–1498 (2008)
18. Akpan, J.P.: Issues associated with inserting computer simulations into biology instruction: a review of the literature. Electron. J. Sci. Educ. **5**(3) (2001)
19. Winn, W., et al.: Learning oceanography from a computer simulation compared with direct experience at sea. J. Res. Sci. Teach. **43**(1), 25–42 (2005)

20. Gelbart, H., Brill, G., Yarden, A.: The impact of a web-based research simulation in bioinformatics on students' understanding of genetics. Res. Sci. Educ. **39**(5), 725–751 (2009)
21. Marshall, J.A., Young, E.S.: Preservice teachers' theory development in physical and simulated environments. J. Res. Sci. Teach. **43**(9), 907–937 (2006)
22. Waight, N., Abd-El-Khalick, F.: The impact of technology on the enactment of inquiry in a technology enthusiast's sixth grade science classroom. J. Res. Sci. Teach. **44**(1), 154–182 (2007)

Author Index

Printed in the United States
By Bookmasters